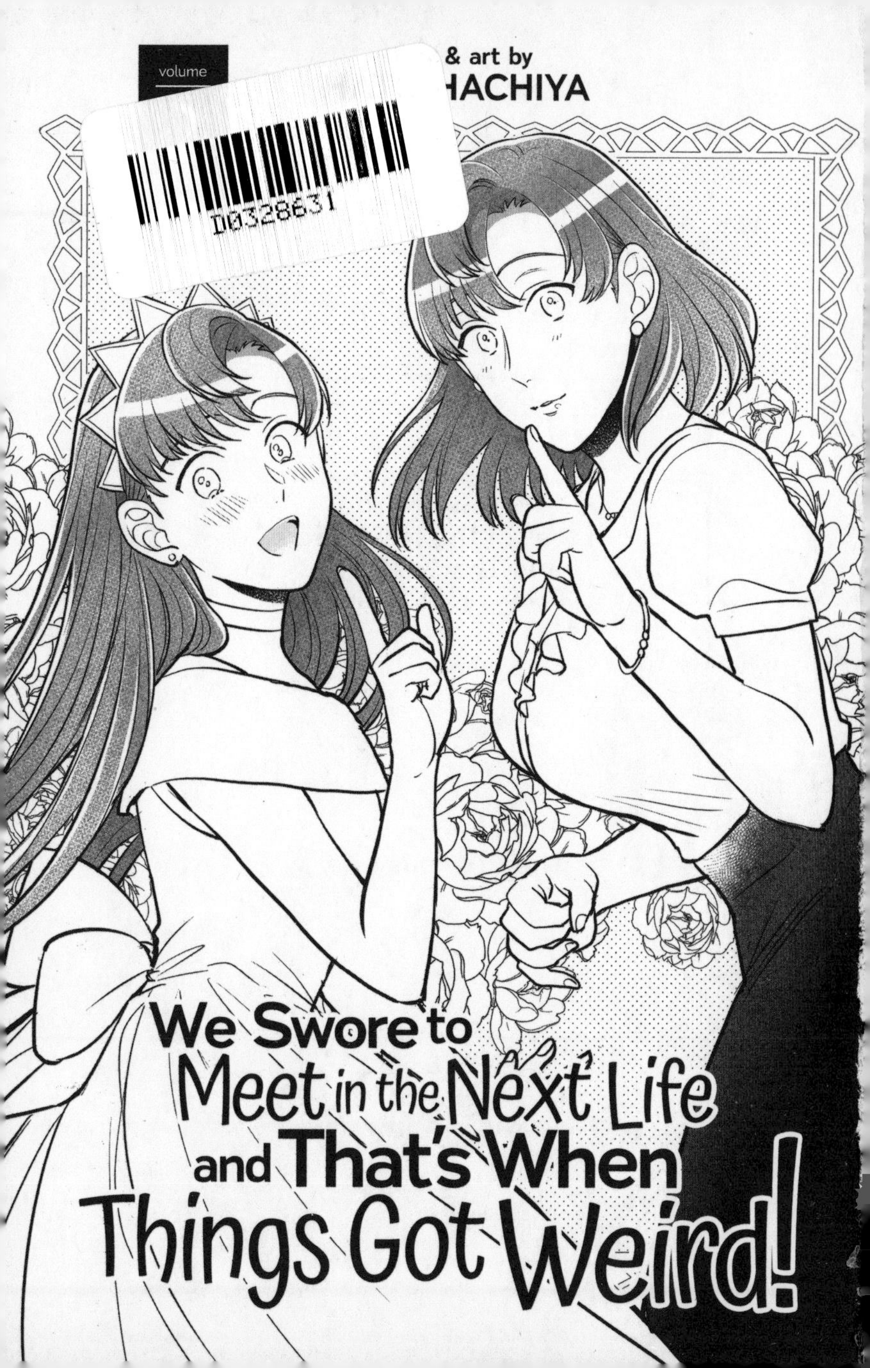
volume
& art by
HACHIYA
We Swore to
Meet in the Next Life
and That's When
Things Got Weird!

CONTENTS

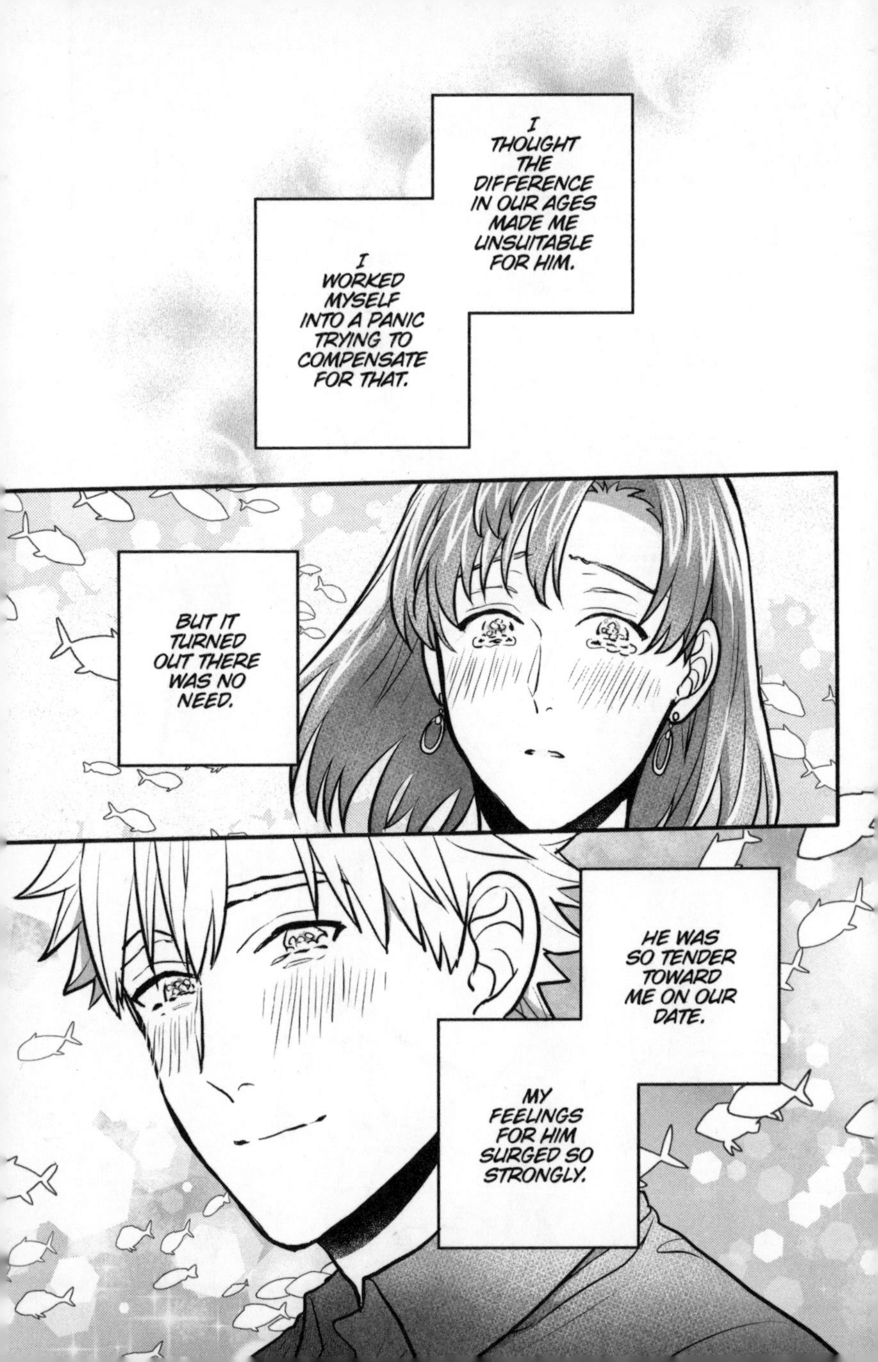
I THOUGHT THE DIFFERENCE IN OUR AGES MADE ME UNSUITABLE FOR HIM.
I WORKED MYSELF INTO A PANIC TRYING TO COMPENSATE FOR THAT.
BUT IT TURNED OUT THERE WAS NO NEED.
HE WAS SO TENDER TOWARD ME ON OUR DATE.
MY FEELINGS FOR HIM SURGED SO STRONGLY.

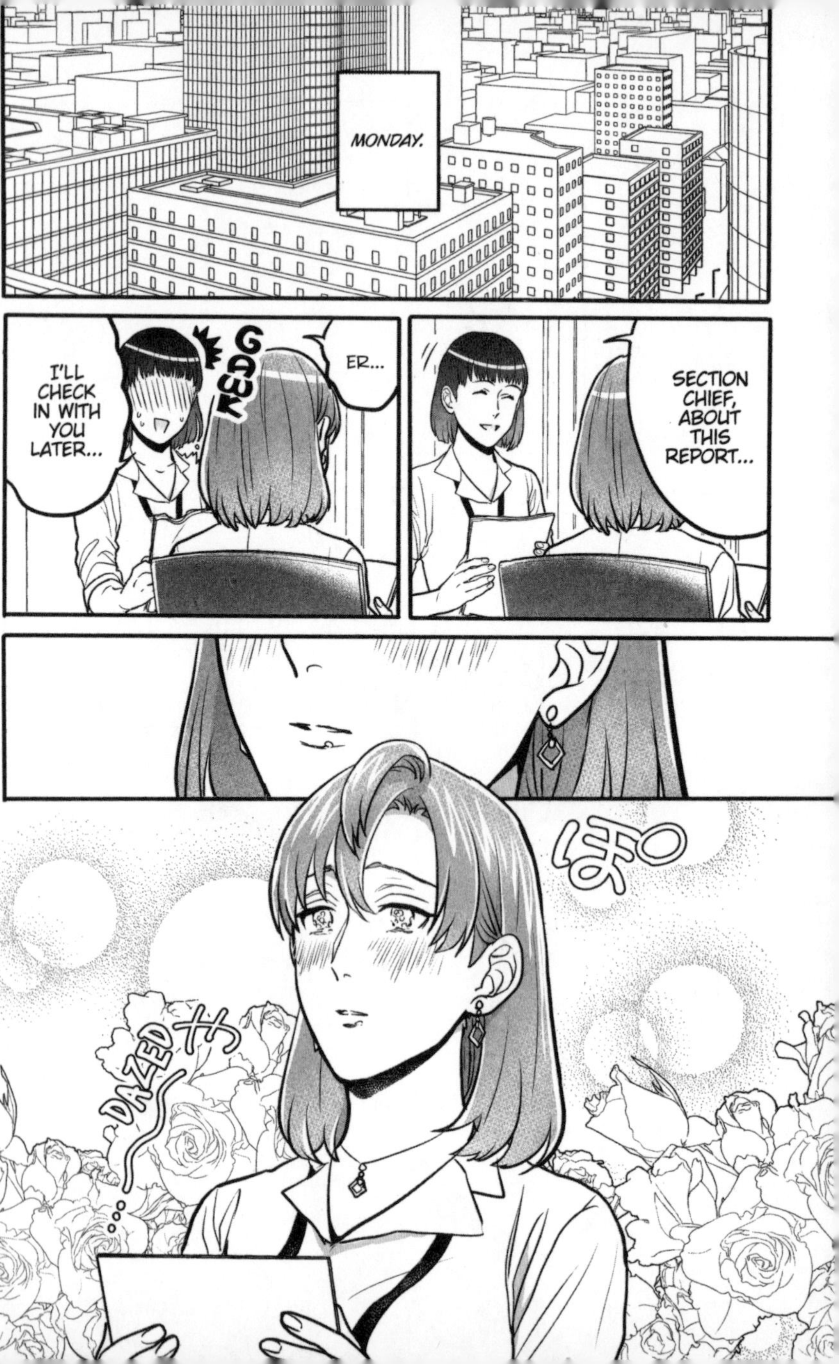
MONDAY.
SECTION CHIEF, ABOUT THIS REPORT...
ER...
GAWK
I'LL CHECK IN WITH YOU LATER...
ぽ
DAZED

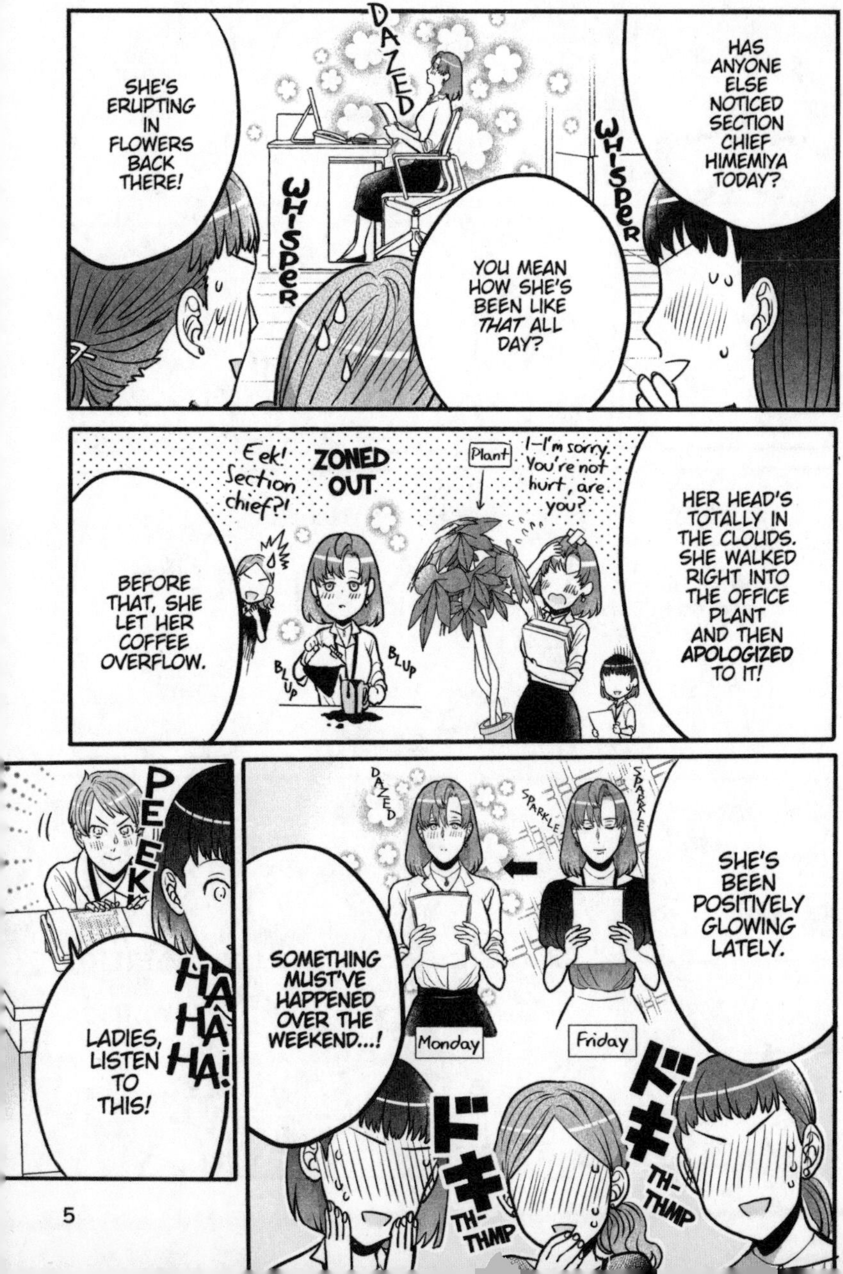
HAS ANYONE ELSE NOTICED SECTION CHIEF HIMEMIYA TODAY?
WHISPER
YOU MEAN HOW SHE'S BEEN LIKE *THAT* ALL DAY?
DAZED
WHISPER
SHE'S ERUPTING IN FLOWERS BACK THERE!
HER HEAD'S TOTALLY IN THE CLOUDS. SHE WALKED RIGHT INTO THE OFFICE PLANT AND THEN **APOLOGIZED** TO IT!
I-I'm sorry. You're not hurt, are you?
Plant
ZONED OUT
Eek! Section chief?!
BEFORE THAT, SHE LET HER COFFEE OVERFLOW.
BLUP
BLUP
SHE'S BEEN POSITIVELY GLOWING LATELY.
SPARKLE
SPARKLE
Friday
DAZED
Monday
SOMETHING MUST'VE HAPPENED OVER THE WEEKEND...!
ドキ
TH-THMP
ドキ
TH-THMP
PEEEK!
HA HA HA!
LADIES, LISTEN TO THIS!

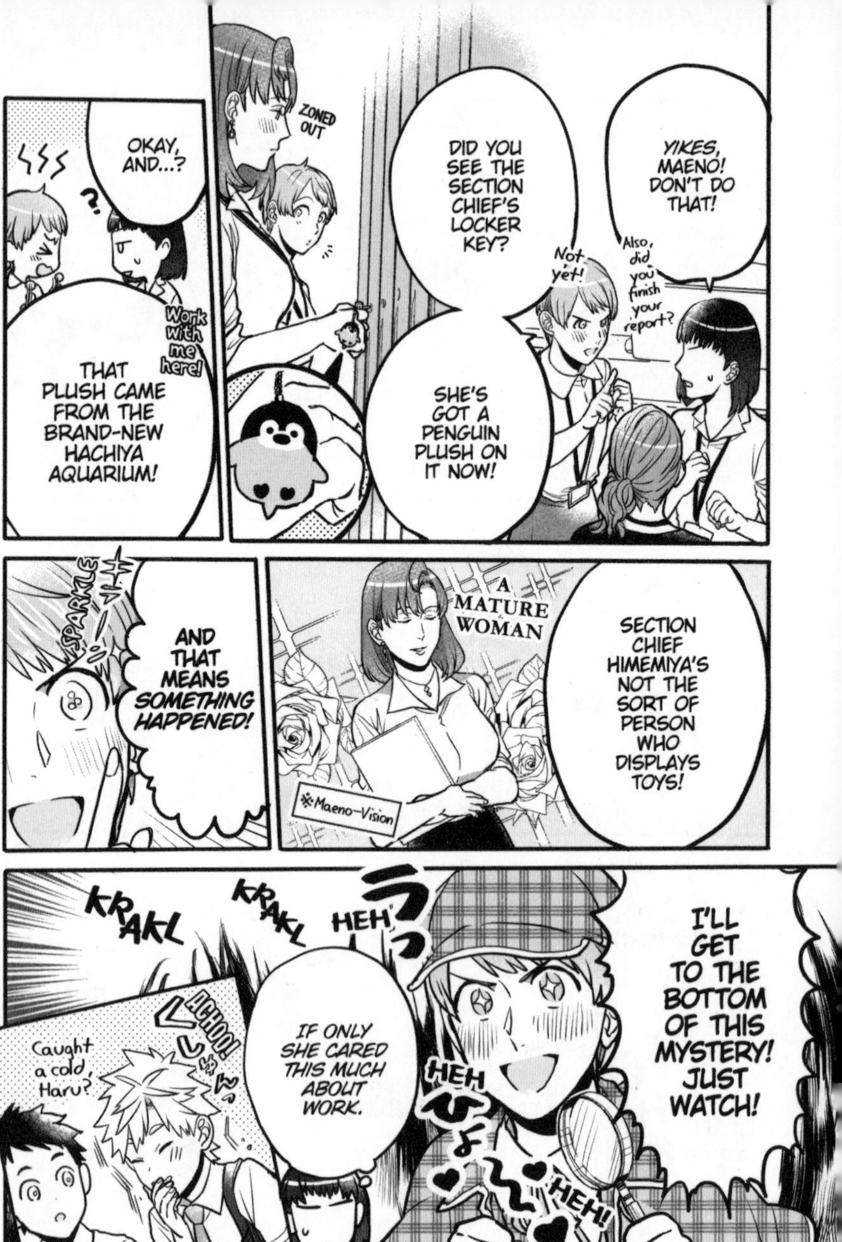
YIKES, MAENO! DON'T DO THAT!
Also, did you finish your report?
Not yet!
DID YOU SEE THE SECTION CHIEF'S LOCKER KEY?
ZONED OUT
SHE'S GOT A PENGUIN PLUSH ON IT NOW!
OKAY, AND...?
?
THAT PLUSH CAME FROM THE BRAND-NEW HACHIYA AQUARIUM!
Work with me here!
SECTION CHIEF HIMEMIYA'S NOT THE SORT OF PERSON WHO DISPLAYS TOYS!
A MATURE WOMAN
※Maeno-Vision
AND THAT MEANS SOMETHING HAPPENED!
SPARKLE
I'LL GET TO THE BOTTOM OF THIS MYSTERY! JUST WATCH!
HEH
HEH
HEH!
KRAKL
KRAKL
IF ONLY SHE CARED THIS MUCH ABOUT WORK.
ACHOO!
Caught a cold, Haru?

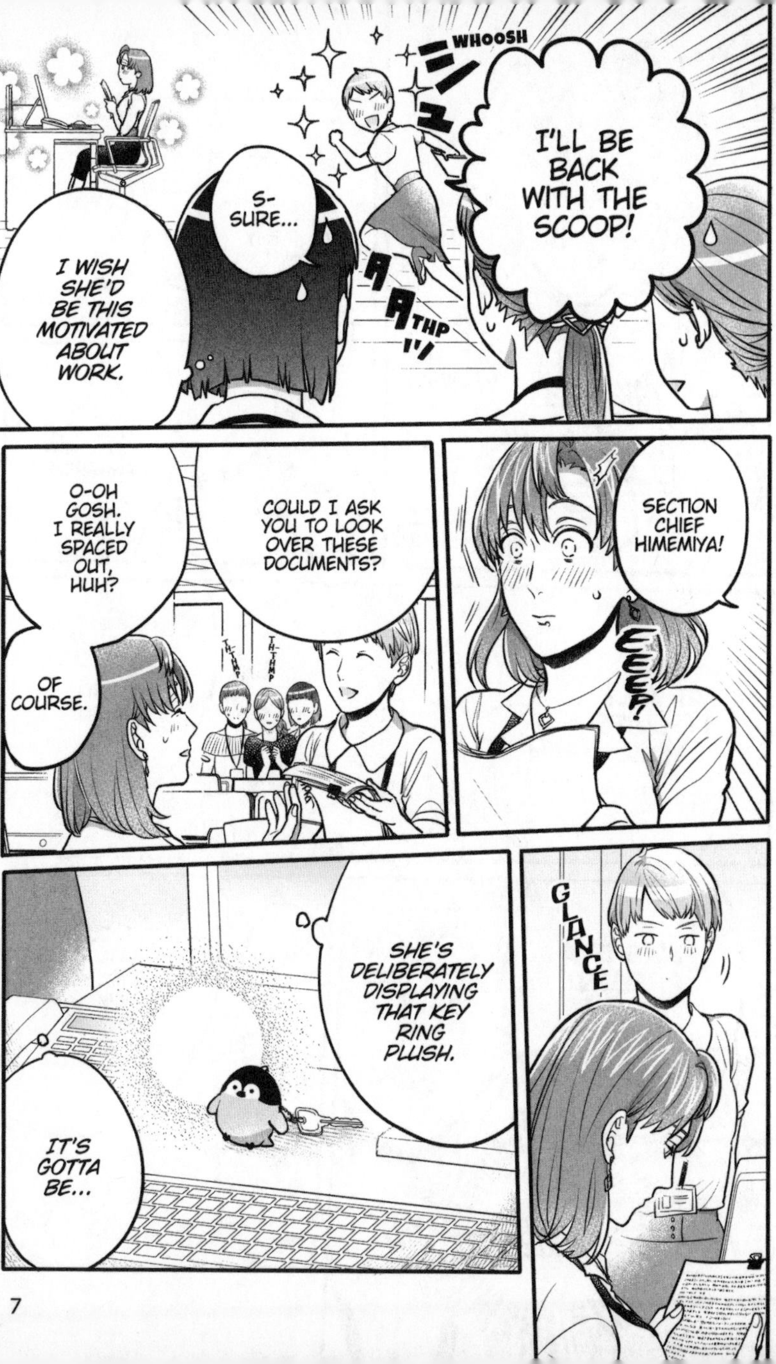
WHOOSH
I'LL BE BACK WITH THE SCOOP!
S-SURE...
THP
I WISH SHE'D BE THIS MOTIVATED ABOUT WORK.
SECTION CHIEF HIMEMIYA!
EEEP!
COULD I ASK YOU TO LOOK OVER THESE DOCUMENTS?
TH-THMP
TH-THMP
O-OH GOSH. I REALLY SPACED OUT, HUH?
OF COURSE.
GLANCE
SHE'S DELIBERATELY DISPLAYING THAT KEY RING PLUSH.
IT'S GOTTA BE...

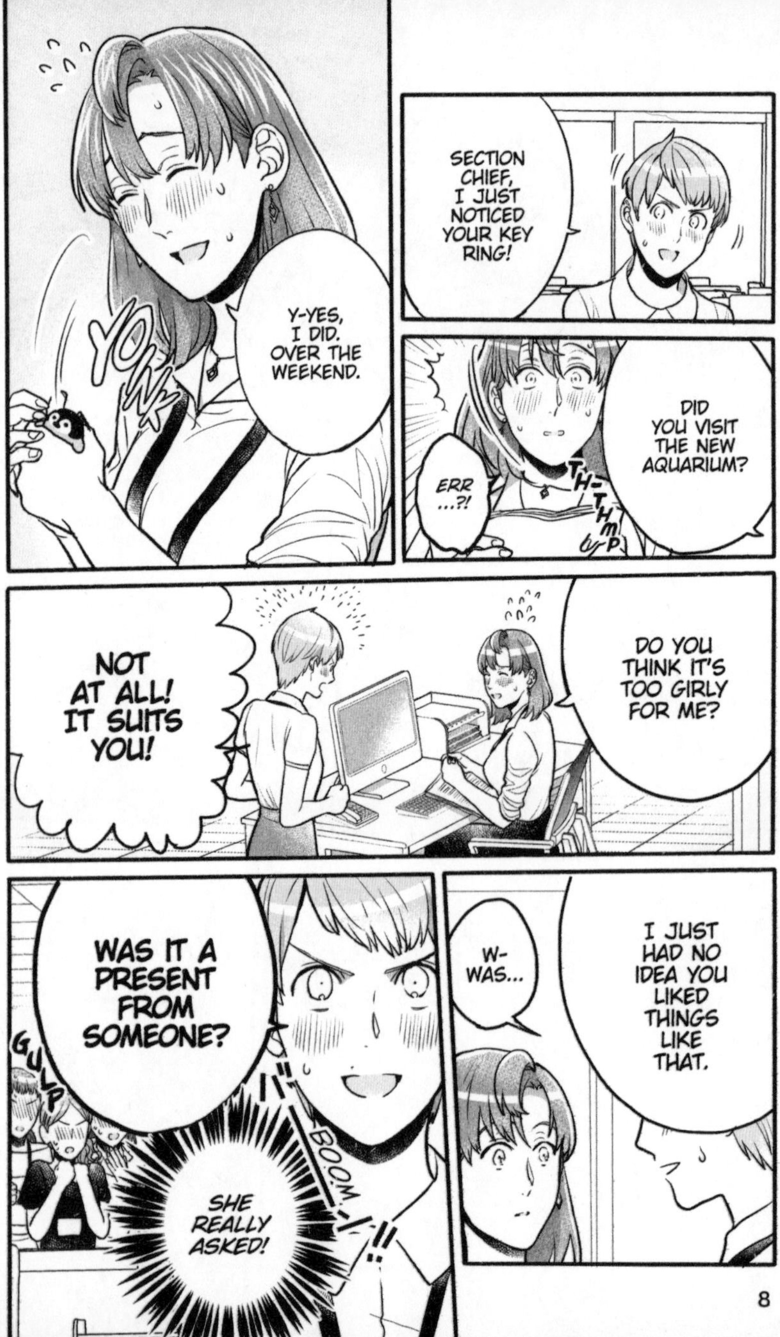
SECTION CHIEF, I JUST NOTICED YOUR KEY RING!
DID YOU VISIT THE NEW AQUARIUM?
ERR ...?!
TH-THUMP
YOINK
Y-YES, I DID. OVER THE WEEKEND.
DO YOU THINK IT'S TOO GIRLY FOR ME?
NOT AT ALL! IT SUITS YOU!
I JUST HAD NO IDEA YOU LIKED THINGS LIKE THAT.
W-WAS...
WAS IT A PRESENT FROM SOMEONE?
GULP
BOOOM
SHE REALLY ASKED!

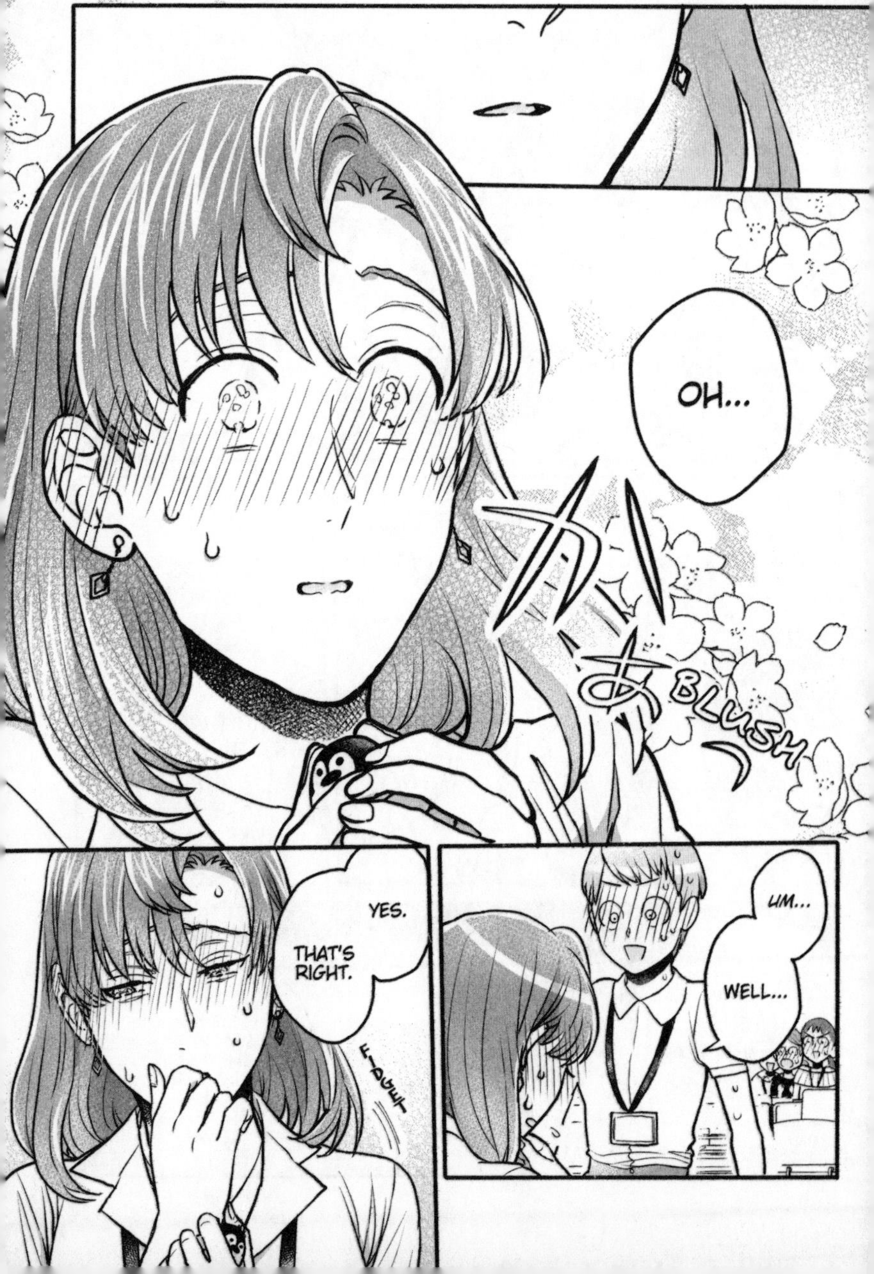
OH...
BLUSH
UM...
WELL...
YES.
THAT'S RIGHT.
FIDGET

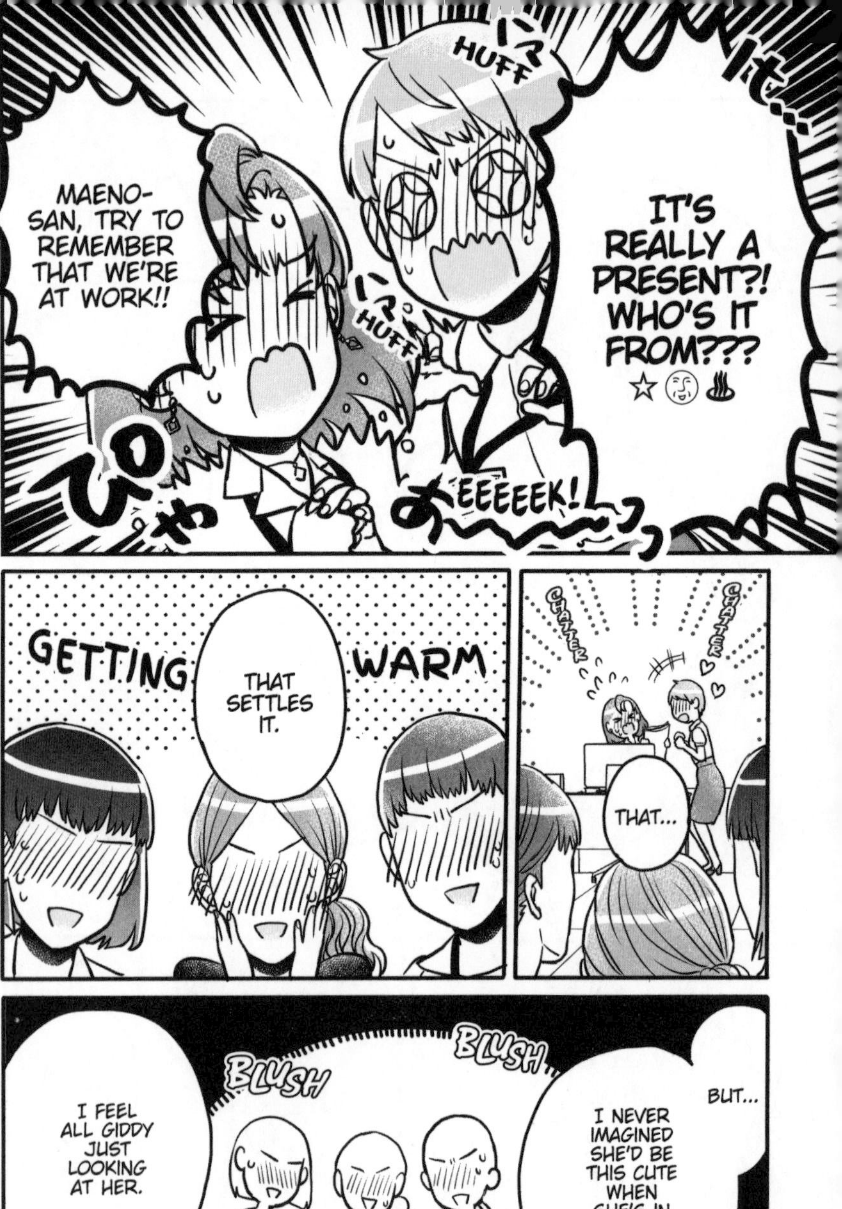
It...
HUFF
IT'S REALLY A PRESENT?! WHO'S IT FROM??? ☆ ♨
HUFF
MAENO-SAN, TRY TO REMEMBER THAT WE'RE AT WORK!!
EEEEEK!
CHATTER
CHATTER
THAT...
GETTING WARM
THAT SETTLES IT.
BUT...
I NEVER IMAGINED SHE'D BE THIS CUTE WHEN SHE'S IN LOVE!
BLUSH
BLUSH
I FEEL ALL GIDDY JUST LOOKING AT HER.

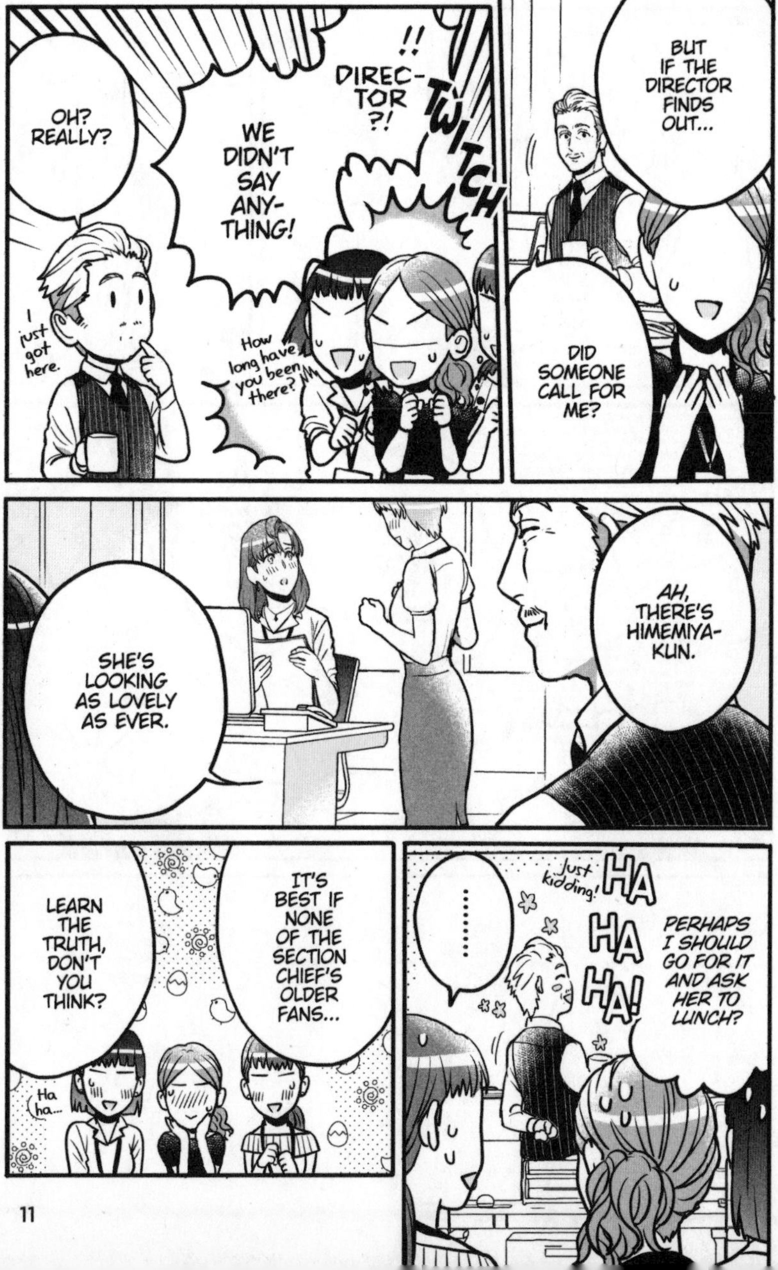
BUT IF THE DIRECTOR FINDS OUT...
DID SOMEONE CALL FOR ME?
!!
DIRECTOR?!
TWITCH
WE DIDN'T SAY ANYTHING!
How long have you been there?
OH? REALLY?
I just got here.
AH, THERE'S HIMEMIYA-KUN.
SHE'S LOOKING AS LOVELY AS EVER.
PERHAPS I SHOULD GO FOR IT AND ASK HER TO LUNCH?
HA HA HA!
Just kidding!
....
IT'S BEST IF NONE OF THE SECTION CHIEF'S OLDER FANS...
LEARN THE TRUTH, DON'T YOU THINK?
Ha ha...

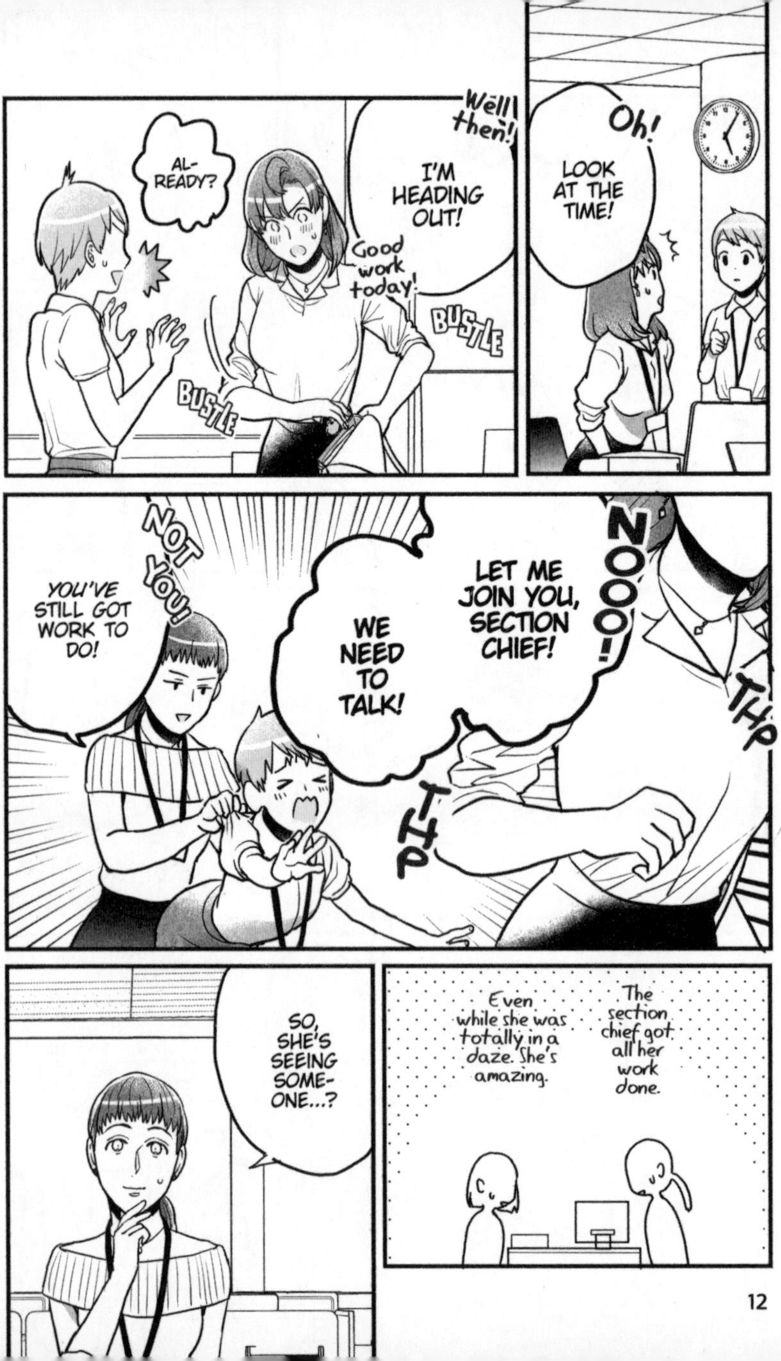
Oh!
LOOK AT THE TIME!
Well then!
I'M HEADING OUT!
Good work today!
BUSTLE
BUSTLE
AL-READY?
NOOOO!
THP
LET ME JOIN YOU, SECTION CHIEF!
WE NEED TO TALK!
THP
NOT YOU!
YOU'VE STILL GOT WORK TO DO!
The section chief got all her work done.
Even while she was totally in a daze. She's amazing.
SO, SHE'S SEEING SOME-ONE...?

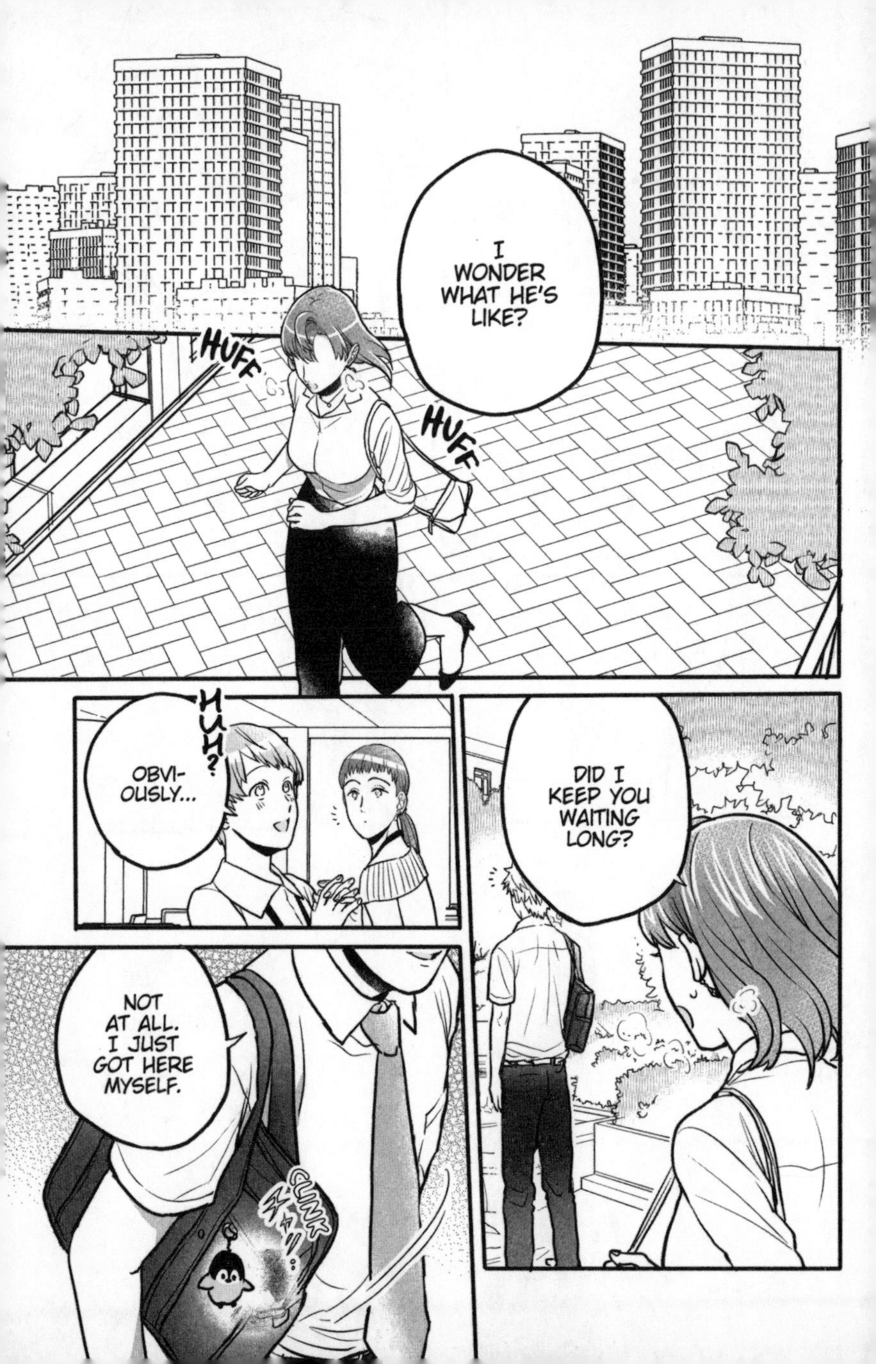
I WONDER WHAT HE'S LIKE?
HUFF
HUFF
DID I KEEP YOU WAITING LONG?
HUH?
OBVI-OUSLY...
NOT AT ALL. I JUST GOT HERE MYSELF.
CLINK

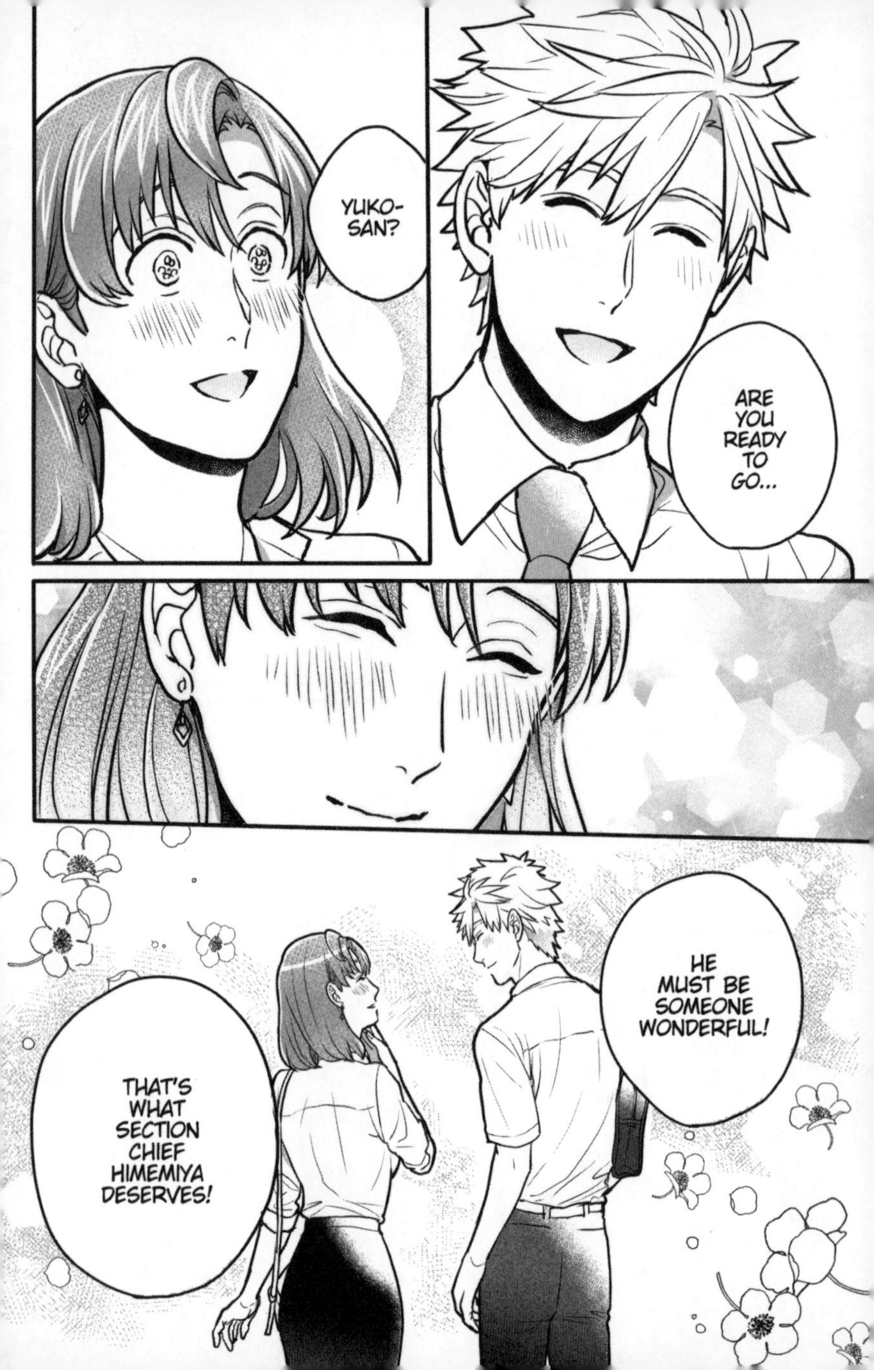
ARE YOU READY TO GO...
YUKO-SAN?
HE MUST BE SOMEONE WONDERFUL!
THAT'S WHAT SECTION CHIEF HIMEMIYA DESERVES!

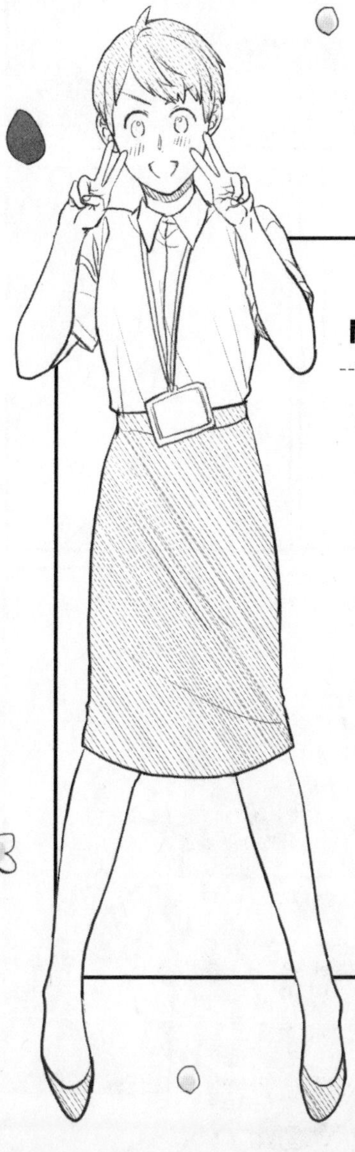

Maeno Yume (23)

The very picture of a bright-eyed new employee. She's always making blunders at work, but her bubbly enthusiasm and chatty nature have earned the affection of her fellow employees...reluctantly.

She's a big fan of the beautiful, talented, and kind section chief Himemiya, and is thrilled to be working in her department. She also admires Himeyama's womanly figure, and often finds herself thinking about it. It's time to focus on work, Maeno-san!

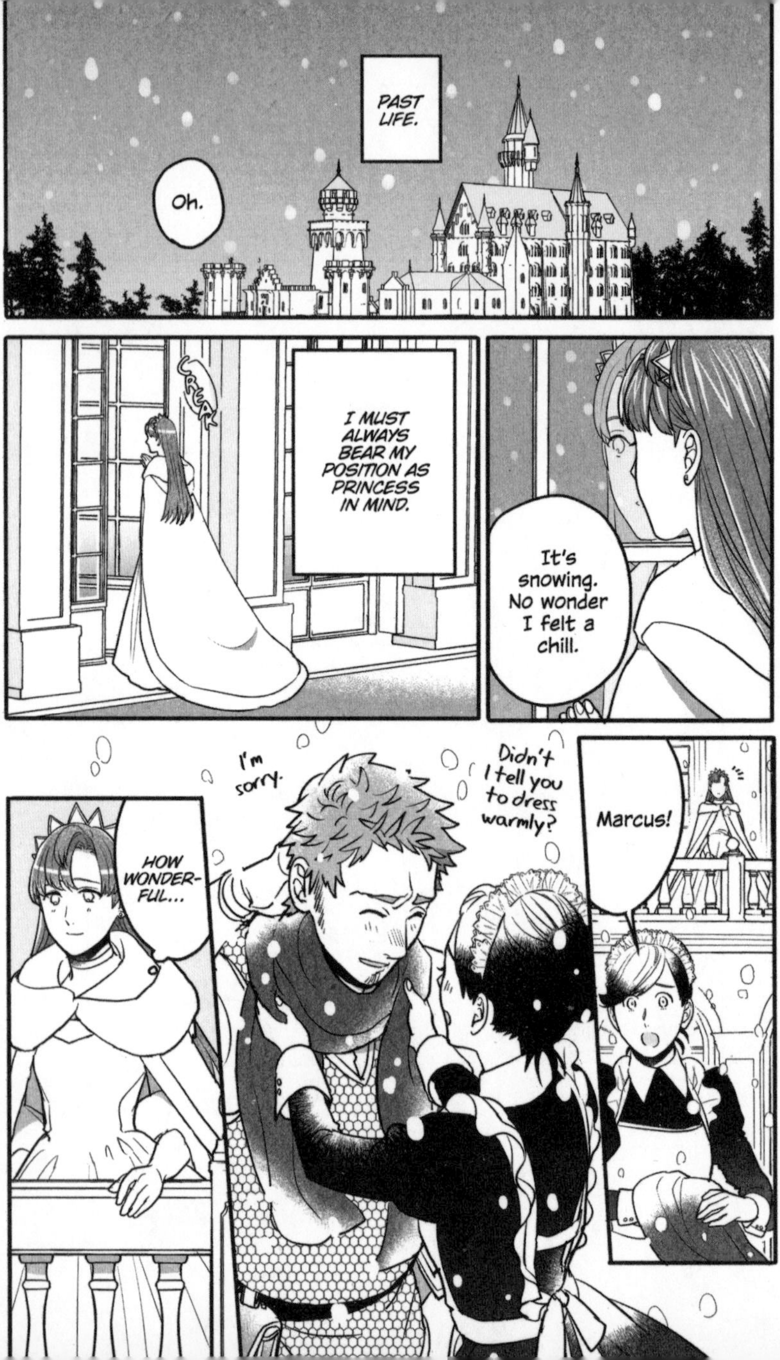
PAST LIFE.
Oh.
It's snowing. No wonder I felt a chill.
I MUST ALWAYS BEAR MY POSITION AS PRINCESS IN MIND.
CREAK
Marcus!
Didn't I tell you to dress warmly?
I'm sorry.
HOW WONDER-FUL...

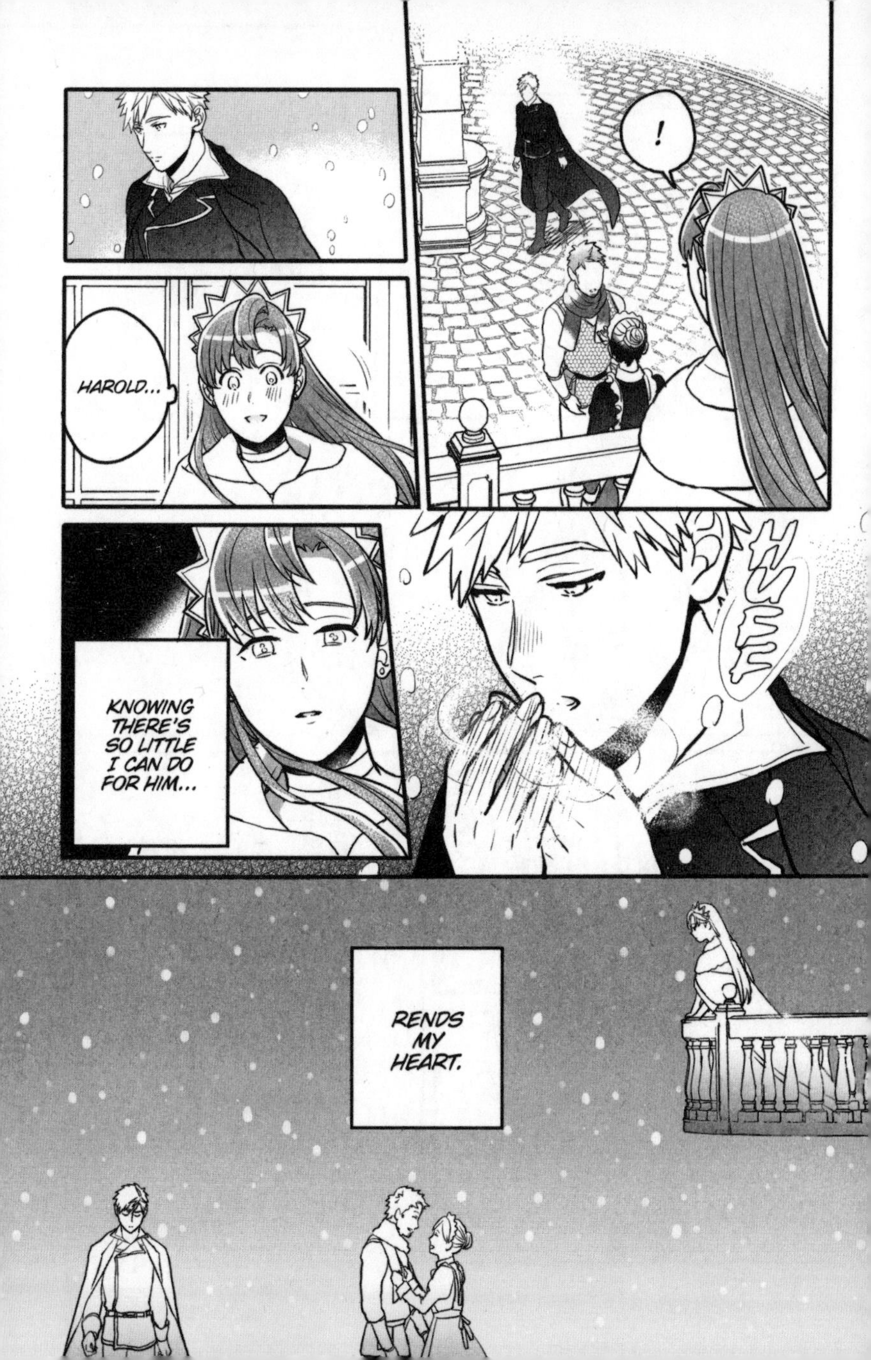
!
HAROLD...
HUFF
KNOWING THERE'S SO LITTLE I CAN DO FOR HIM...
RENDS MY HEART.

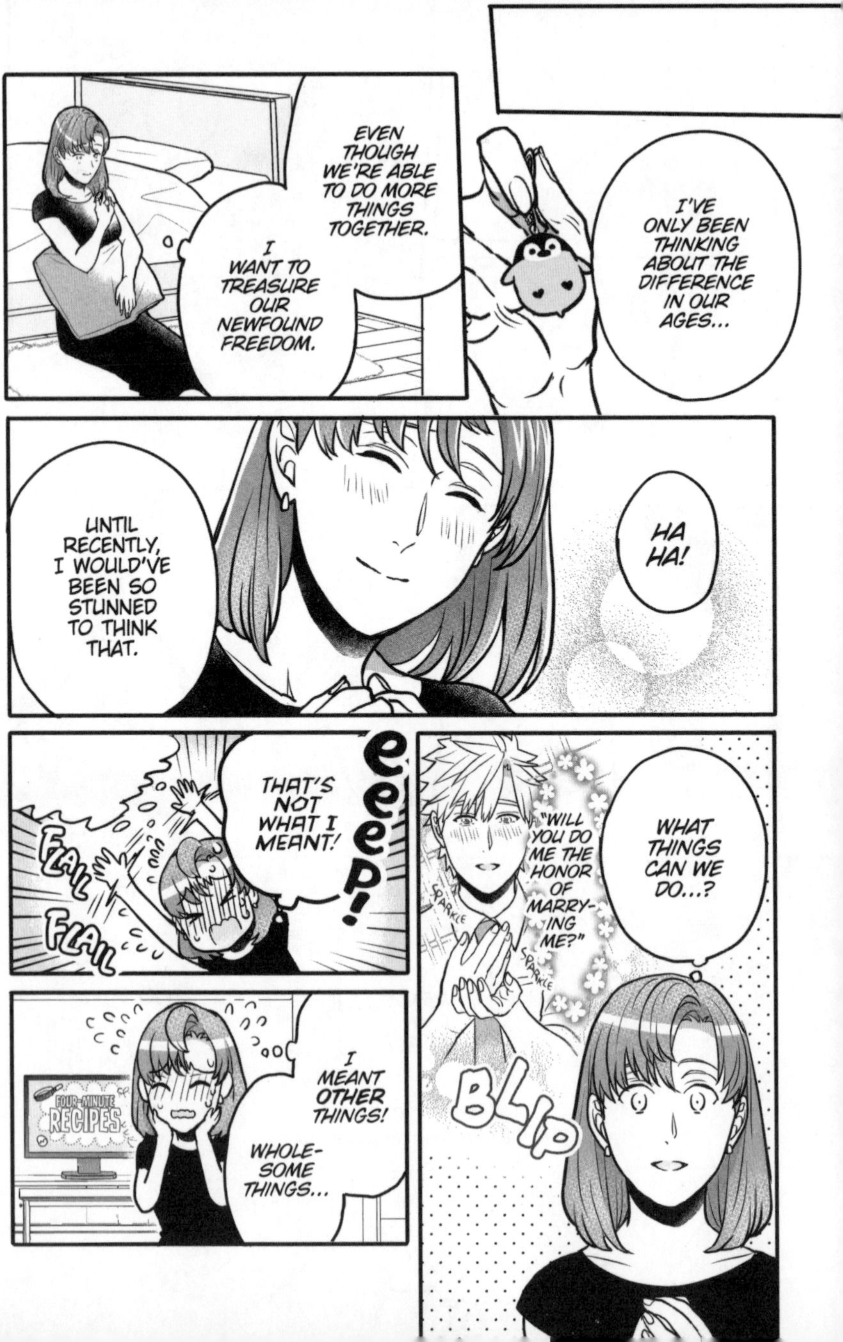
I'VE ONLY BEEN THINKING ABOUT THE DIFFERENCE IN OUR AGES...
EVEN THOUGH WE'RE ABLE TO DO MORE THINGS TOGETHER.
I WANT TO TREASURE OUR NEWFOUND FREEDOM.
HA HA!
UNTIL RECENTLY, I WOULD'VE BEEN SO STUNNED TO THINK THAT.
WHAT THINGS CAN WE DO...?
"WILL YOU DO ME THE HONOR OF MARRY-ING ME?"
SPARKLE
SPARKLE
BLIP
EEEEP!
THAT'S NOT WHAT I MEANT!
FLAIL
FLAIL
I MEANT OTHER THINGS!
WHOLE-SOME THINGS...
FOUR-MINUTE RECIPES

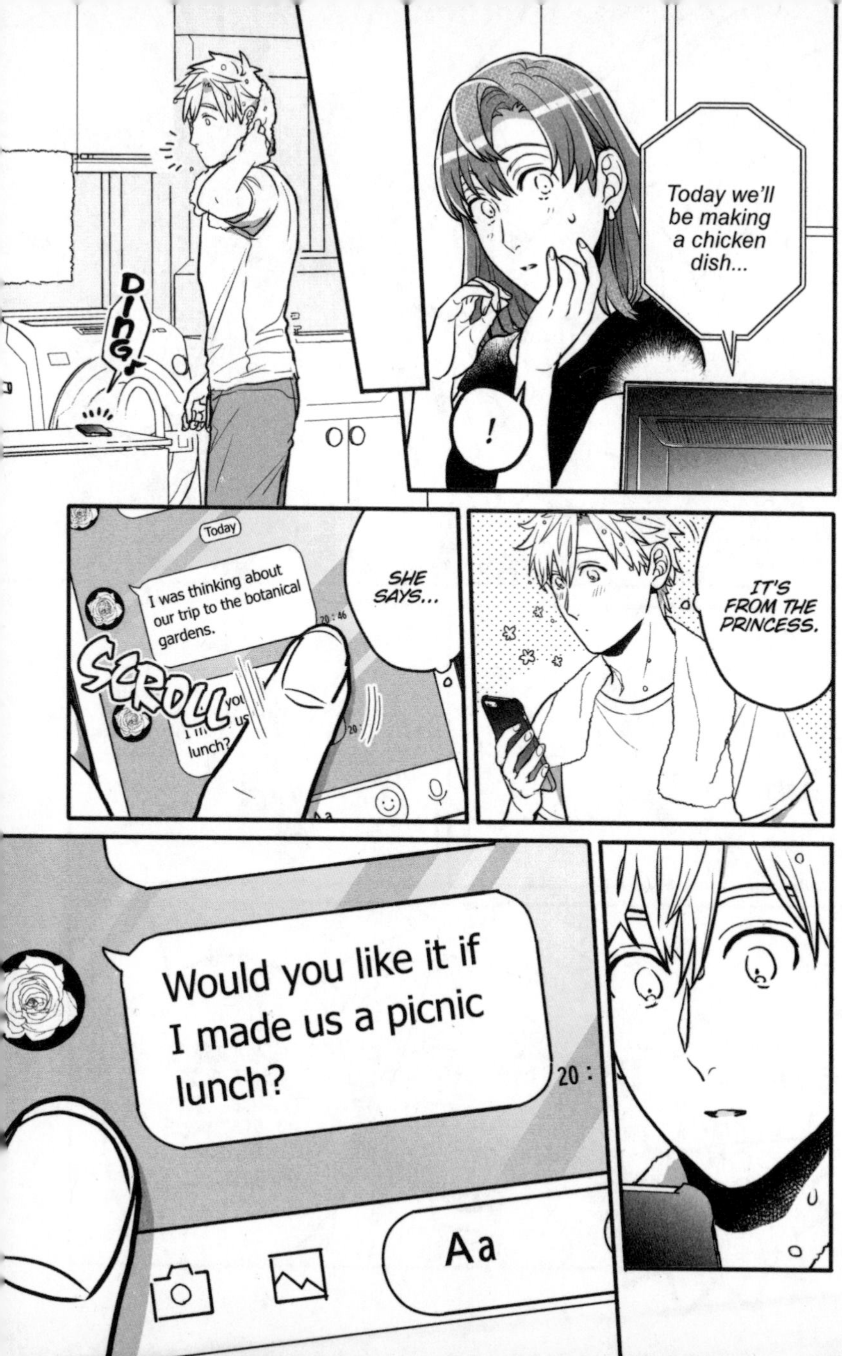
Today we'll be making a chicken dish...
!
DING♪
IT'S FROM THE PRINCESS.
SHE SAYS...
Today
I was thinking about our trip to the botanical gardens.
20 : 46
SCROLL
Would you like it if I made us a picnic lunch?
20 :
Aa

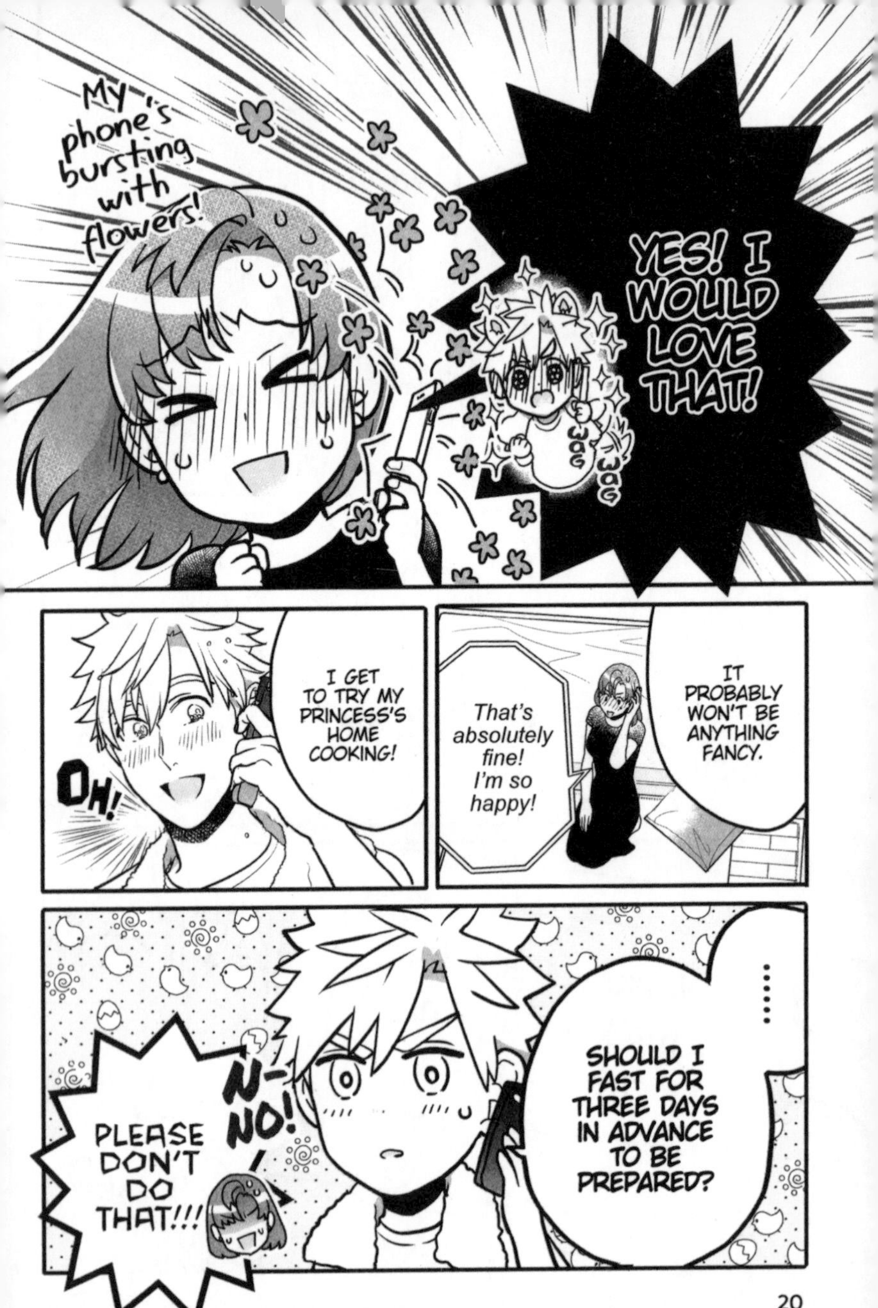
YES! I WOULD LOVE THAT!
WAG WAG
My phone's bursting with flowers!
IT PROBABLY WON'T BE ANYTHING FANCY.
That's absolutely fine! I'm so happy!
I GET TO TRY MY PRINCESS'S HOME COOKING!
OH!
......
SHOULD I FAST FOR THREE DAYS IN ADVANCE TO BE PREPARED?
N-NO!
PLEASE DON'T DO THAT!!!

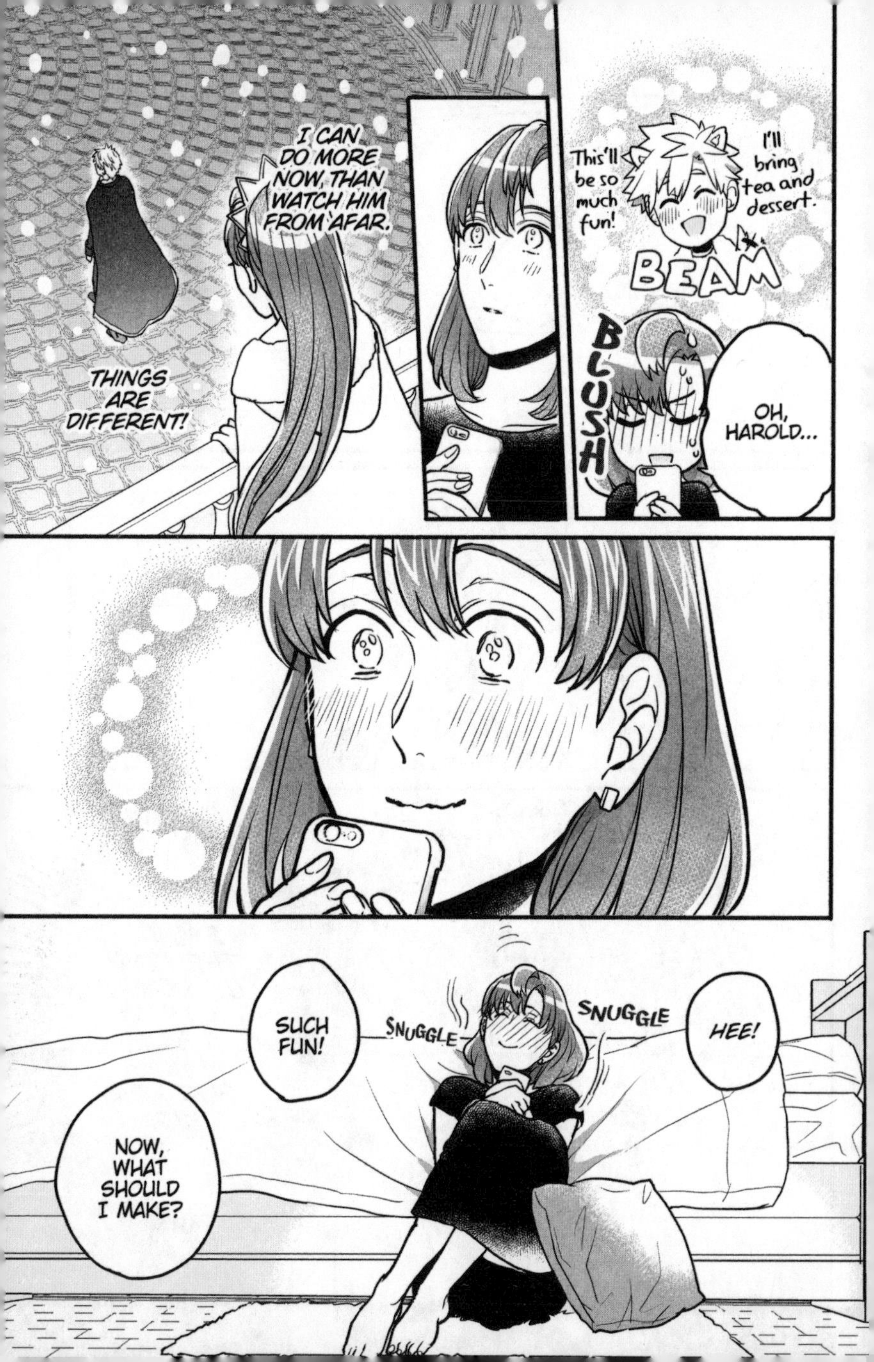
I'll bring tea and dessert.
This'll be so much fun!
BEAM
OH, HAROLD...
BLUSH
I CAN DO MORE NOW, THAN WATCH HIM FROM AFAR.
THINGS ARE DIFFERENT!
HEE!
SNUGGLE
SUCH FUN!
SNUGGLE
NOW, WHAT SHOULD I MAKE?

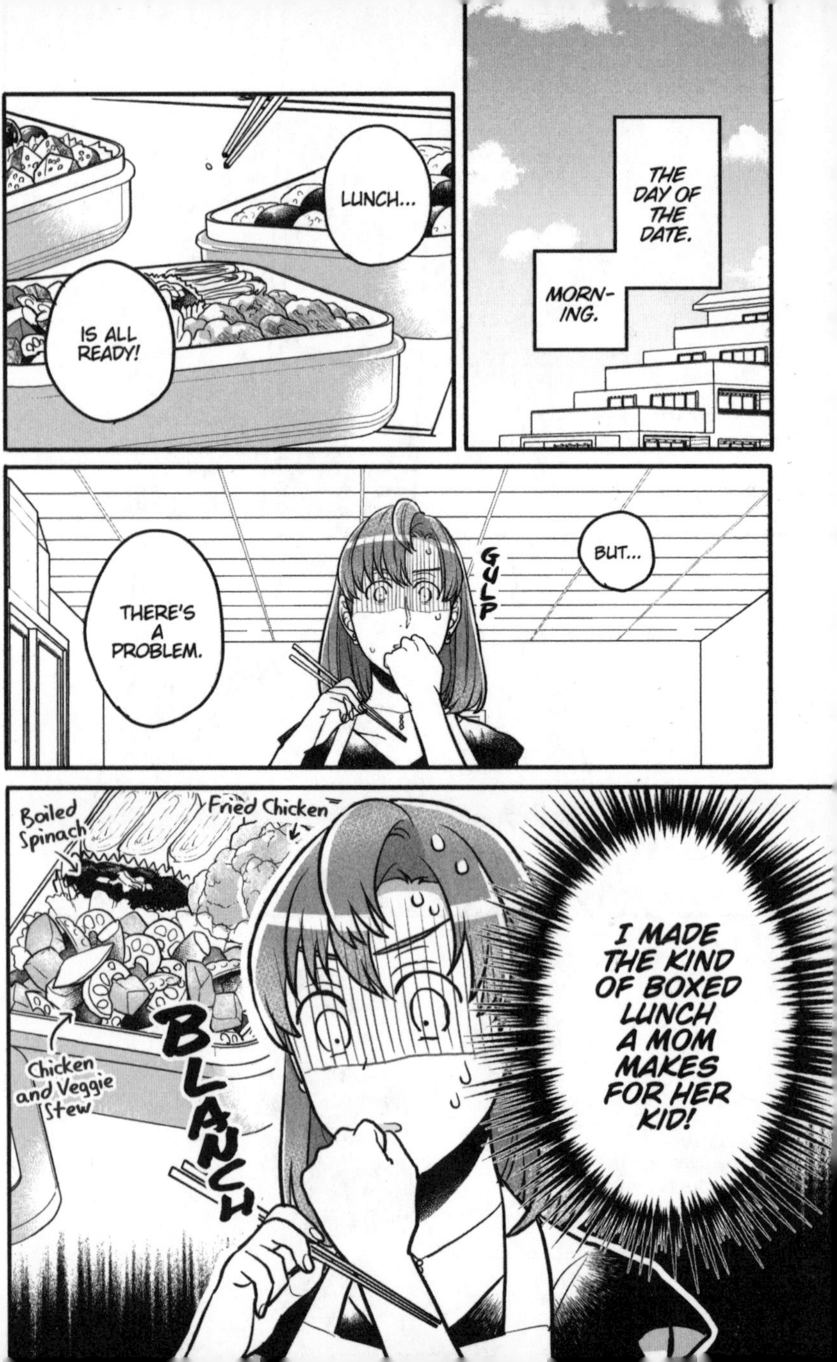
THE DAY OF THE DATE.
MORN-ING.
LUNCH...
IS ALL READY!
BUT...
GULP
THERE'S A PROBLEM.
I MADE THE KIND OF BOXED LUNCH A MOM MAKES FOR HER KID!
Fried Chicken
Boiled Spinach
BLANCH
Chicken and Veggie Stew

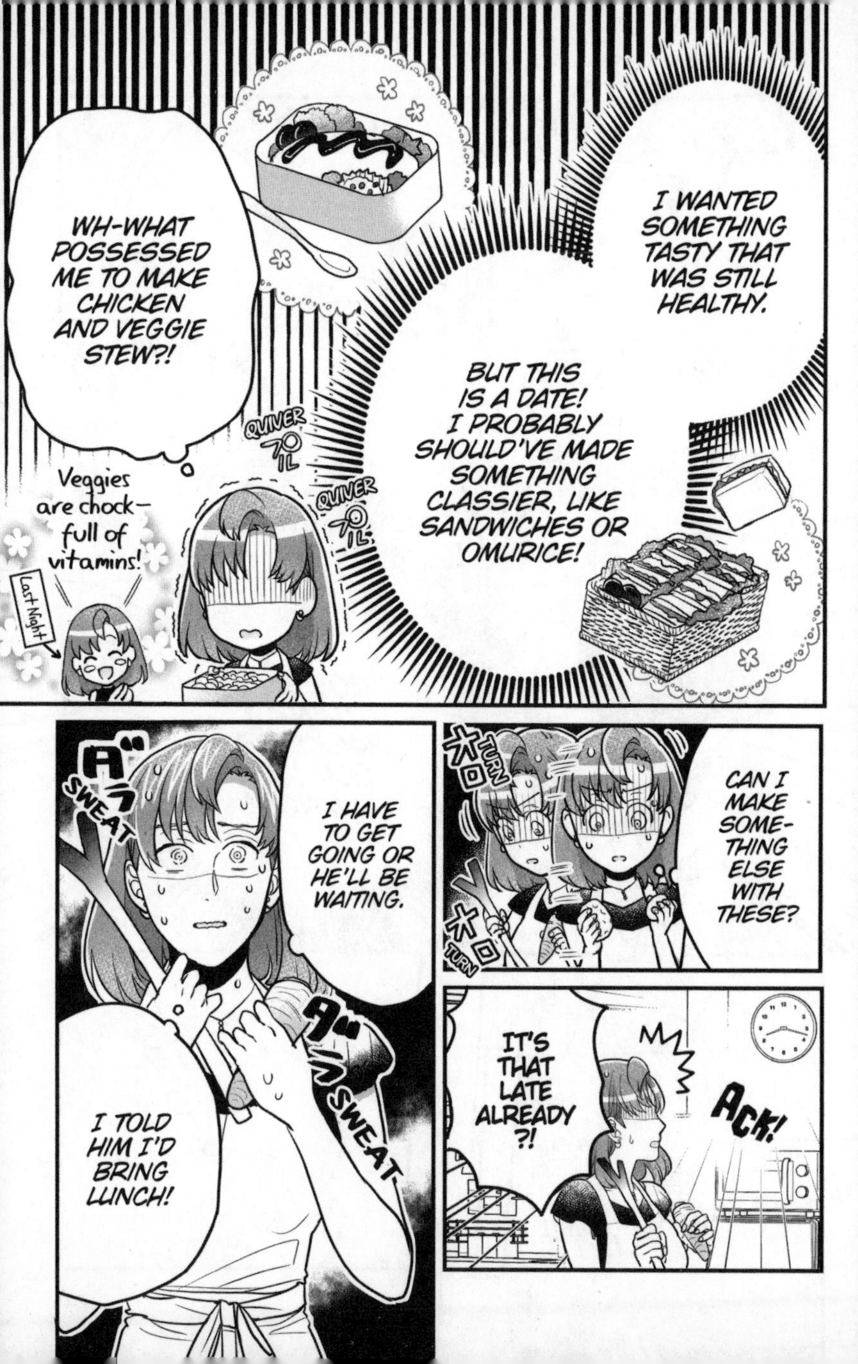
I WANTED SOMETHING TASTY THAT WAS STILL HEALTHY.
BUT THIS IS A DATE! I PROBABLY SHOULD'VE MADE SOMETHING CLASSIER, LIKE SANDWICHES OR OMURICE!
WH-WHAT POSSESSED ME TO MAKE CHICKEN AND VEGGIE STEW?!
QUIVER
QUIVER
Veggies are chock-full of vitamins!
Last Night
TURN
TURN
CAN I MAKE SOME-THING ELSE WITH THESE?
IT'S THAT LATE ALREADY?!
ACK!
SWEAT
I HAVE TO GET GOING OR HE'LL BE WAITING.
I TOLD HIM I'D BRING LUNCH!
SWEAT

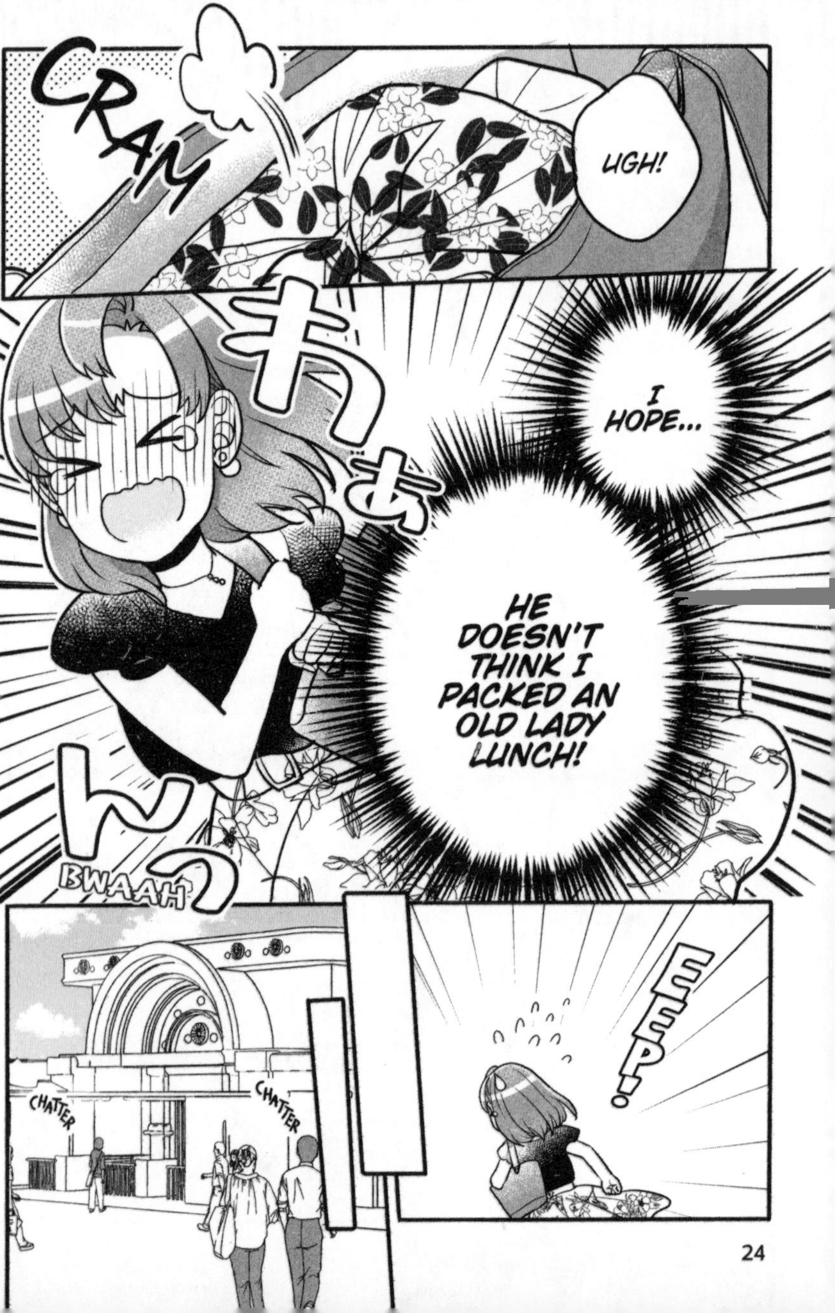
UGH!
CRAM
I HOPE...
HE DOESN'T THINK I PACKED AN OLD LADY LUNCH!
わぁんっ
BWAAH
EEEP!
CHATTER
CHATTER

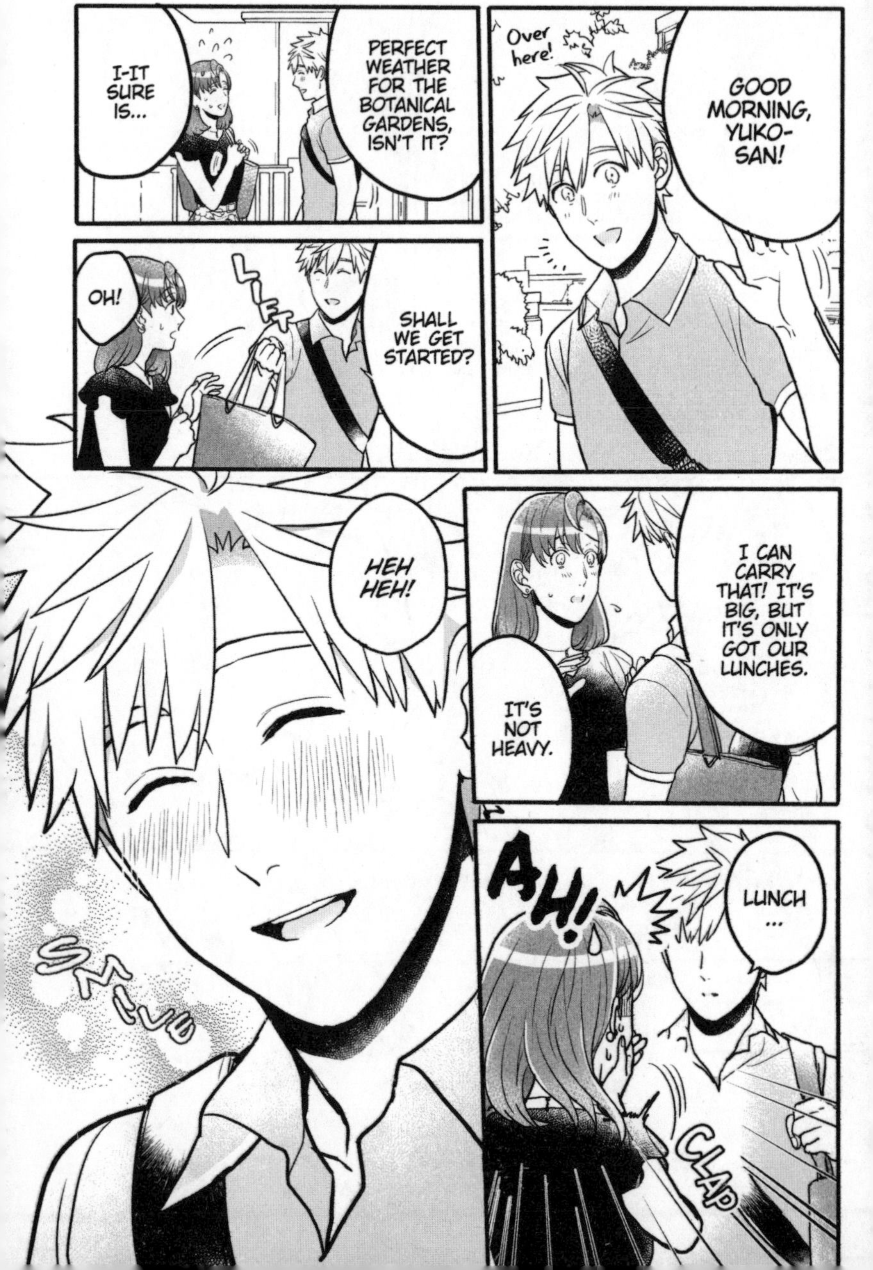
Over here!
GOOD MORNING, YUKO-SAN!
PERFECT WEATHER FOR THE BOTANICAL GARDENS, ISN'T IT?
I-IT SURE IS...
SHALL WE GET STARTED?
LIFT
OH!
I CAN CARRY THAT! IT'S BIG, BUT IT'S ONLY GOT OUR LUNCHES.
IT'S NOT HEAVY.
LUNCH ...
AH!
CLAP
HEH HEH!
SMILE

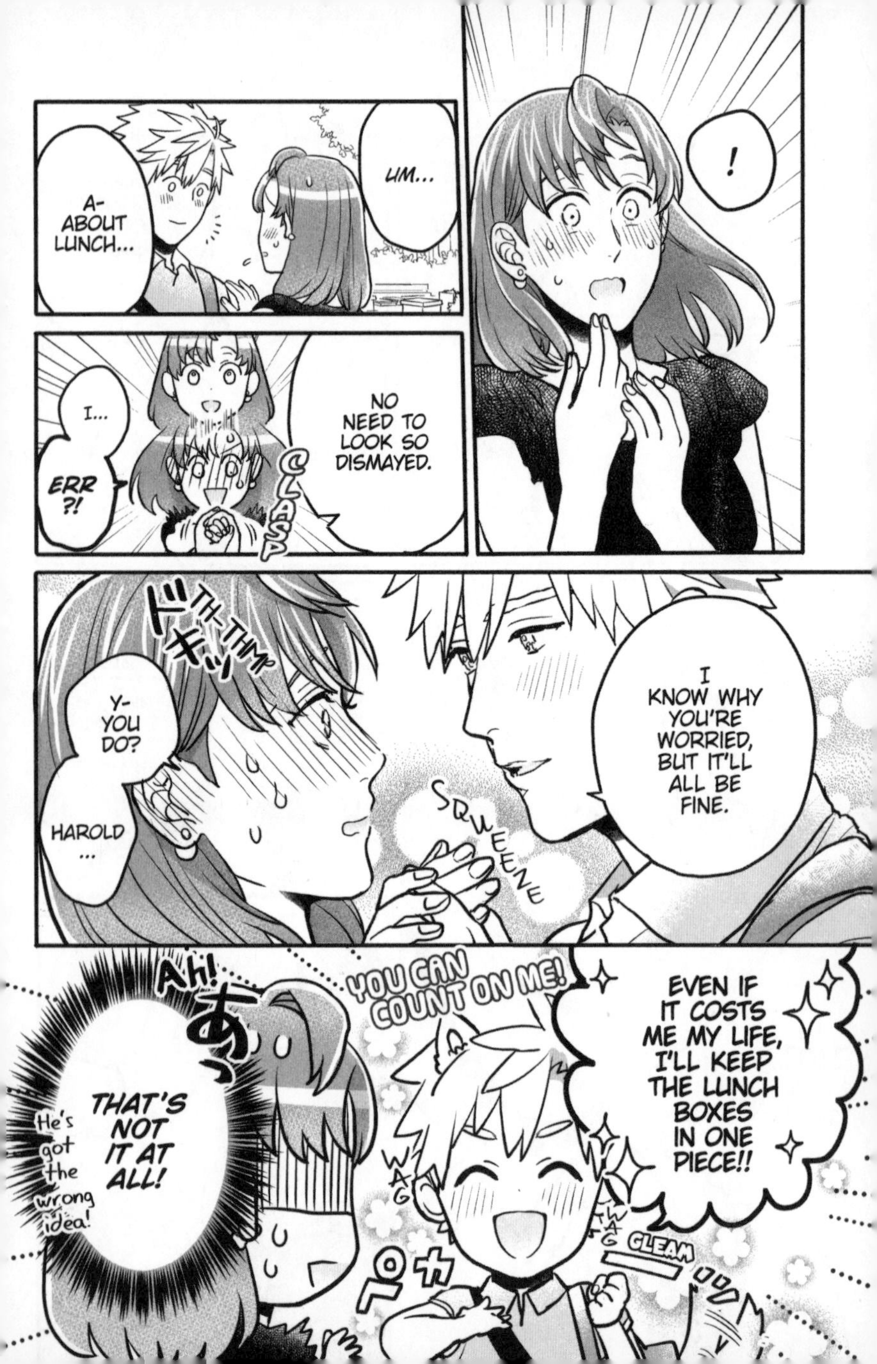
!
UM...
A-ABOUT LUNCH...
NO NEED TO LOOK SO DISMAYED.
CLASP
I...
ERR?!
I KNOW WHY YOU'RE WORRIED, BUT IT'LL ALL BE FINE.
TH-THMP
SQUEEZE
Y-YOU DO?
HAROLD...
EVEN IF IT COSTS ME MY LIFE, I'LL KEEP THE LUNCH BOXES IN ONE PIECE!!
YOU CAN COUNT ON ME!
WAG WAG
GLEAM
Ah!
THAT'S NOT IT AT ALL!
He's got the wrong idea!

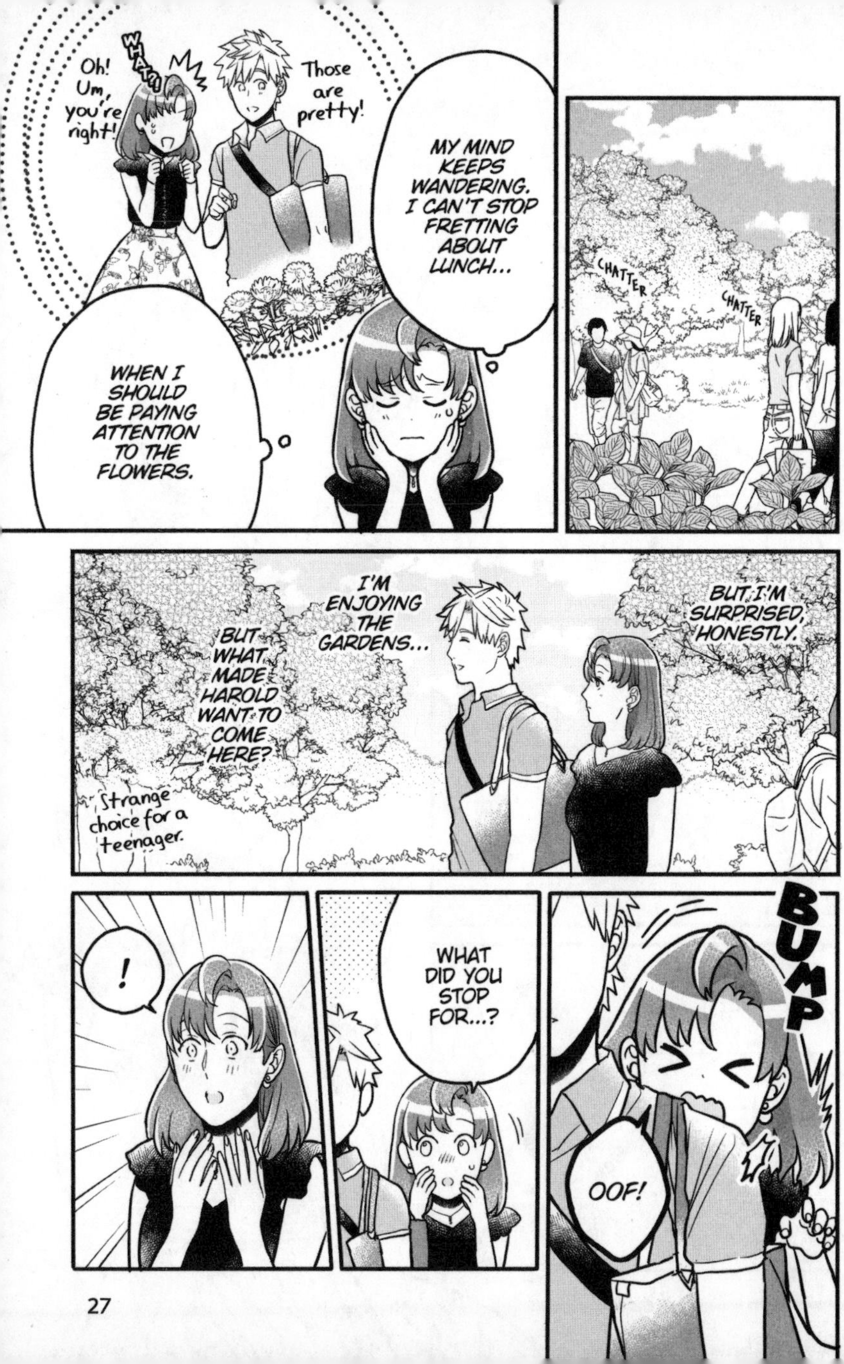
CHATTER
CHATTER
MY MIND KEEPS WANDERING. I CAN'T STOP FRETTING ABOUT LUNCH...
Those are pretty!
WHAT?!
Oh! Um, you're right!
WHEN I SHOULD BE PAYING ATTENTION TO THE FLOWERS.
BUT I'M SURPRISED, HONESTLY.
I'M ENJOYING THE GARDENS...
BUT WHAT MADE HAROLD WANT TO COME HERE?
Strange choice for a teenager.
BUMP
OOF!
WHAT DID YOU STOP FOR...?
!

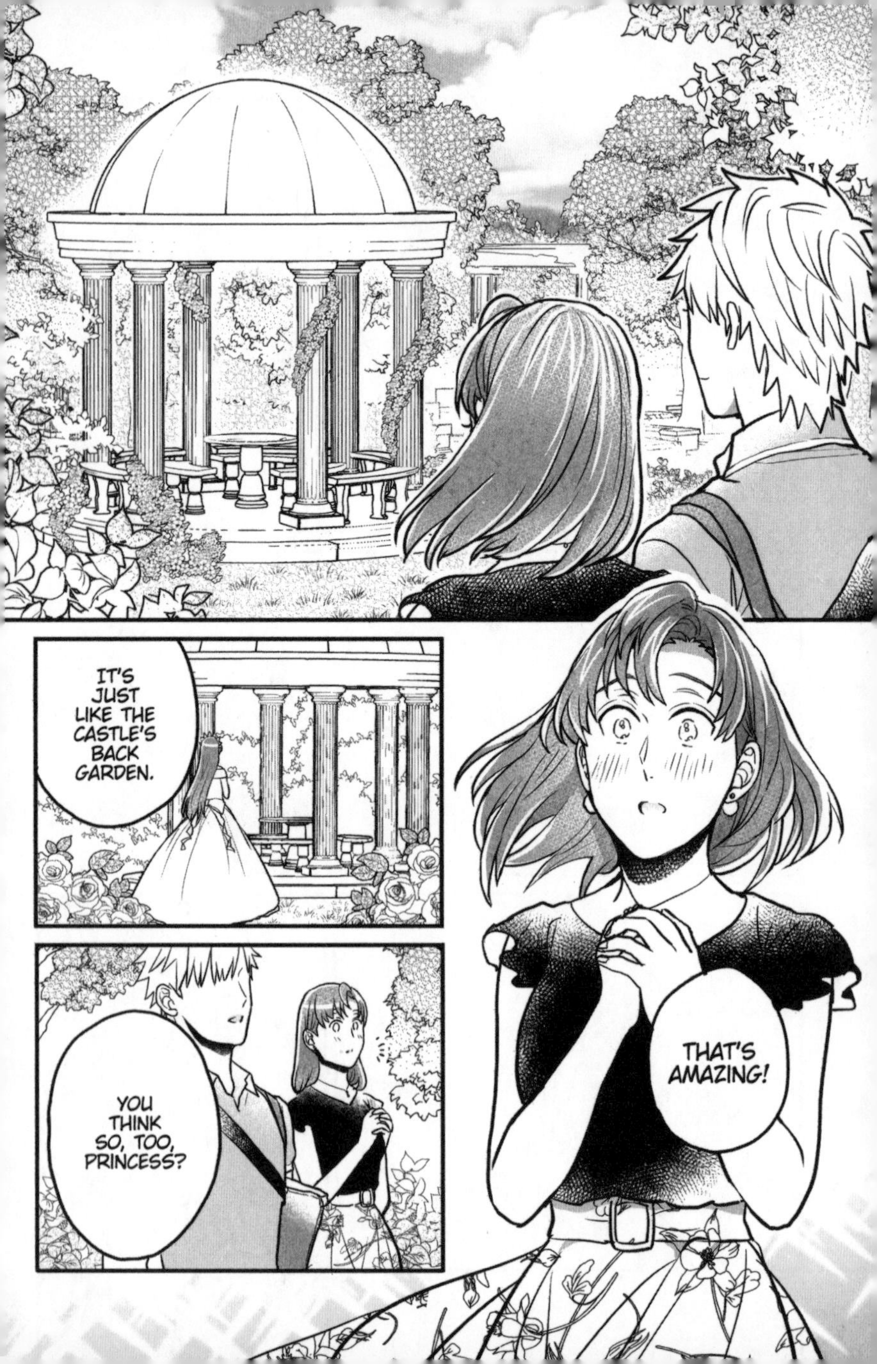
THAT'S AMAZING!
IT'S JUST LIKE THE CASTLE'S BACK GARDEN.
YOU THINK SO, TOO, PRINCESS?

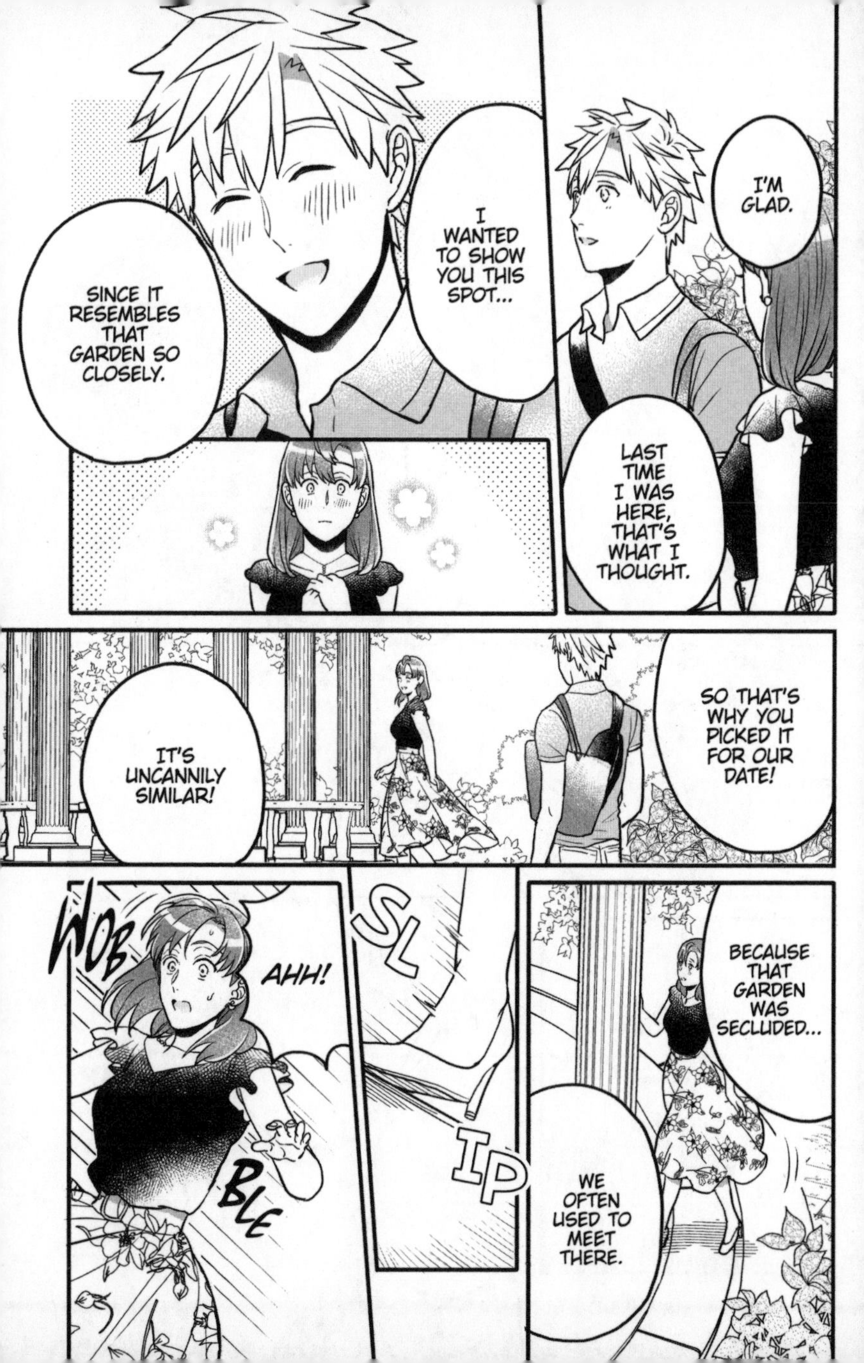
I'M GLAD.
LAST TIME I WAS HERE, THAT'S WHAT I THOUGHT.
I WANTED TO SHOW YOU THIS SPOT...
SINCE IT RESEMBLES THAT GARDEN SO CLOSELY.
SO THAT'S WHY YOU PICKED IT FOR OUR DATE!
IT'S UNCANNILY SIMILAR!
BECAUSE THAT GARDEN WAS SECLUDED...
WE OFTEN USED TO MEET THERE.
SL
IP
WOB
AHH!
BLE

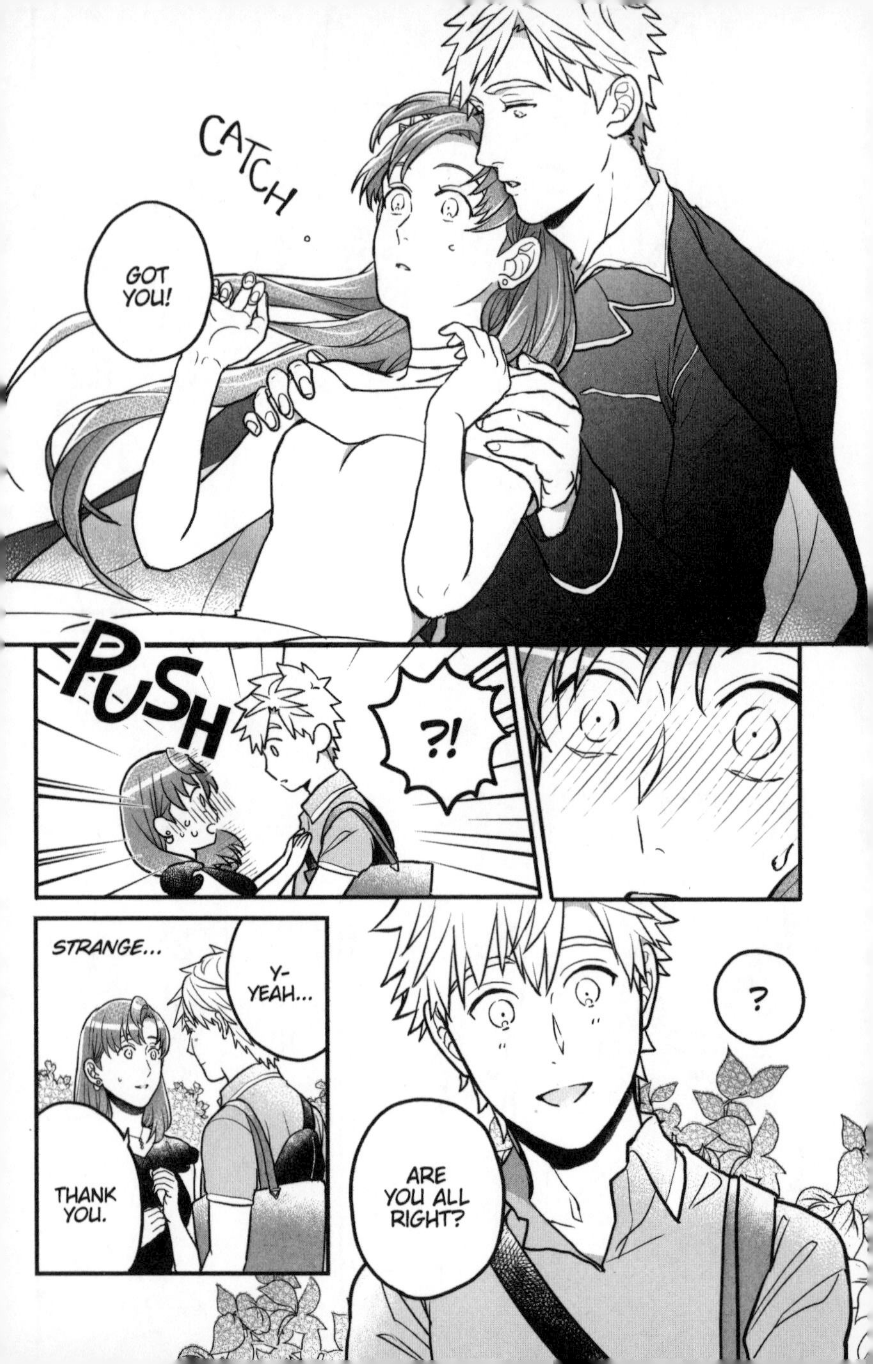
CATCH
GOT YOU!
PUSH
?!
?
ARE YOU ALL RIGHT?
Y-YEAH...
STRANGE...
THANK YOU.

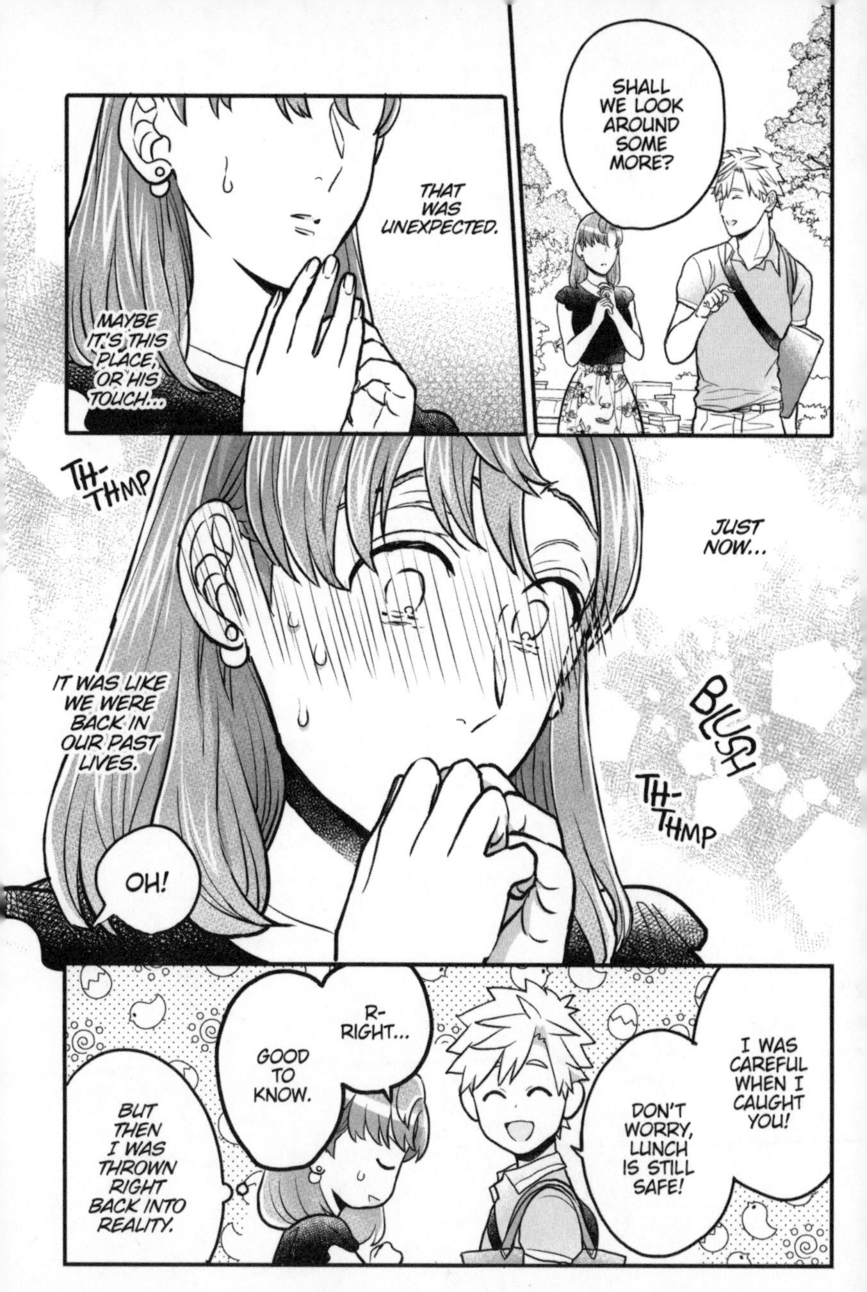
SHALL WE LOOK AROUND SOME MORE?
THAT WAS UNEXPECTED.
MAYBE IT'S THIS PLACE, OR HIS TOUCH...
JUST NOW...
BLUSH
TH-THMP
TH-THMP
IT WAS LIKE WE WERE BACK IN OUR PAST LIVES.
OH!
I WAS CAREFUL WHEN I CAUGHT YOU!
DON'T WORRY, LUNCH IS STILL SAFE!
R-RIGHT...
GOOD TO KNOW.
BUT THEN I WAS THROWN RIGHT BACK INTO REALITY.

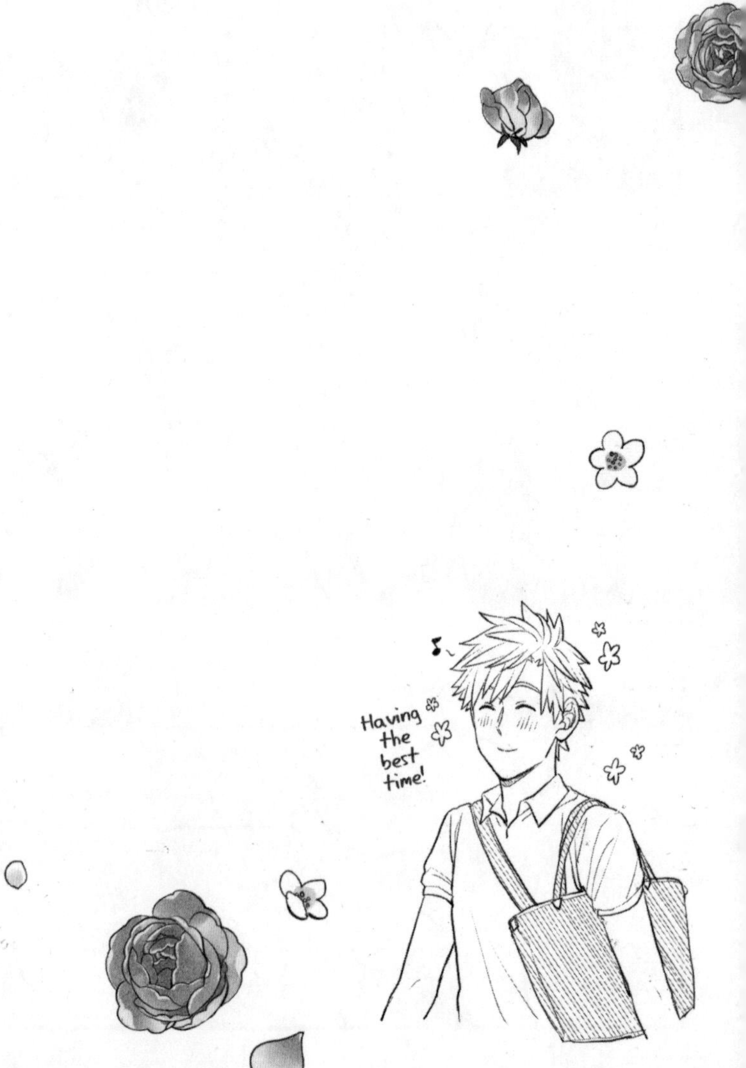
Having the best time!

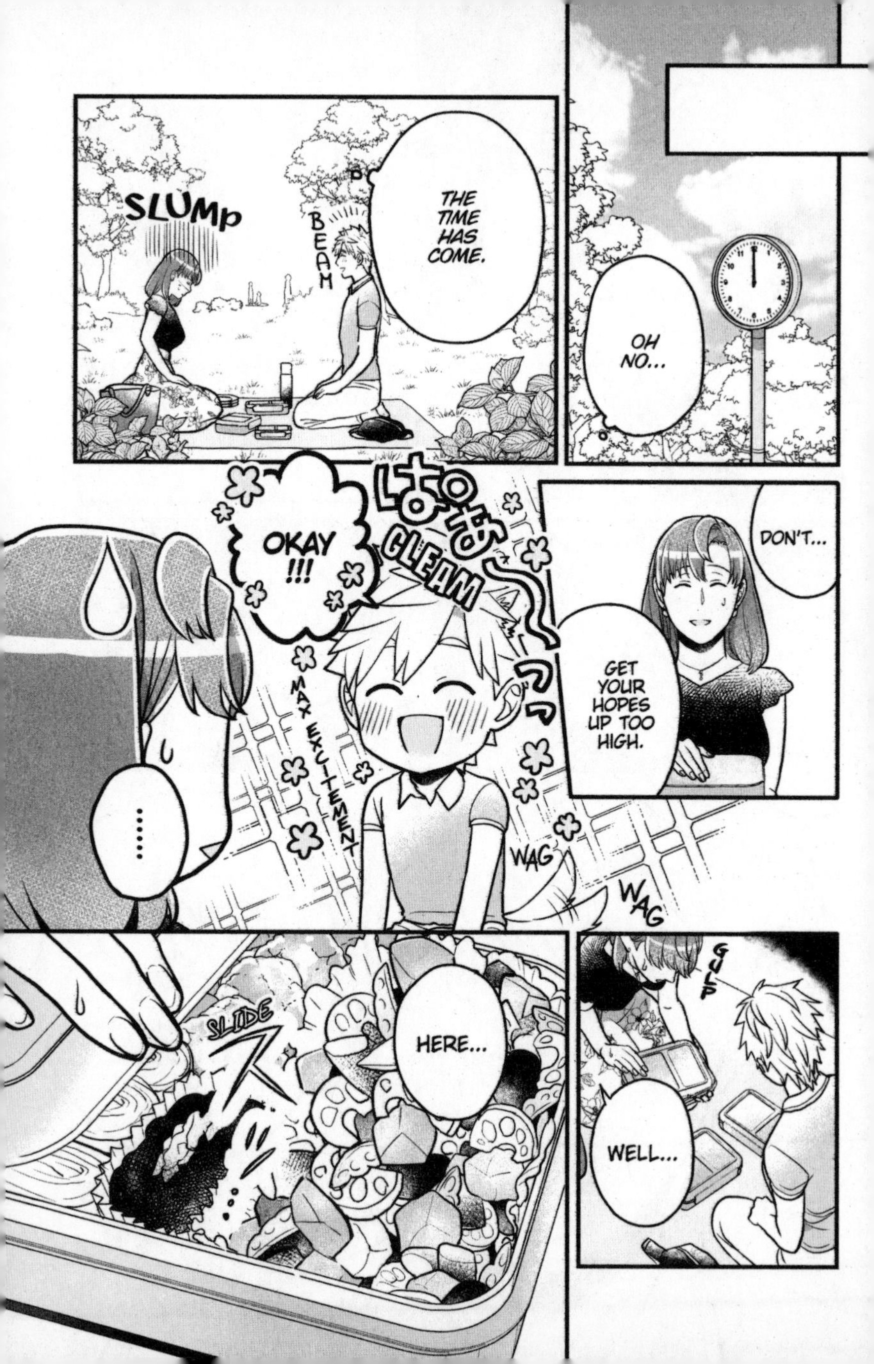
OH NO...
THE TIME HAS COME.
SLUMP
BEAM
DON'T...
GET YOUR HOPES UP TOO HIGH.
はぁ〜っ
GLEAM
OKAY!!!
MAX EXCITEMENT
WAG
WAG
......
GULP
WELL...
HERE...
SLIDE
...

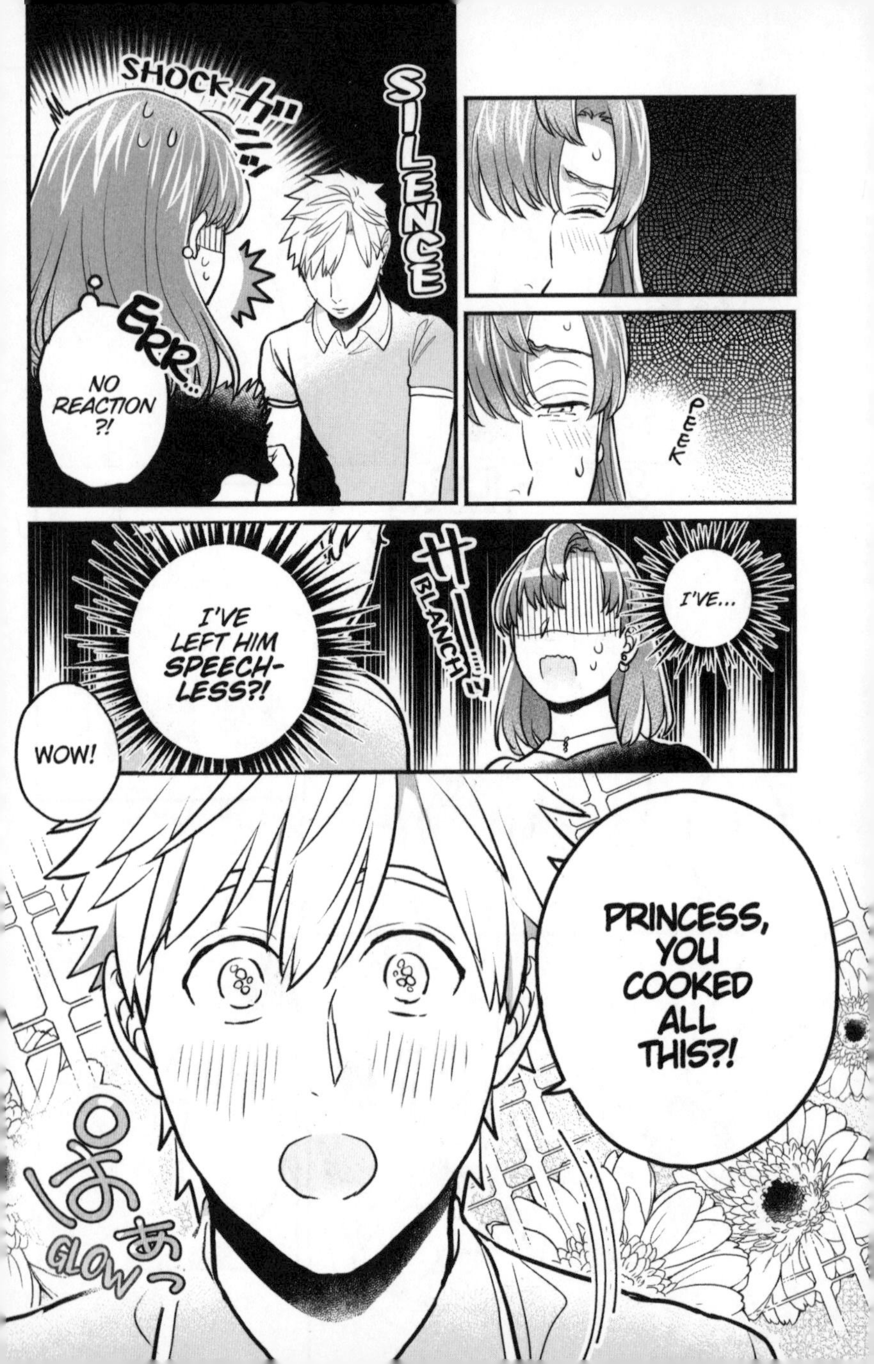
PEEK
SILENCE
SHOCK
ERR...
NO REACTION?!
I'VE...
BLANCH
I'VE LEFT HIM SPEECHLESS?!
WOW!
PRINCESS, YOU COOKED ALL THIS?!
GLOW

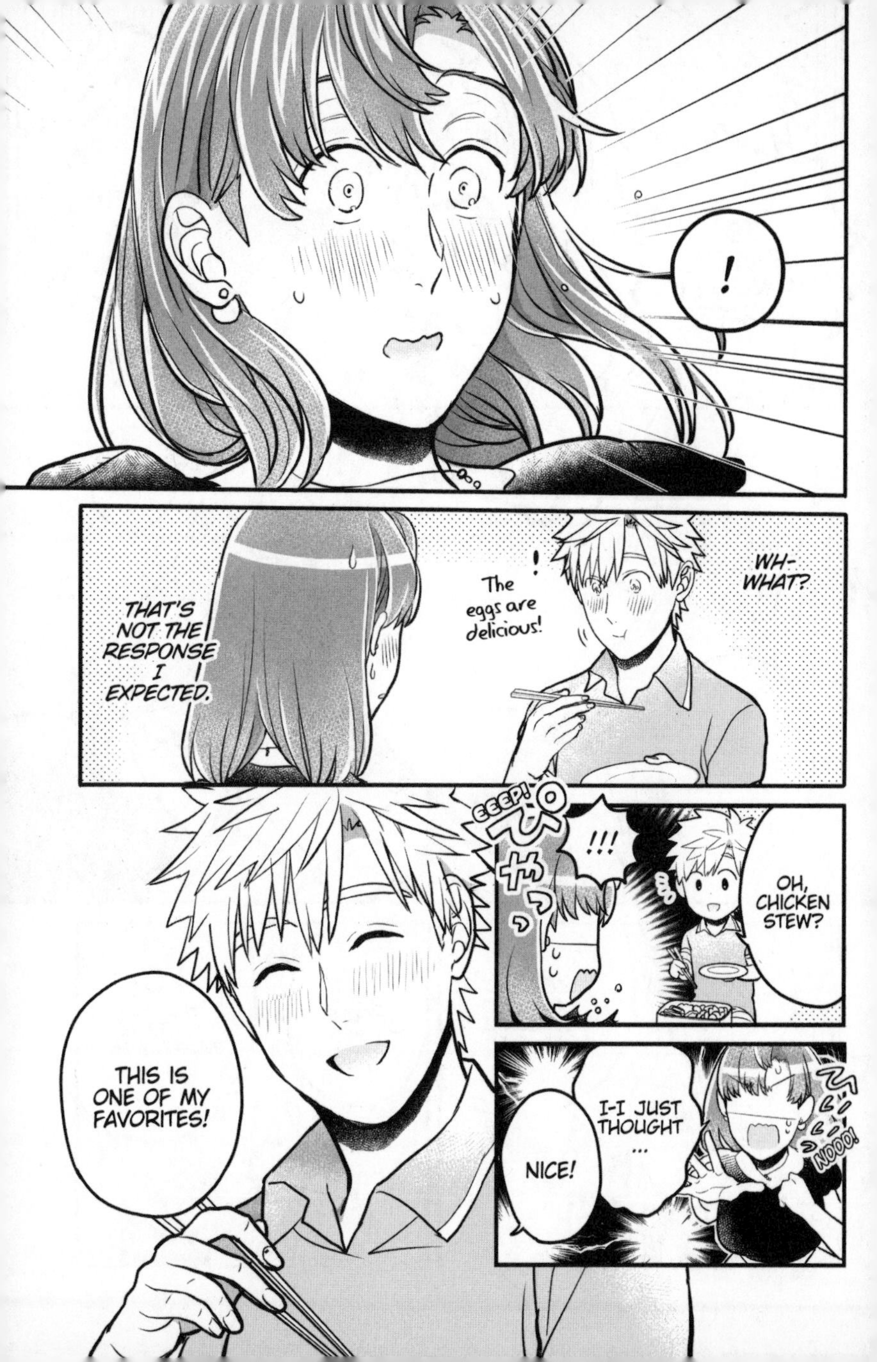
!
WH-WHAT?
!
The eggs are delicious!
THAT'S NOT THE RESPONSE I EXPECTED.
OH, CHICKEN STEW?
!!!
EEEP!
I-I JUST THOUGHT ...
NICE!
NOOO!
THIS IS ONE OF MY FAVORITES!

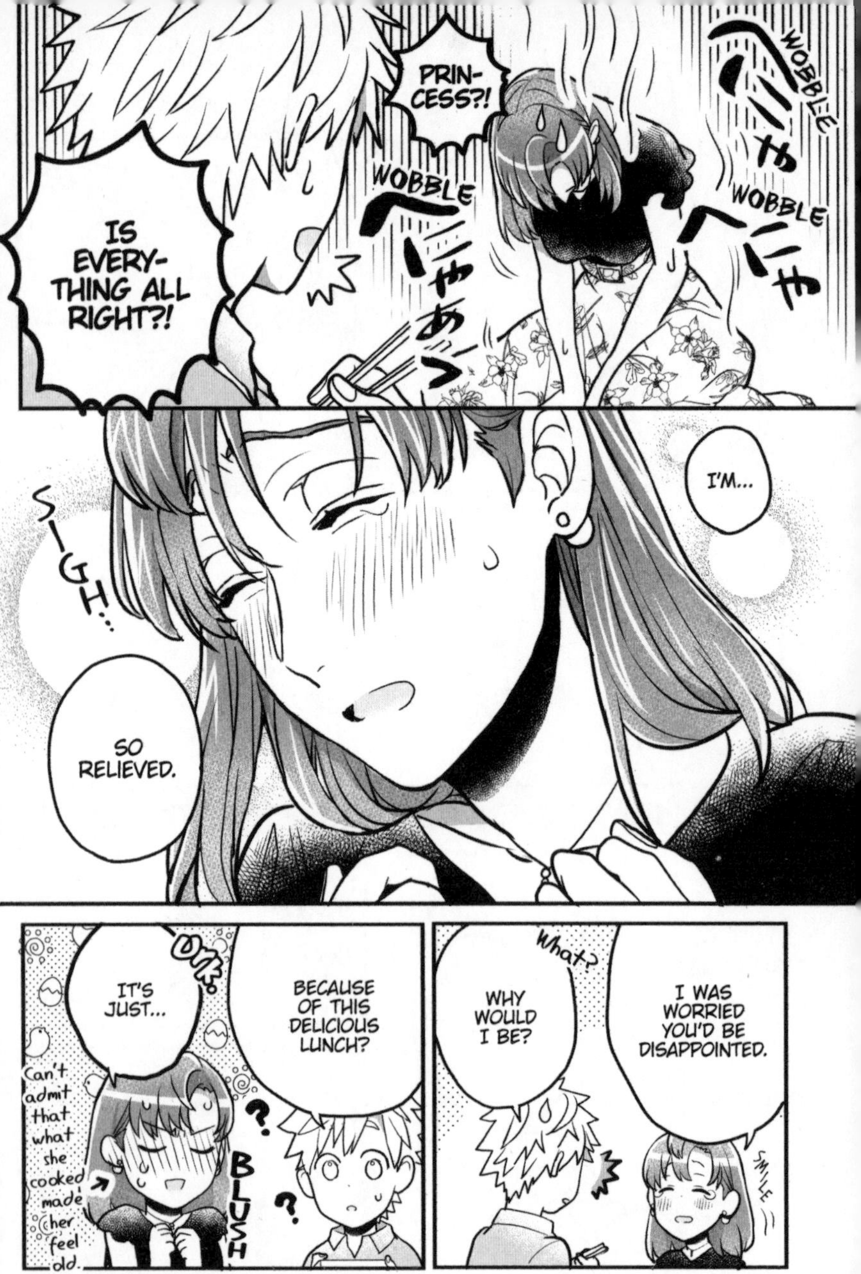
WOBBLE
PRIN-CESS?!
WOBBLE
WOBBLE
IS EVERYTHING ALL RIGHT?!
I'M...
SIGH...
SO RELIEVED.
I WAS WORRIED YOU'D BE DISAPPOINTED.
SMILE
What?
WHY WOULD I BE?
BECAUSE OF THIS DELICIOUS LUNCH?
Urk.
IT'S JUST...
BLUSH
Can't admit that what she cooked made her feel old.

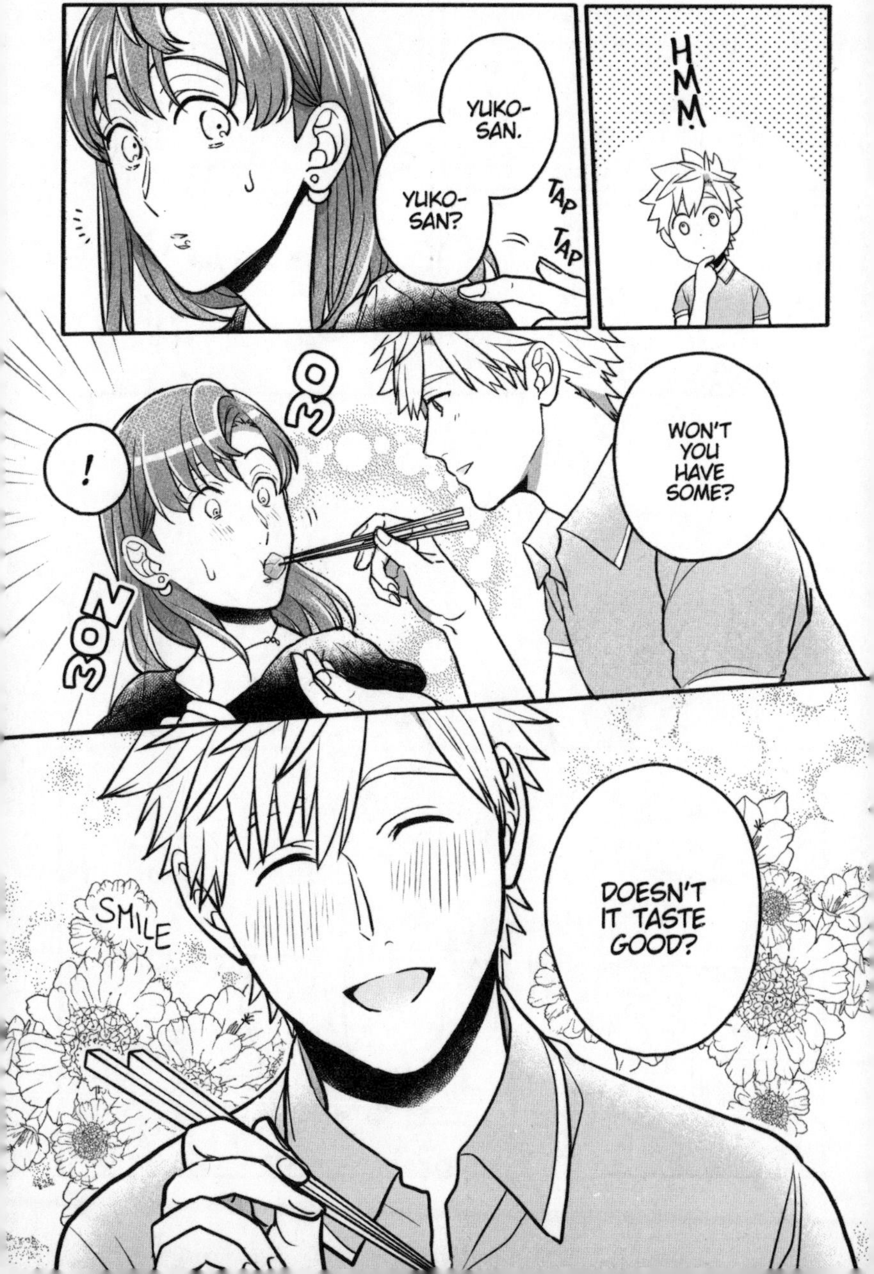
HMM.
YUKO-SAN.
YUKO-SAN?
TAP TAP
WON'T YOU HAVE SOME?
!
DOESN'T IT TASTE GOOD?
SMILE

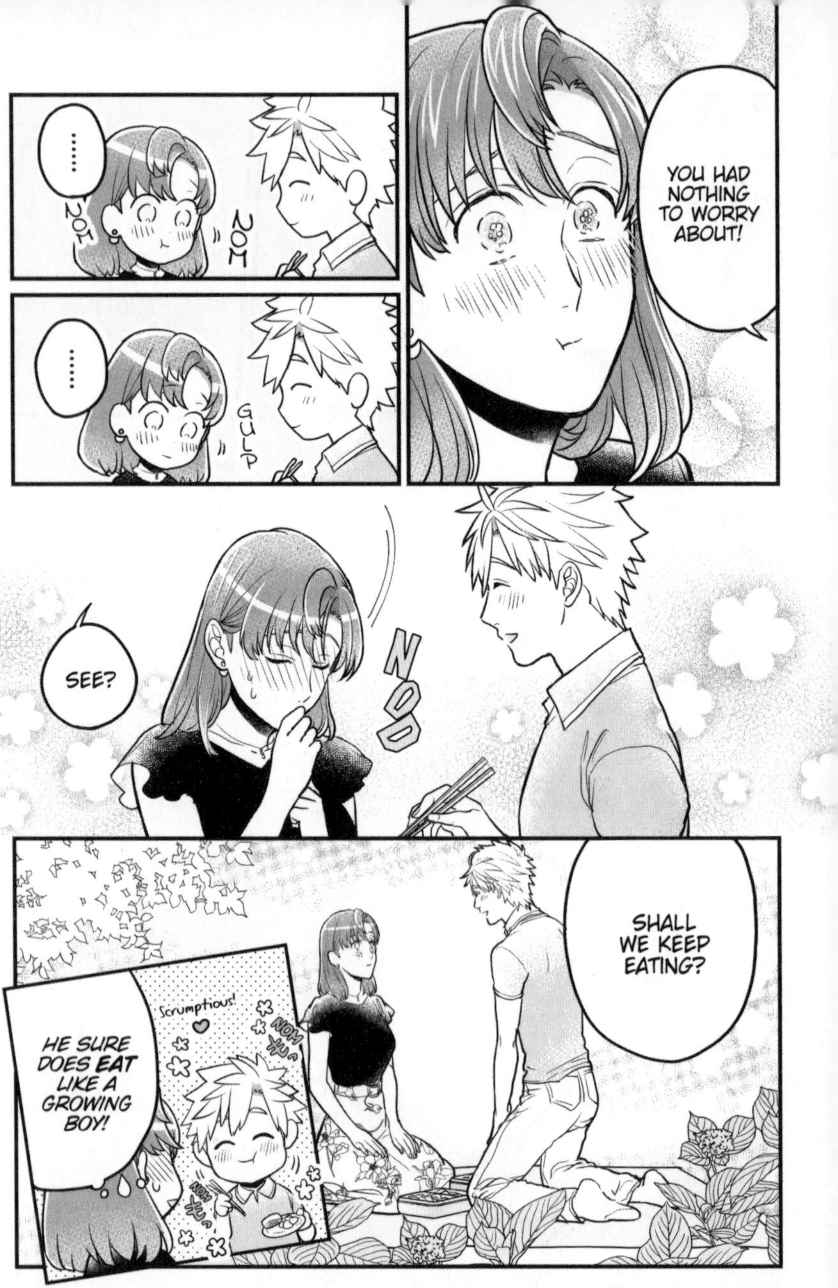
YOU HAD NOTHING TO WORRY ABOUT!
......
NOM
NOM
......
GULP
NOD
SEE?
SHALL WE KEEP EATING?
HE SURE DOES EAT LIKE A GROWING BOY!
Scrumptious!
NOM
NOM

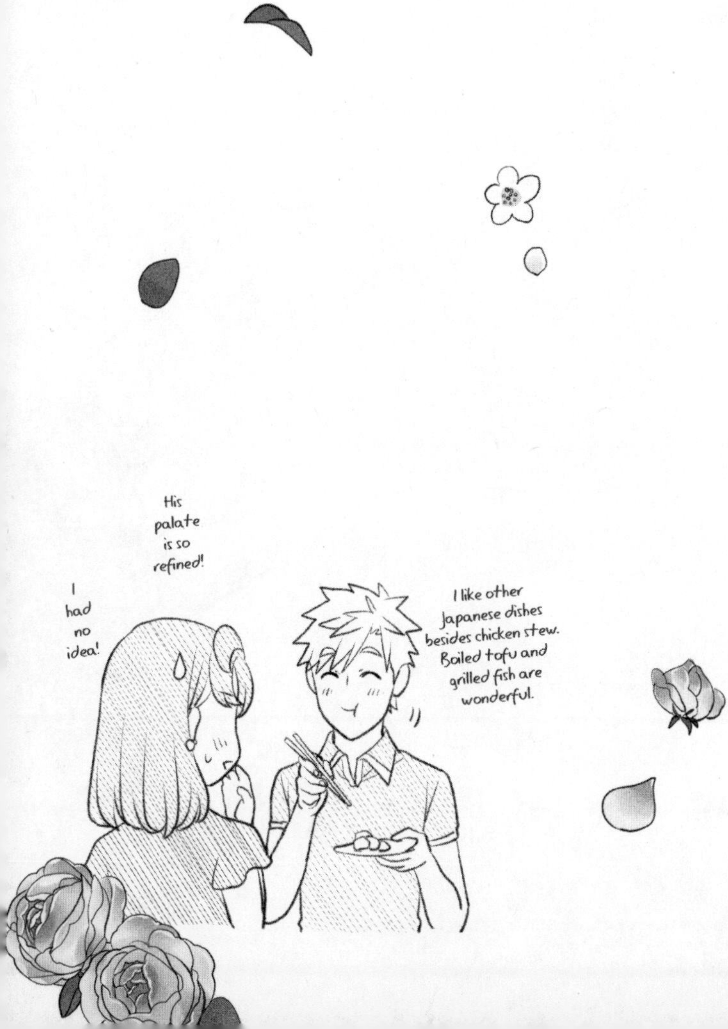
I like other Japanese dishes besides chicken stew. Boiled tofu and grilled fish are wonderful.
His palate is so refined!
I had no idea!

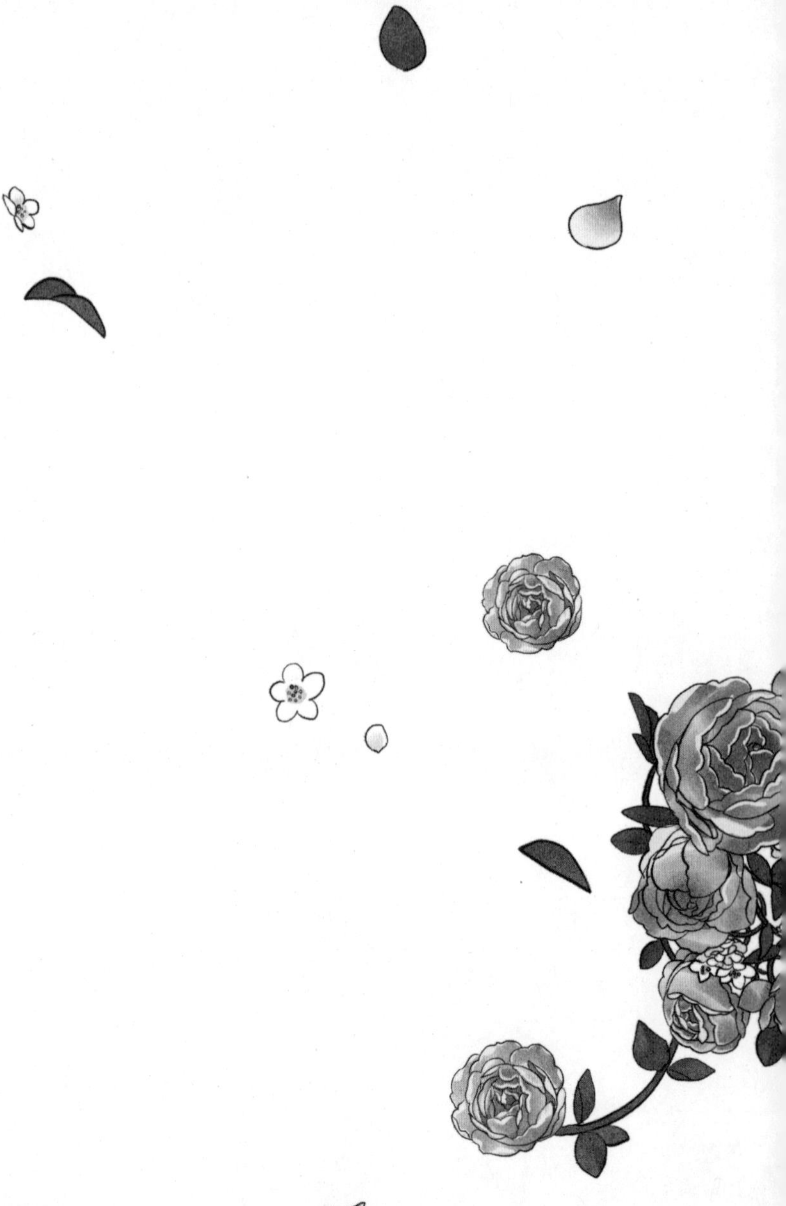

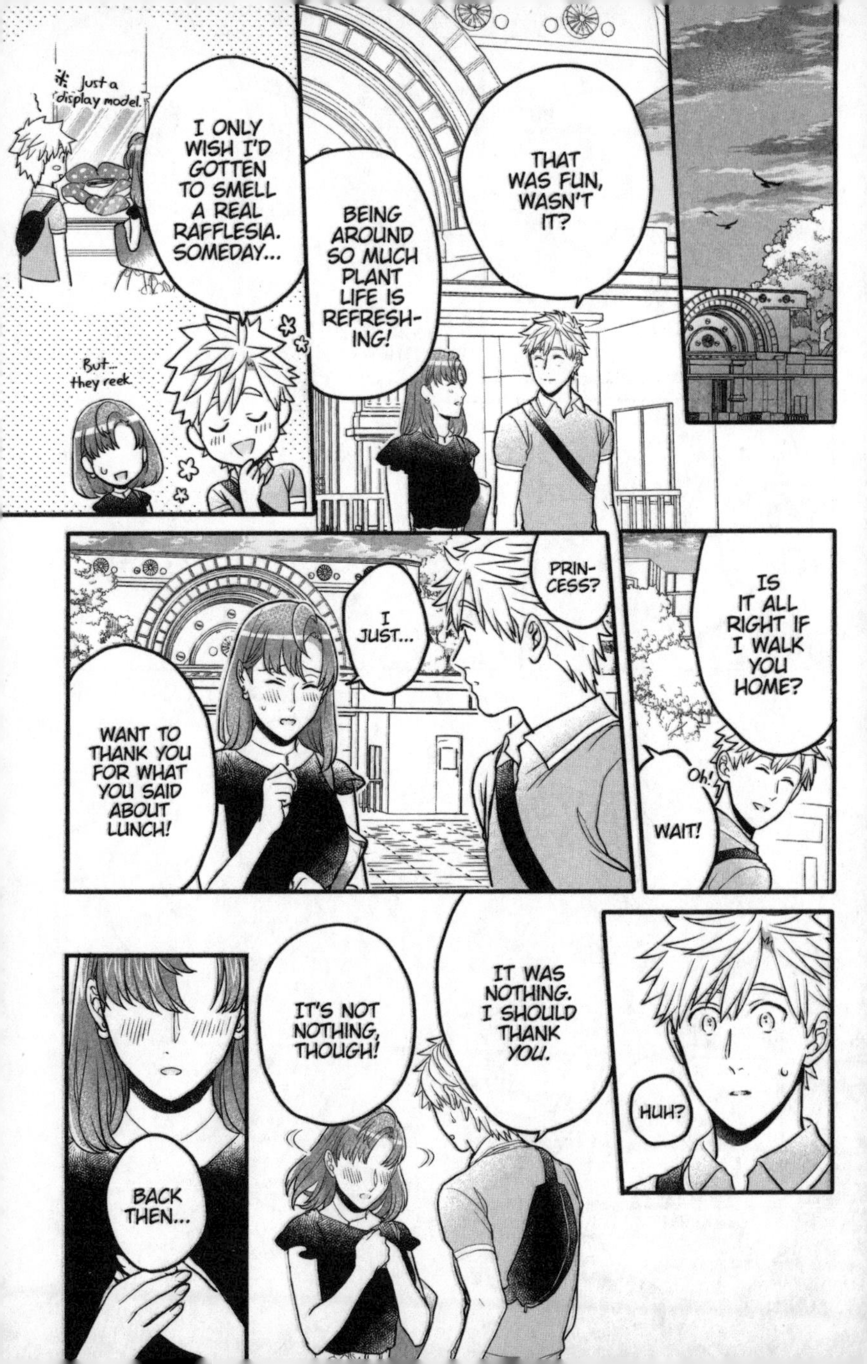
THAT WAS FUN, WASN'T IT?
BEING AROUND SO MUCH PLANT LIFE IS REFRESH-ING!
I ONLY WISH I'D GOTTEN TO SMELL A REAL RAFFLESIA. SOMEDAY...
※ Just a display model.
But... they reek.
IS IT ALL RIGHT IF I WALK YOU HOME?
Oh!
WAIT!
PRIN-CESS?
I JUST...
WANT TO THANK YOU FOR WHAT YOU SAID ABOUT LUNCH!
HUH?
IT WAS NOTHING. I SHOULD THANK YOU.
IT'S NOT NOTHING, THOUGH!
BACK THEN...

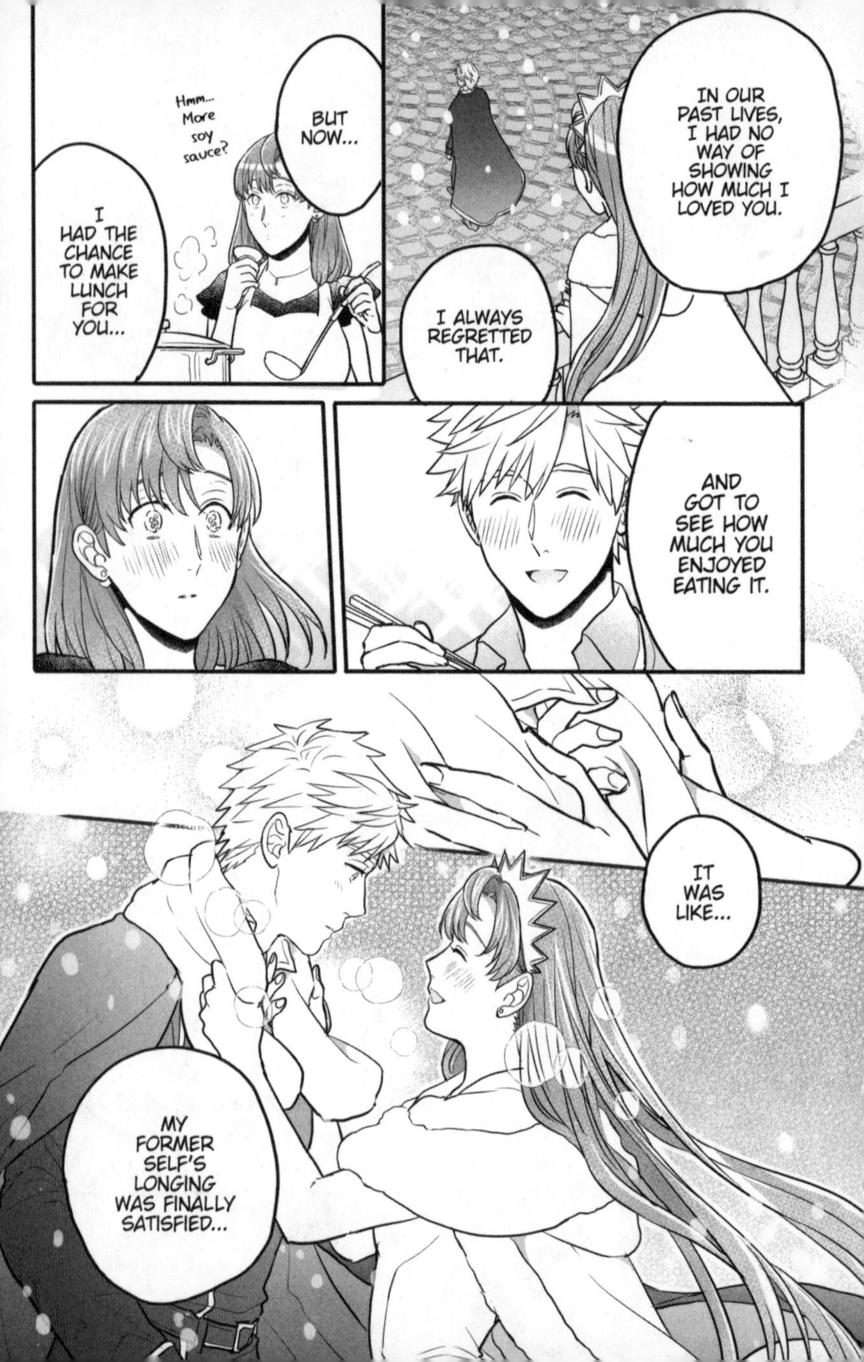
IN OUR PAST LIVES, I HAD NO WAY OF SHOWING HOW MUCH I LOVED YOU.
I ALWAYS REGRETTED THAT.
BUT NOW...
Hmm... More soy sauce?
I HAD THE CHANCE TO MAKE LUNCH FOR YOU...
AND GOT TO SEE HOW MUCH YOU ENJOYED EATING IT.
IT WAS LIKE...
MY FORMER SELF'S LONGING WAS FINALLY SATISFIED...

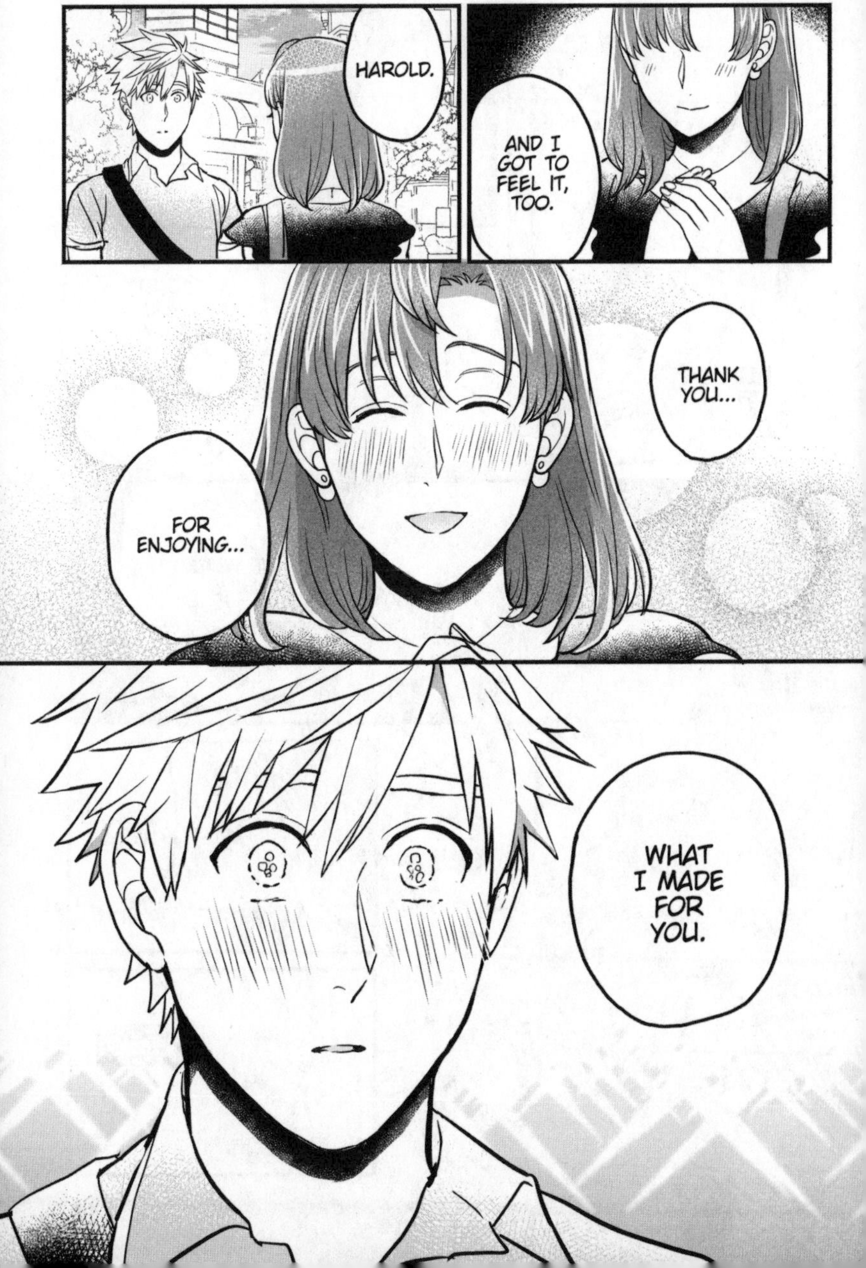
AND I GOT TO FEEL IT, TOO.
HAROLD.
THANK YOU...
FOR ENJOYING...
WHAT I MADE FOR YOU.

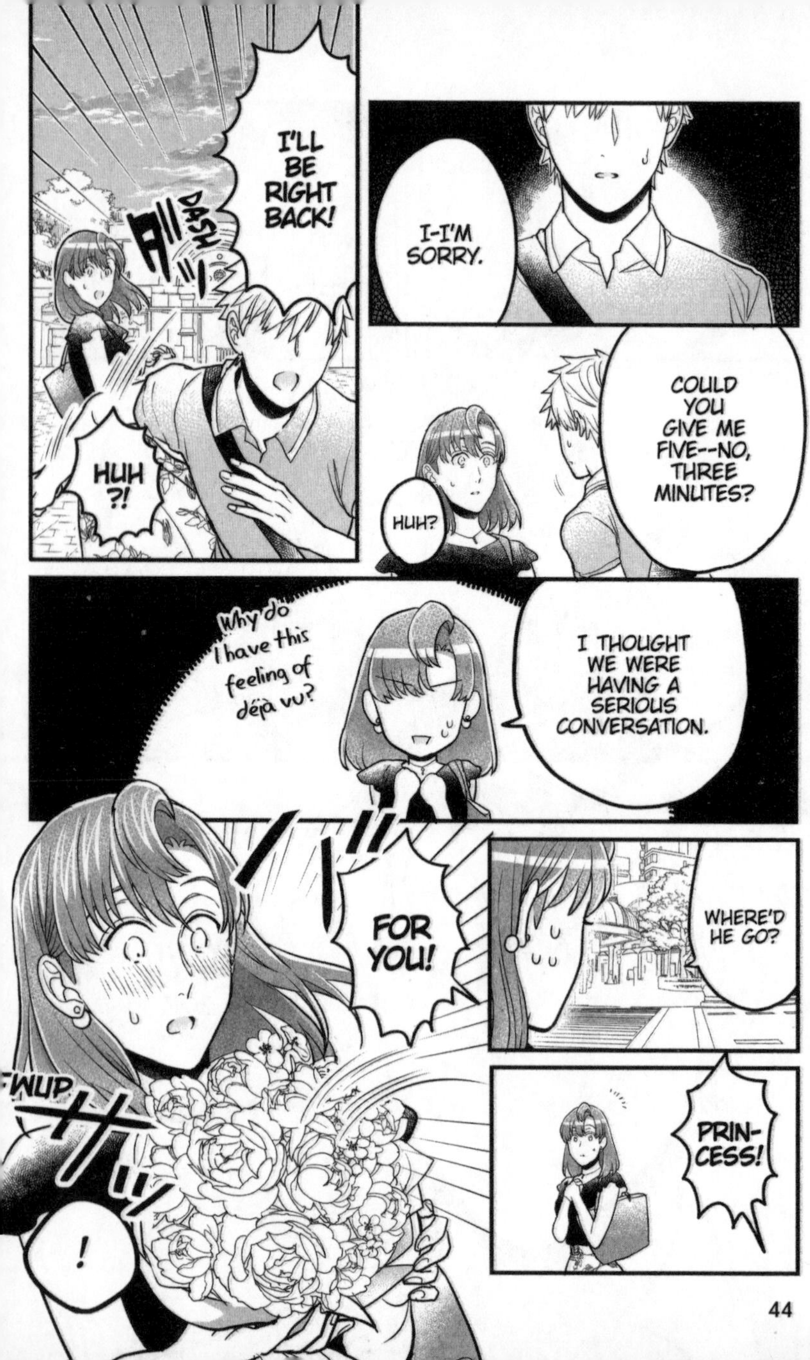
I-I'M SORRY.
COULD YOU GIVE ME FIVE--NO, THREE MINUTES?
HUH?
I'LL BE RIGHT BACK!
DASH
HUH ?!
I THOUGHT WE WERE HAVING A SERIOUS CONVERSATION.
Why do I have this feeling of déjà vu?
WHERE'D HE GO?
PRIN-CESS!
FOR YOU!
FWUP
!

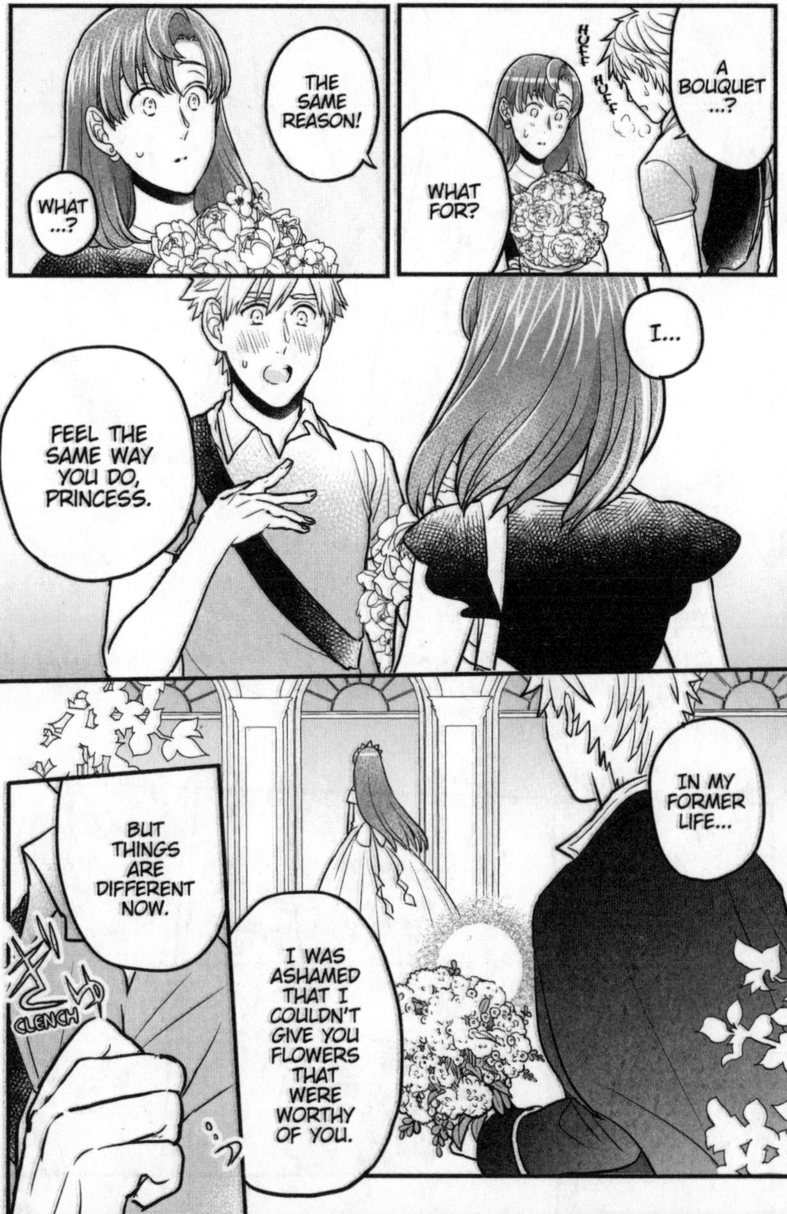
A BOUQUET ...?
HUFF HUFF
WHAT FOR?
THE SAME REASON!
WHAT ...?
I...
FEEL THE SAME WAY YOU DO, PRINCESS.
IN MY FORMER LIFE...
I WAS ASHAMED THAT I COULDN'T GIVE YOU FLOWERS THAT WERE WORTHY OF YOU.
BUT THINGS ARE DIFFERENT NOW.
CLENCH

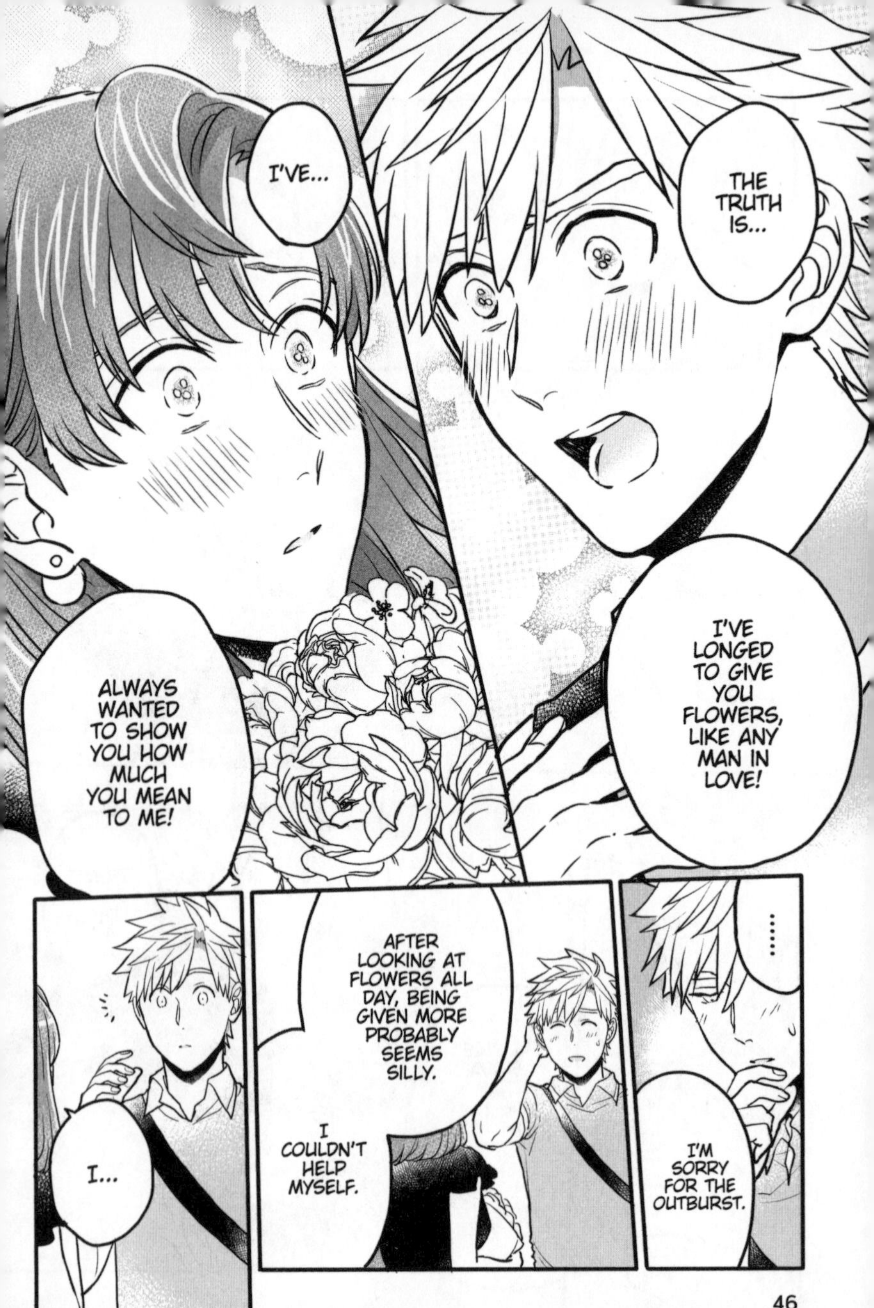
THE TRUTH IS...
I'VE LONGED TO GIVE YOU FLOWERS, LIKE ANY MAN IN LOVE!
I'VE...
ALWAYS WANTED TO SHOW YOU HOW MUCH YOU MEAN TO ME!
......
I'M SORRY FOR THE OUTBURST.
AFTER LOOKING AT FLOWERS ALL DAY, BEING GIVEN MORE PROBABLY SEEMS SILLY.
I COULDN'T HELP MYSELF.
I...

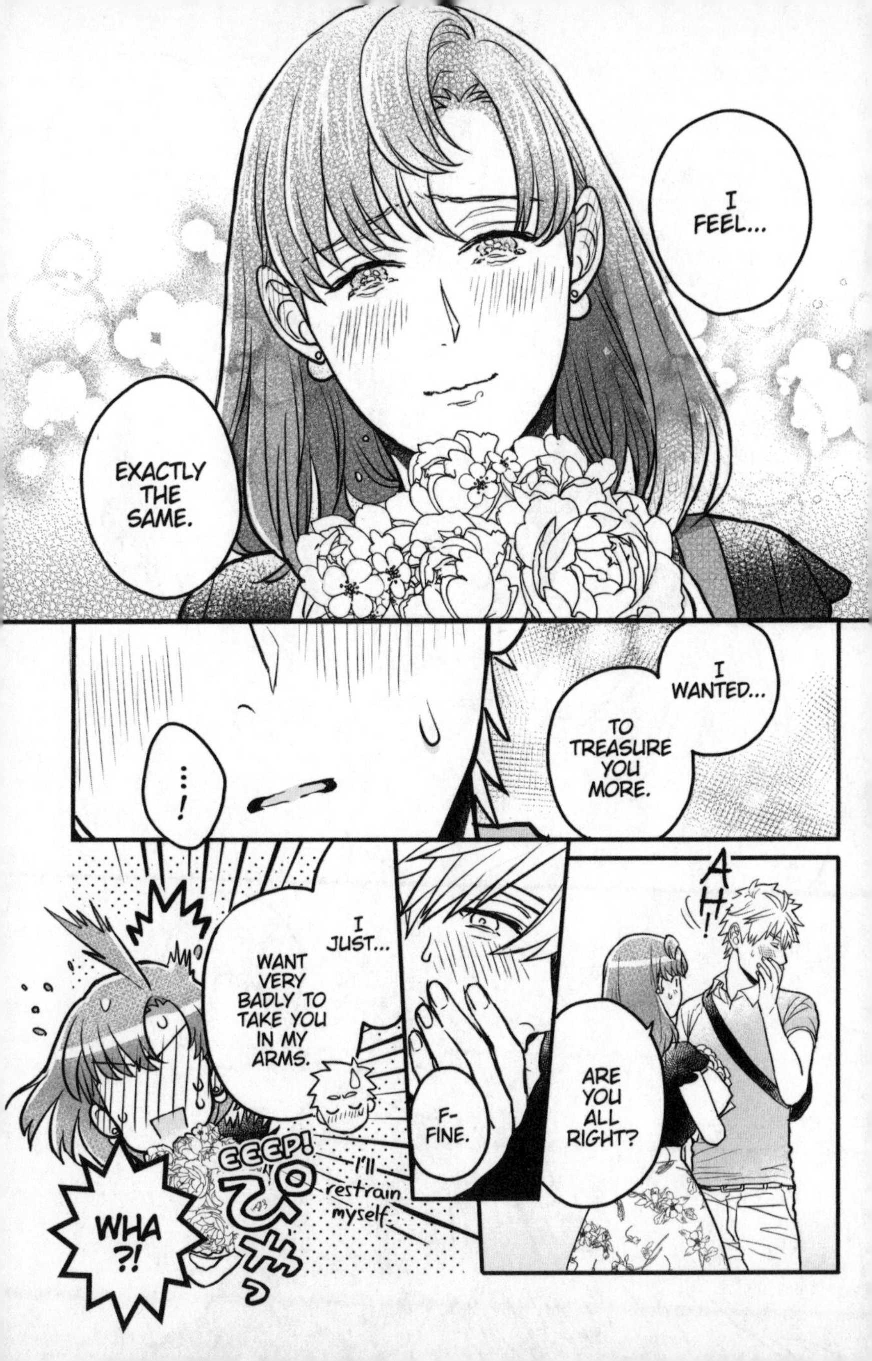
I FEEL...
EXACTLY THE SAME.
I WANTED... TO TREASURE YOU MORE.
...!
AH!
ARE YOU ALL RIGHT?
F- FINE.
I JUST... WANT VERY BADLY TO TAKE YOU IN MY ARMS.
I'll restrain myself
EEEP!
WHA?!

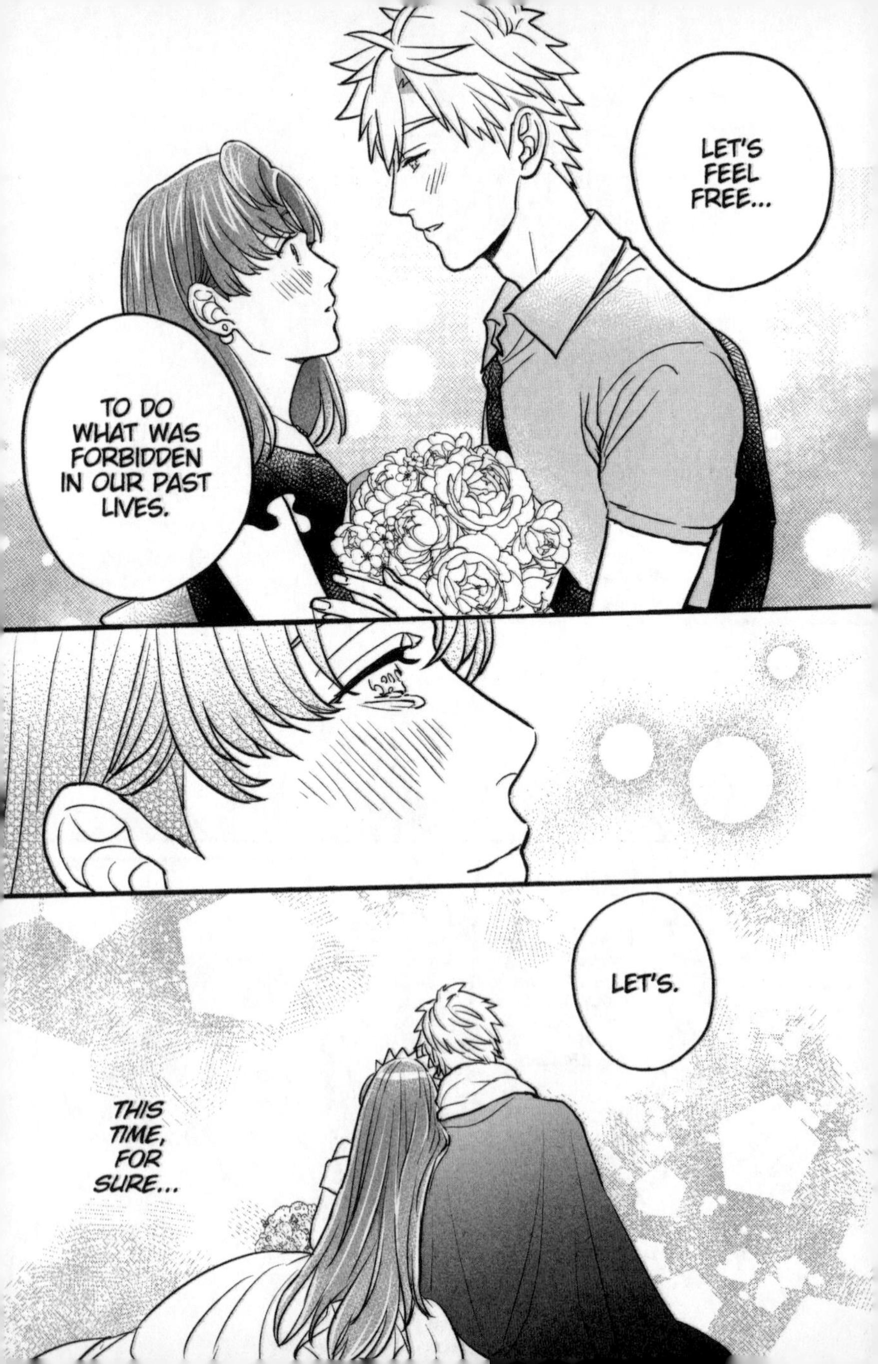
LET'S FEEL FREE...
TO DO WHAT WAS FORBIDDEN IN OUR PAST LIVES.
LET'S.
THIS TIME, FOR SURE...

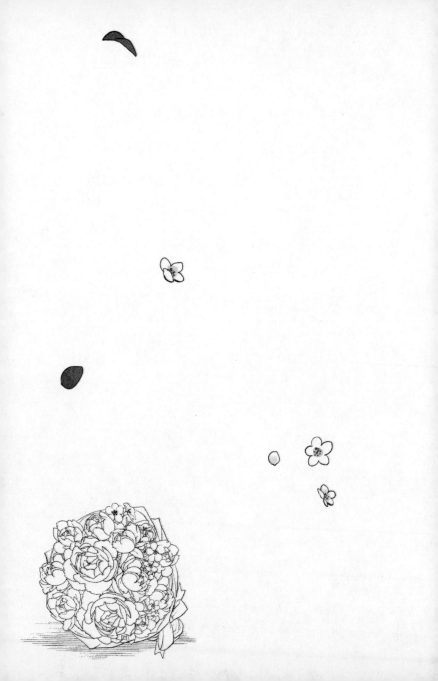

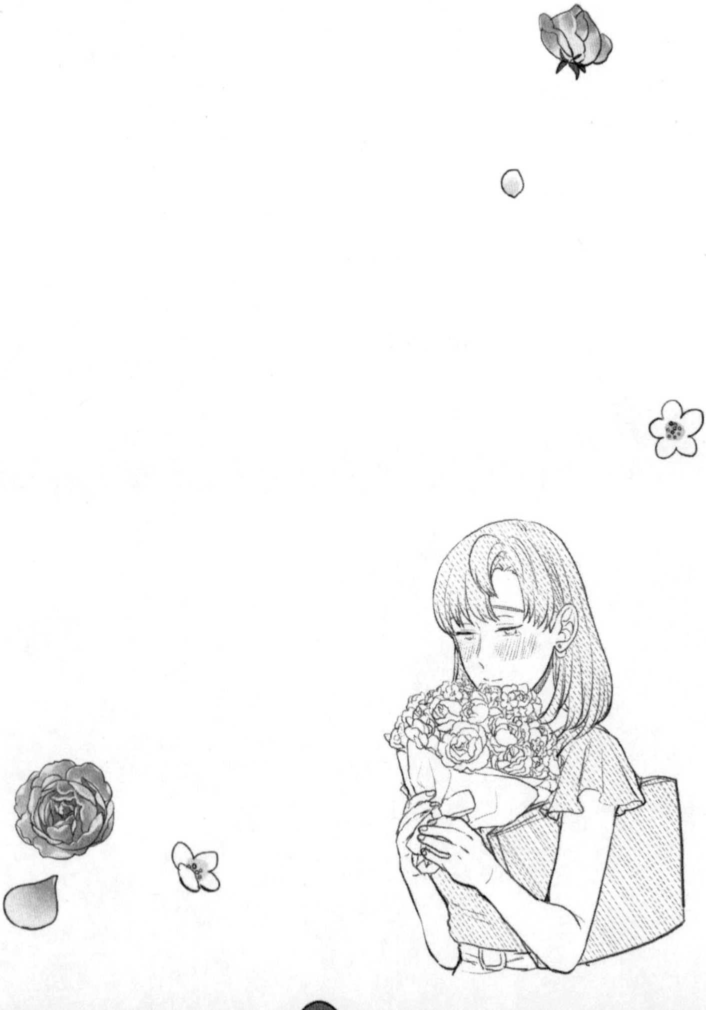

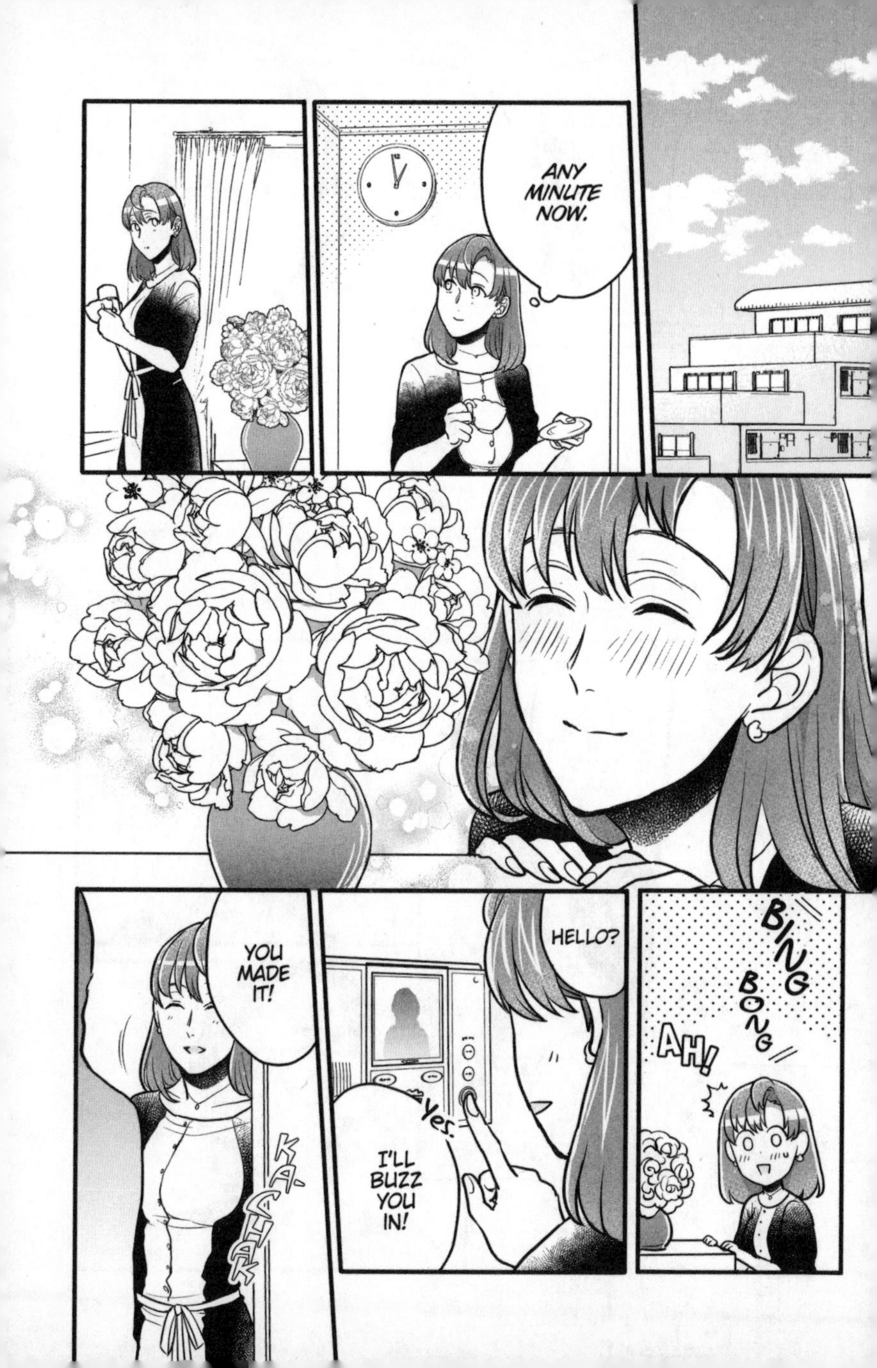

ANY MINUTE NOW.
BING BONG
AH!
HELLO?
YES.
I'LL BUZZ YOU IN!
YOU MADE IT!
KA-CHAK

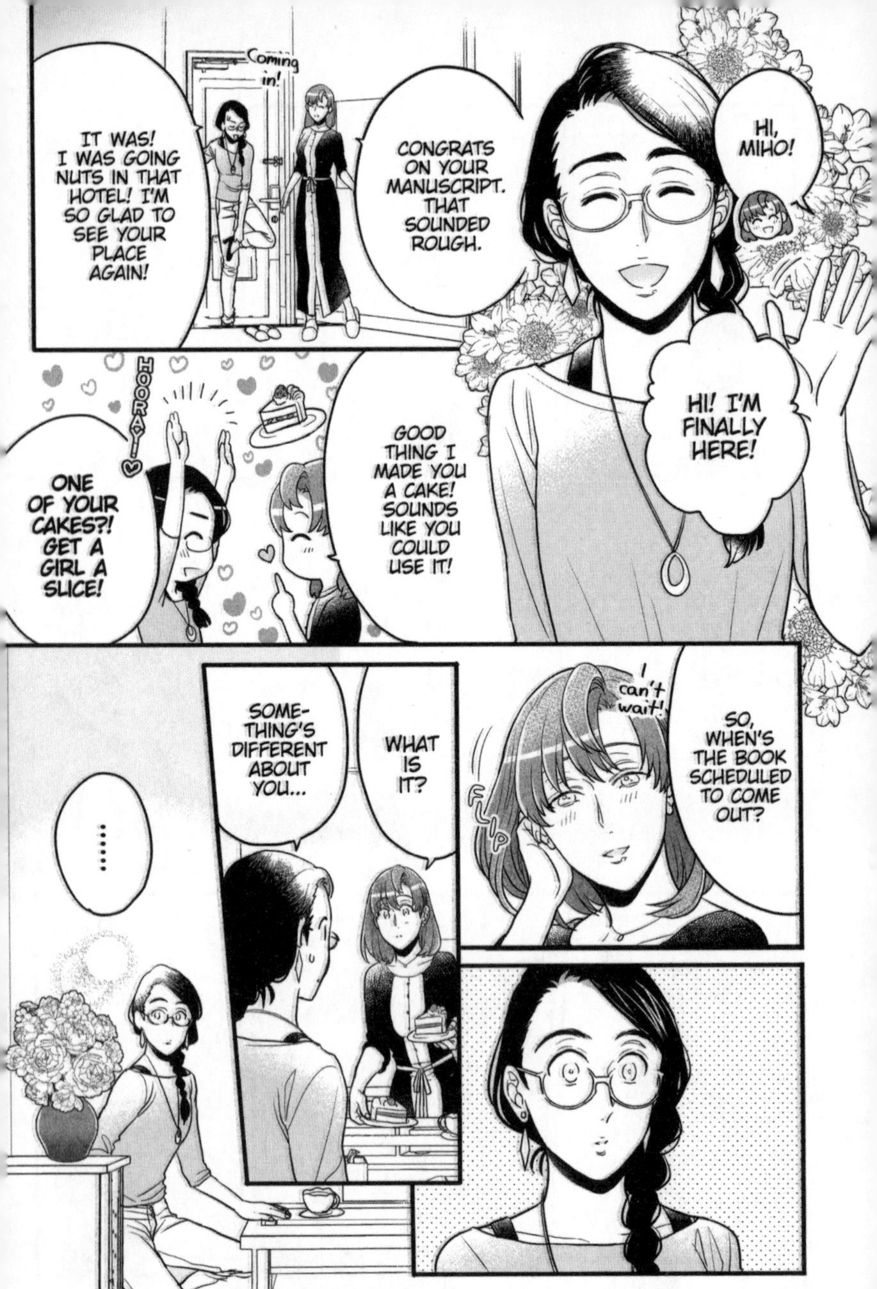
HI, MIHO!
HI! I'M FINALLY HERE!
Coming in!
CONGRATS ON YOUR MANUSCRIPT. THAT SOUNDED ROUGH.
IT WAS! I WAS GOING NUTS IN THAT HOTEL! I'M SO GLAD TO SEE YOUR PLACE AGAIN!
GOOD THING I MADE YOU A CAKE! SOUNDS LIKE YOU COULD USE IT!
HOORAY!
ONE OF YOUR CAKES?! GET A GIRL A SLICE!
I can't wait!
SO, WHEN'S THE BOOK SCHEDULED TO COME OUT?
FLIP
WHAT IS IT?
SOME-THING'S DIFFERENT ABOUT YOU...
......

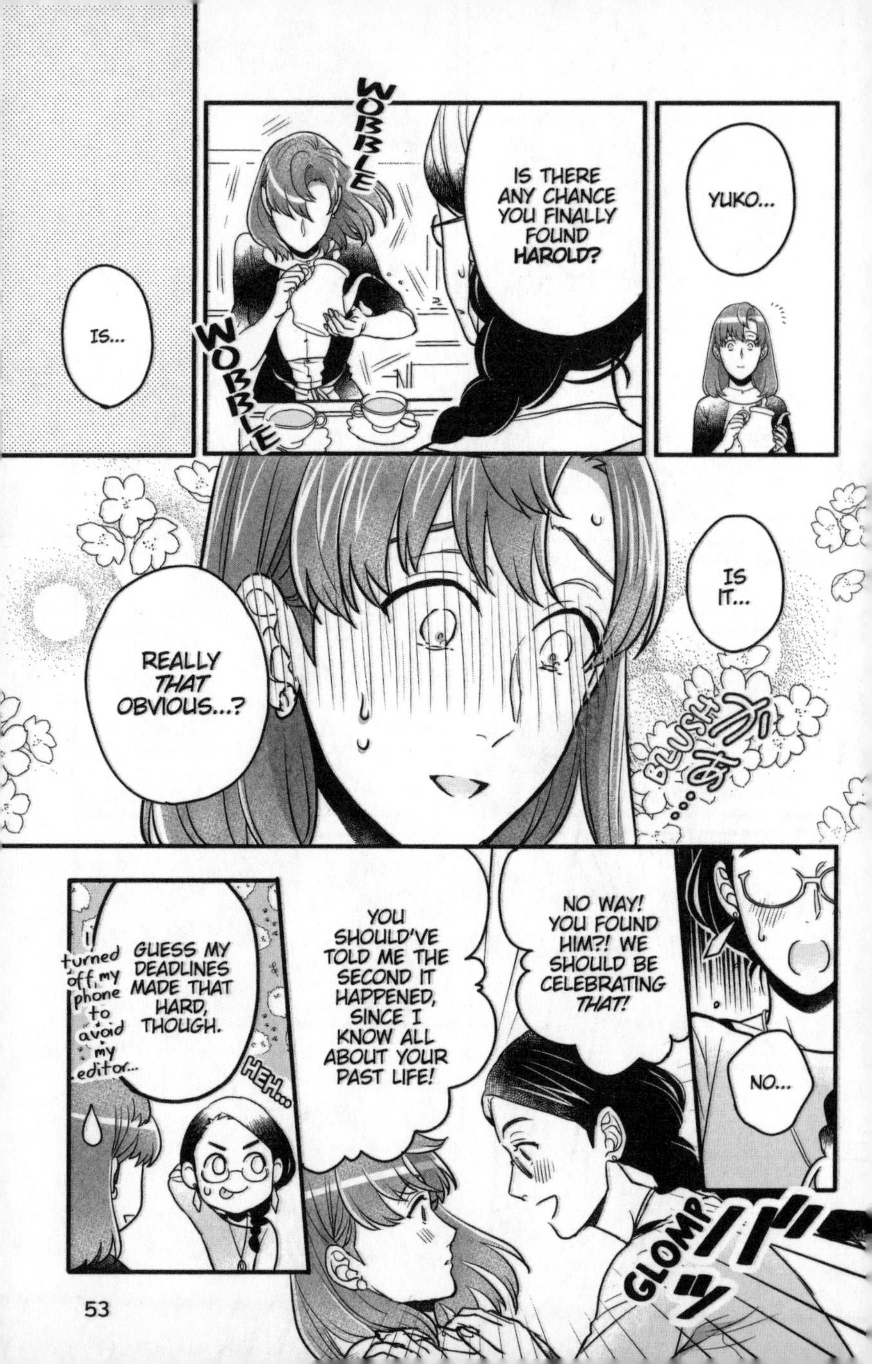
YUKO...
IS THERE ANY CHANCE YOU FINALLY FOUND HAROLD?
WOBBLE
WOBBLE
IS...
IS IT...
REALLY *THAT* OBVIOUS...?
BLUSH
NO...
NO WAY! YOU FOUND HIM?! WE SHOULD BE CELEBRATING *THAT*!
YOU SHOULD'VE TOLD ME THE SECOND IT HAPPENED, SINCE I KNOW ALL ABOUT YOUR PAST LIFE!
GLOMP
GUESS MY DEADLINES MADE THAT HARD, THOUGH.
turned off my phone to avoid my editor...
HEH...

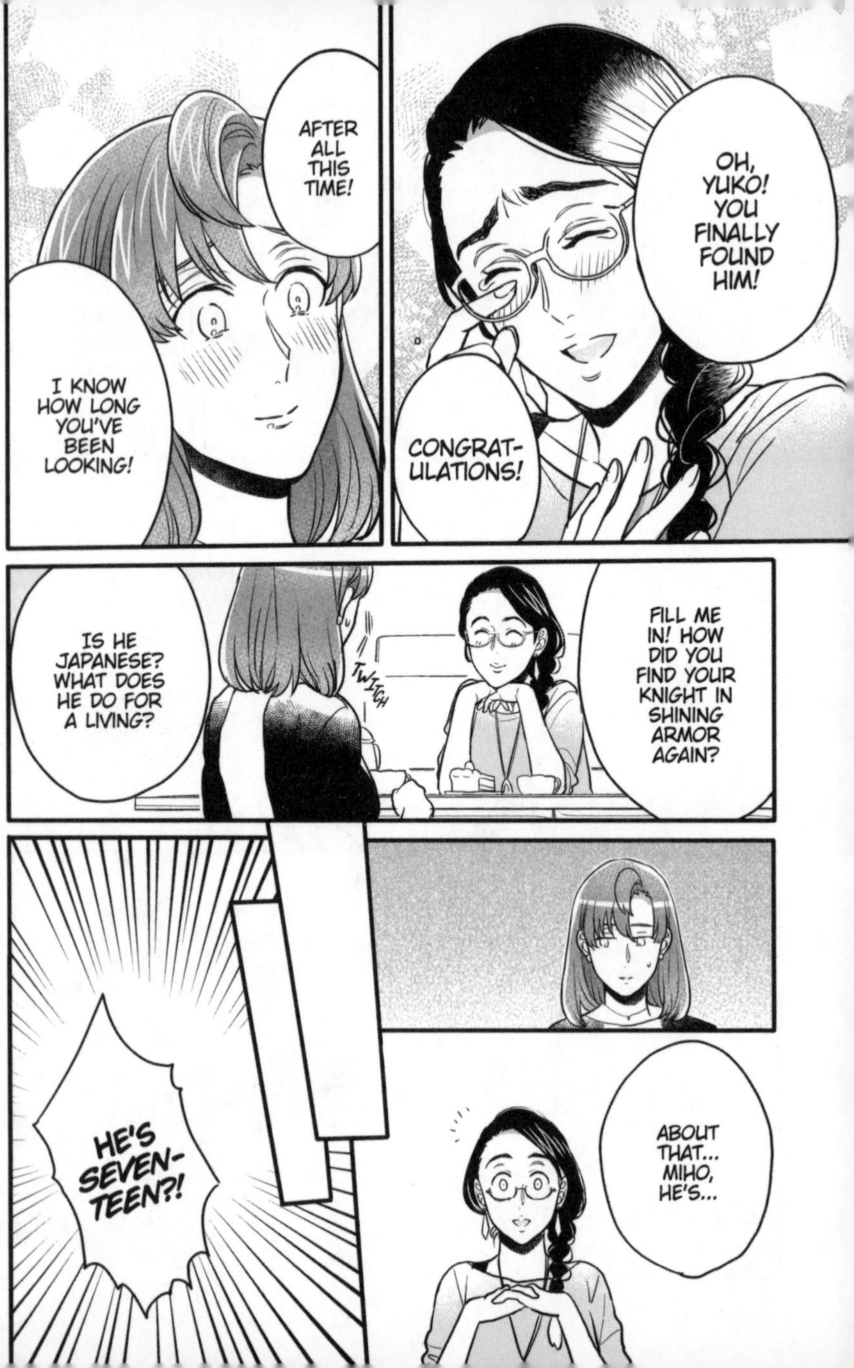
OH, YUKO! YOU FINALLY FOUND HIM!
CONGRAT-ULATIONS!
AFTER ALL THIS TIME!
I KNOW HOW LONG YOU'VE BEEN LOOKING!
FILL ME IN! HOW DID YOU FIND YOUR KNIGHT IN SHINING ARMOR AGAIN?
TWITCH
IS HE JAPANESE? WHAT DOES HE DO FOR A LIVING?
ABOUT THAT... MIHO, HE'S...
HE'S SEVEN-TEEN?!

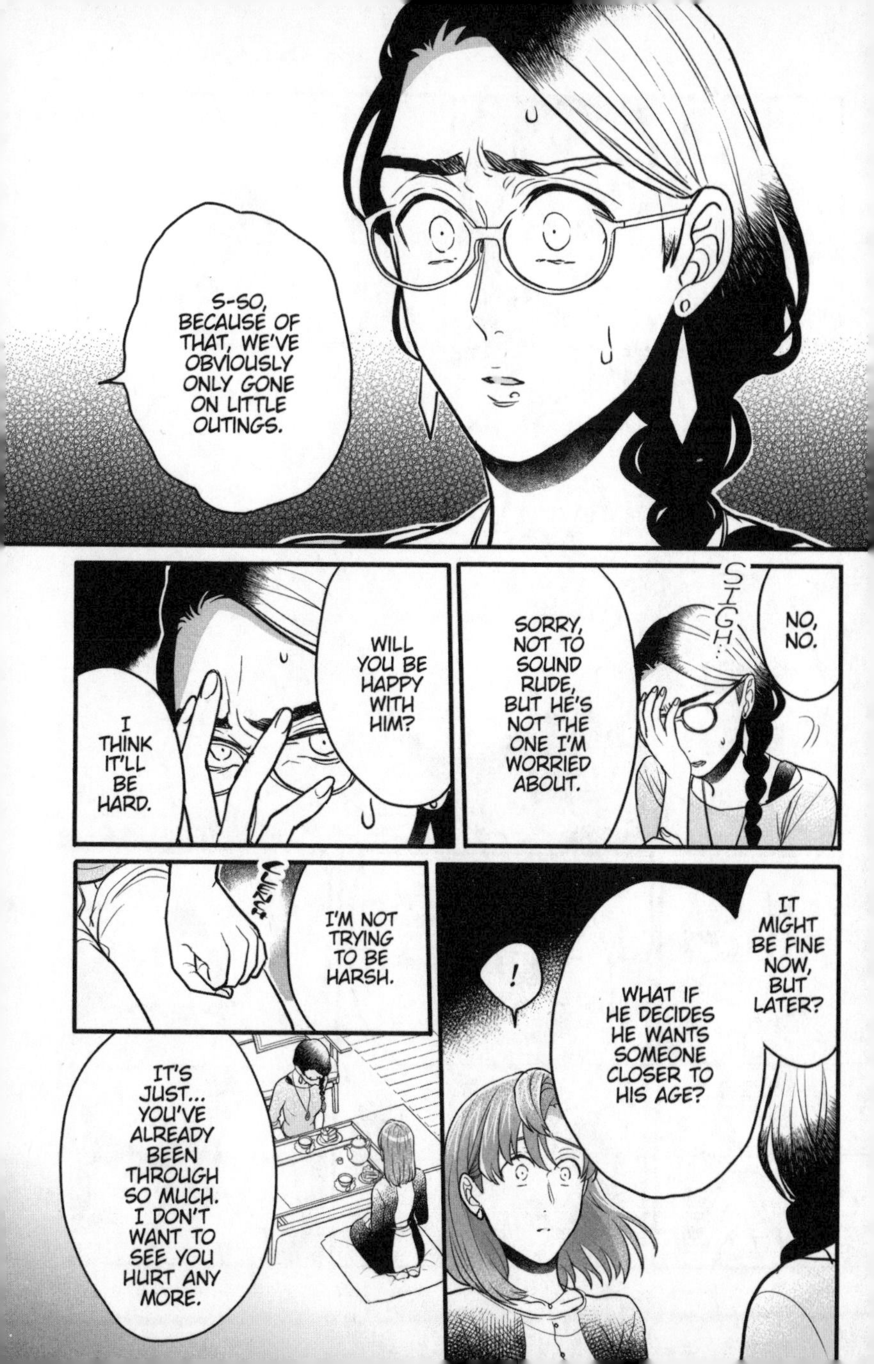
S-SO, BECAUSE OF THAT, WE'VE OBVIOUSLY ONLY GONE ON LITTLE OUTINGS.
SIGH...
NO, NO.
SORRY, NOT TO SOUND RUDE, BUT HE'S NOT THE ONE I'M WORRIED ABOUT.
WILL YOU BE HAPPY WITH HIM?
I THINK IT'LL BE HARD.
IT MIGHT BE FINE NOW, BUT LATER?
WHAT IF HE DECIDES HE WANTS SOMEONE CLOSER TO HIS AGE?
!
I'M NOT TRYING TO BE HARSH.
IT'S JUST... YOU'VE ALREADY BEEN THROUGH SO MUCH. I DON'T WANT TO SEE YOU HURT ANY MORE.

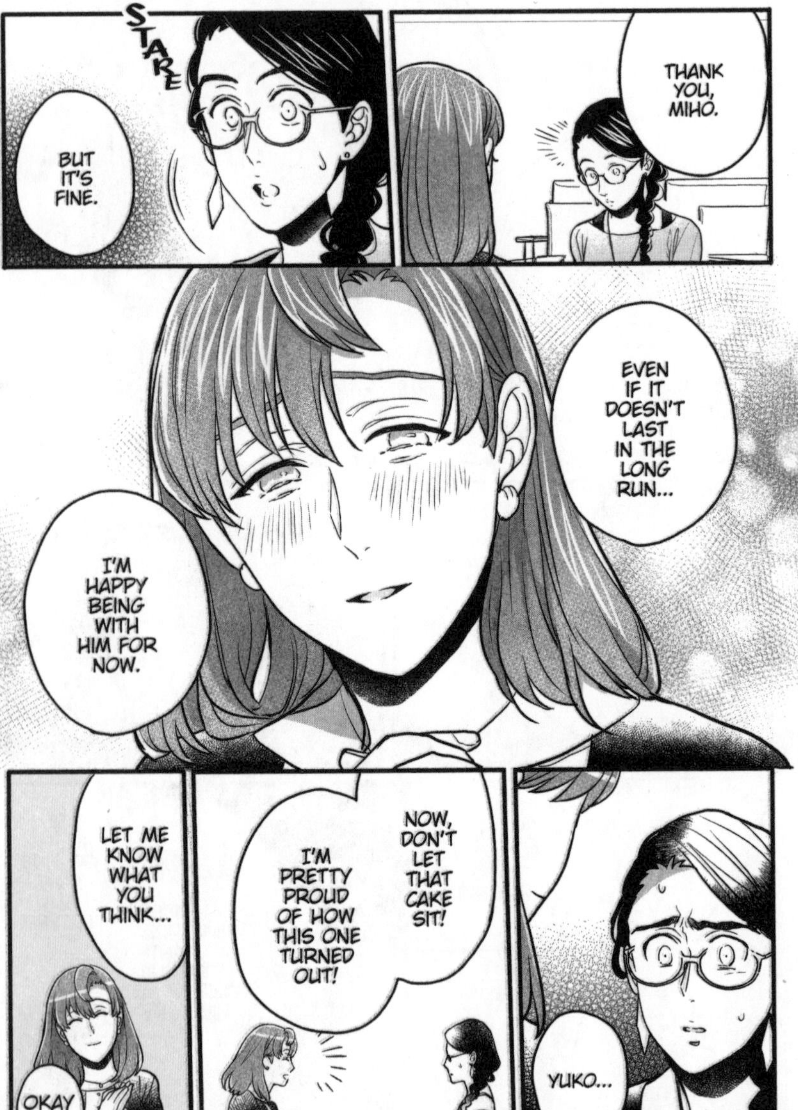
THANK YOU, MIHO.
STARE
BUT IT'S FINE.
EVEN IF IT DOESN'T LAST IN THE LONG RUN...
I'M HAPPY BEING WITH HIM FOR NOW.
YUKO...
NOW, DON'T LET THAT CAKE SIT!
I'M PRETTY PROUD OF HOW THIS ONE TURNED OUT!
LET ME KNOW WHAT YOU THINK...
OKAY?

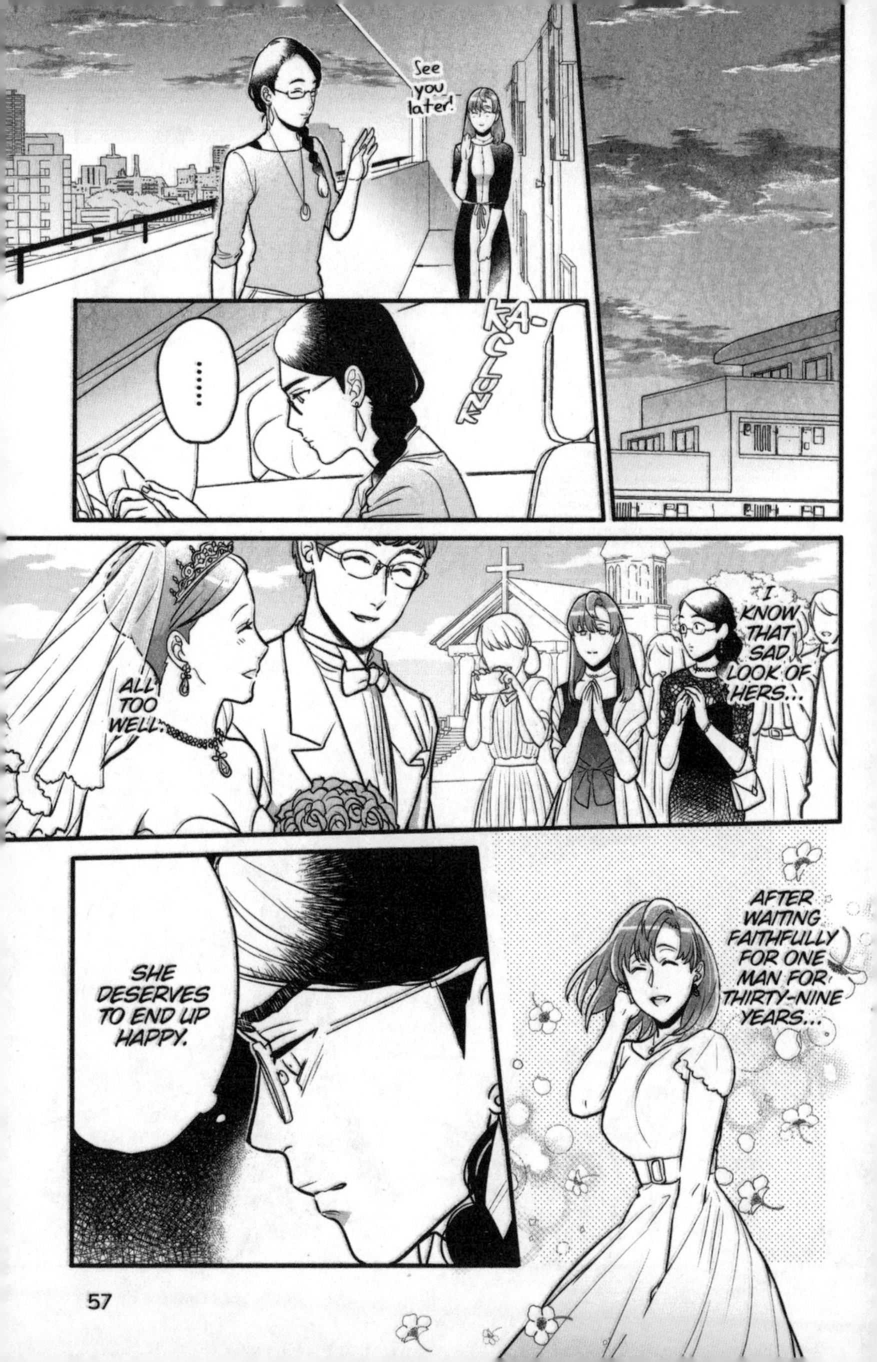
See you later!
......
KA-CLUNK
I KNOW THAT SAD LOOK OF HERS...
ALL TOO WELL.
AFTER WAITING FAITHFULLY FOR ONE MAN FOR THIRTY-NINE YEARS...
SHE DESERVES TO END UP HAPPY.

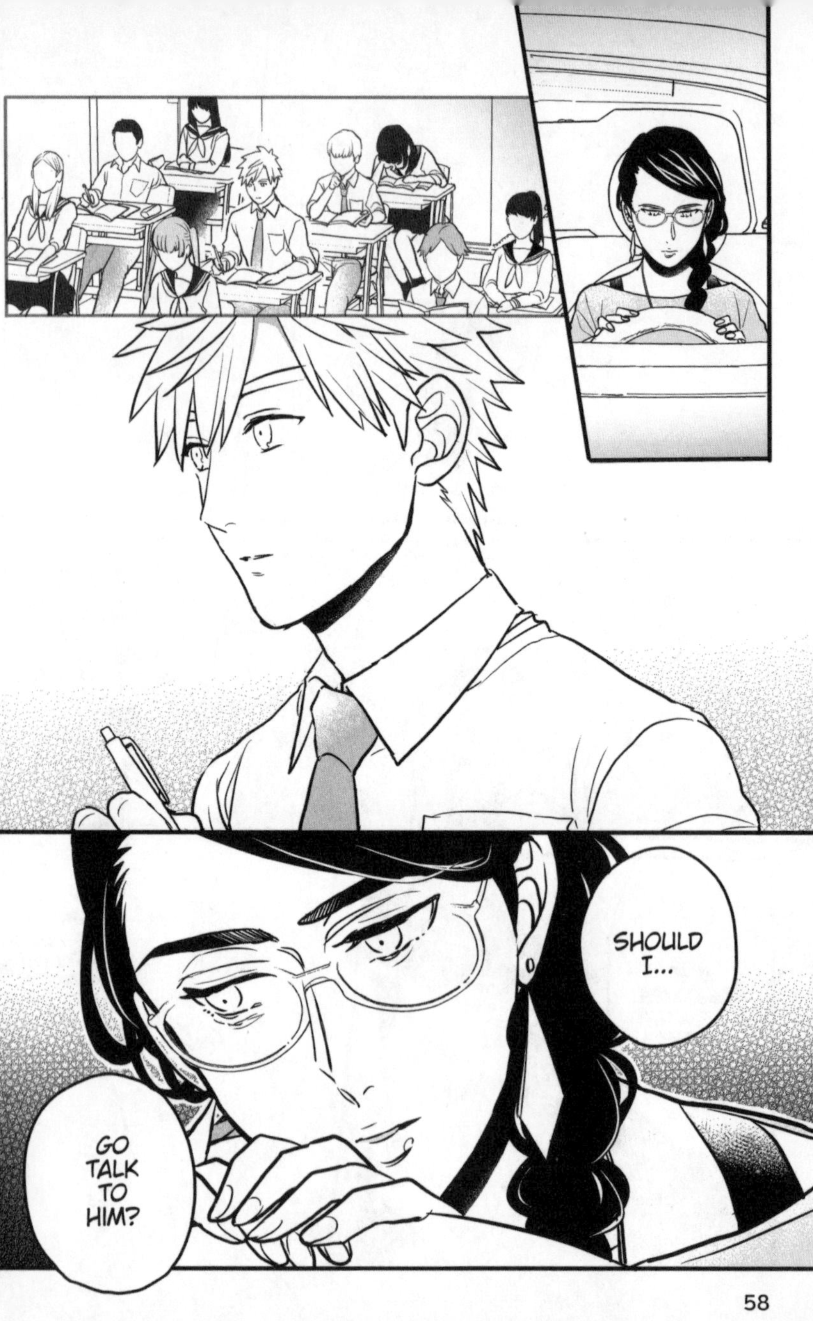
SHOULD I...
GO TALK TO HIM?

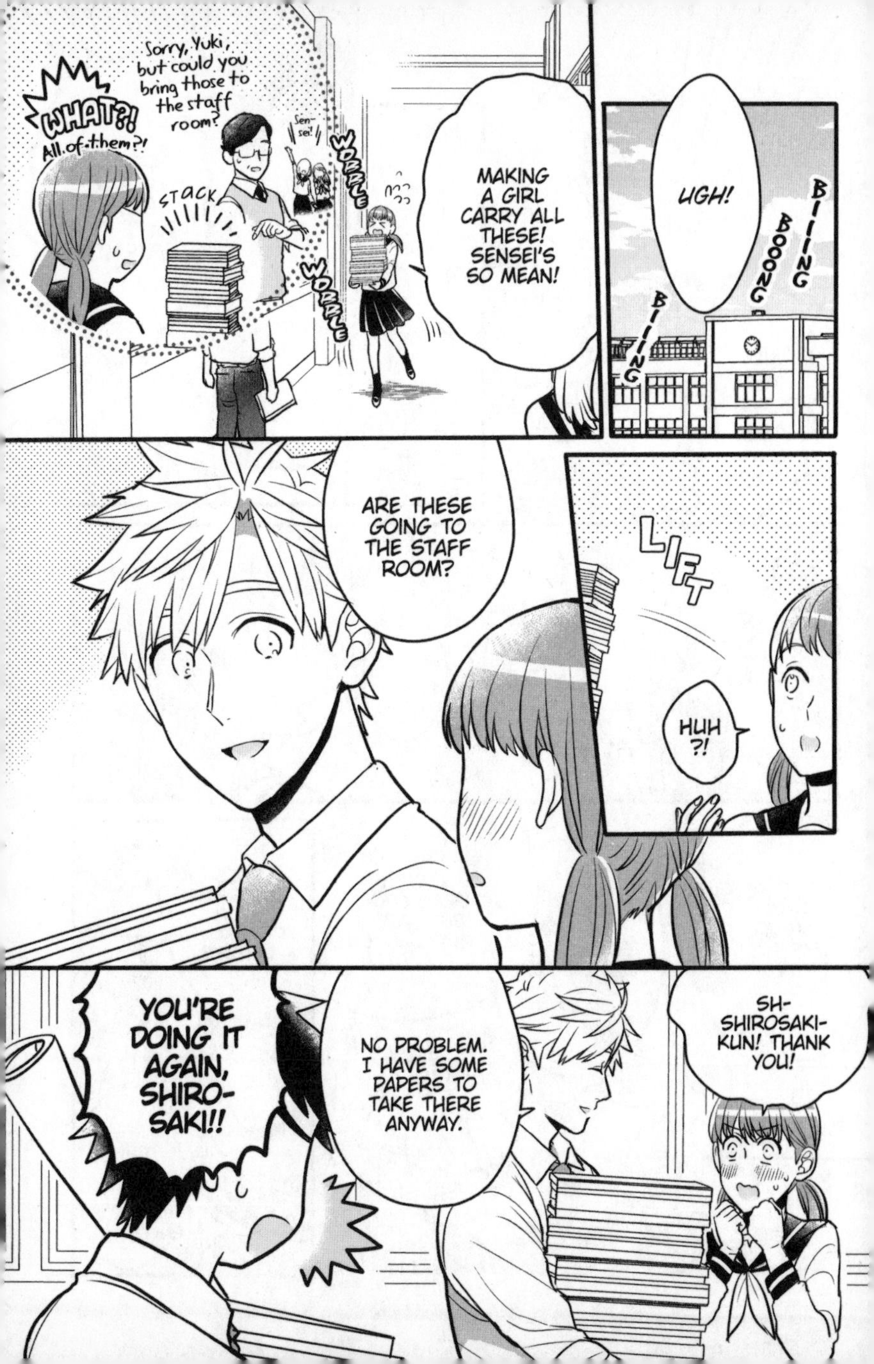
BIIING BOOONG BIIING
UGH!
MAKING A GIRL CARRY ALL THESE! SENSEI'S SO MEAN!
Sorry, Yuki, but could you bring those to the staff room?
WHAT?! All of them?!
Sen-sei!
WOBBLE
STACK
WOBBLE
LIFT
HUH?!
ARE THESE GOING TO THE STAFF ROOM?
SH-SHIROSAKI-KUN! THANK YOU!
NO PROBLEM. I HAVE SOME PAPERS TO TAKE THERE ANYWAY.
YOU'RE DOING IT AGAIN, SHIRO-SAKI!!

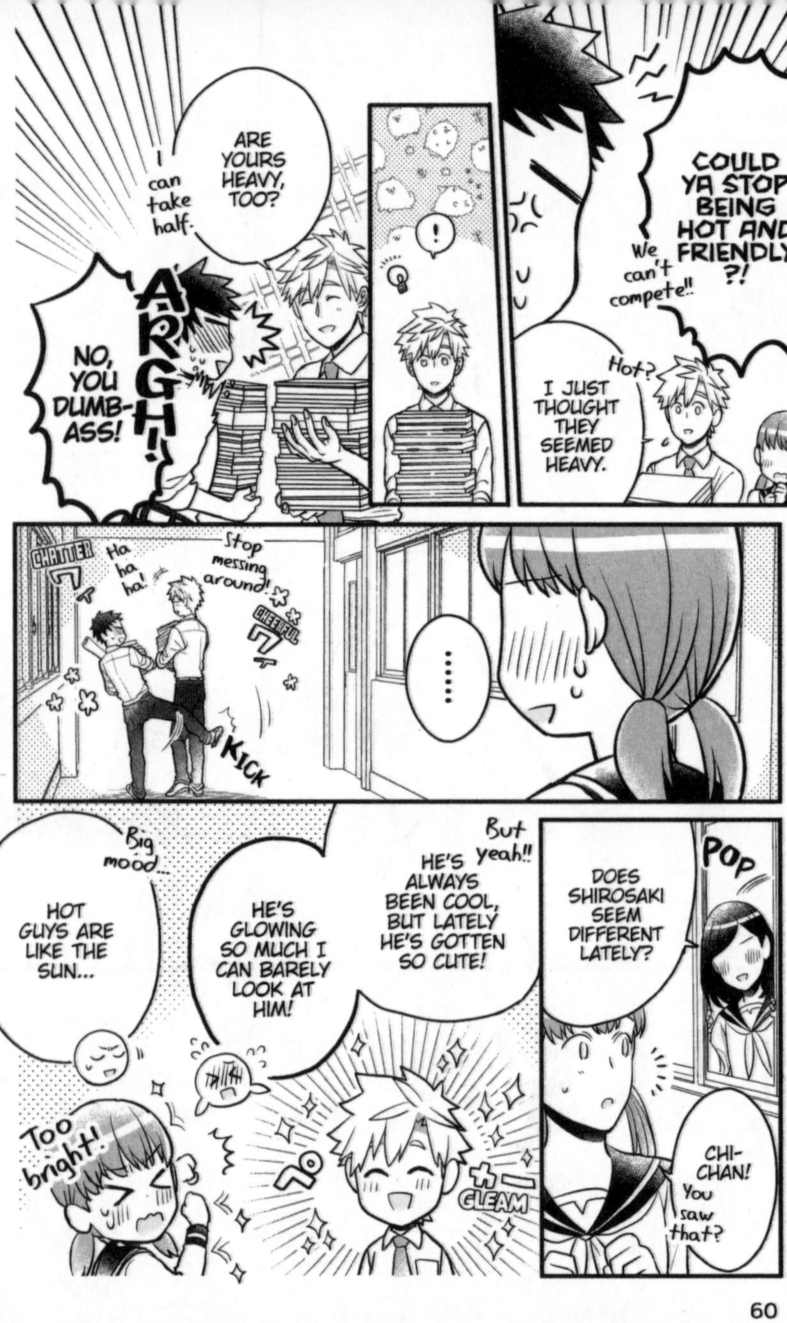
COULD YA STOP BEING HOT AND FRIENDLY?!
We can't compete!!
Hot?
I JUST THOUGHT THEY SEEMED HEAVY.
!
ARE YOURS HEAVY, TOO?
I can take half.
ARGH!!
NO, YOU DUMB-ASS!
......
Stop messing around!
CHEERFUL
Ha ha ha!
CHATTER
KICK
POP
DOES SHIROSAKI SEEM DIFFERENT LATELY?
CHI-CHAN!
You saw that?
But yeah!!
HE'S ALWAYS BEEN COOL, BUT LATELY HE'S GOTTEN SO CUTE!
HE'S GLOWING SO MUCH I CAN BARELY LOOK AT HIM!
Big mood...
HOT GUYS ARE LIKE THE SUN...
GLEAM
Too bright!

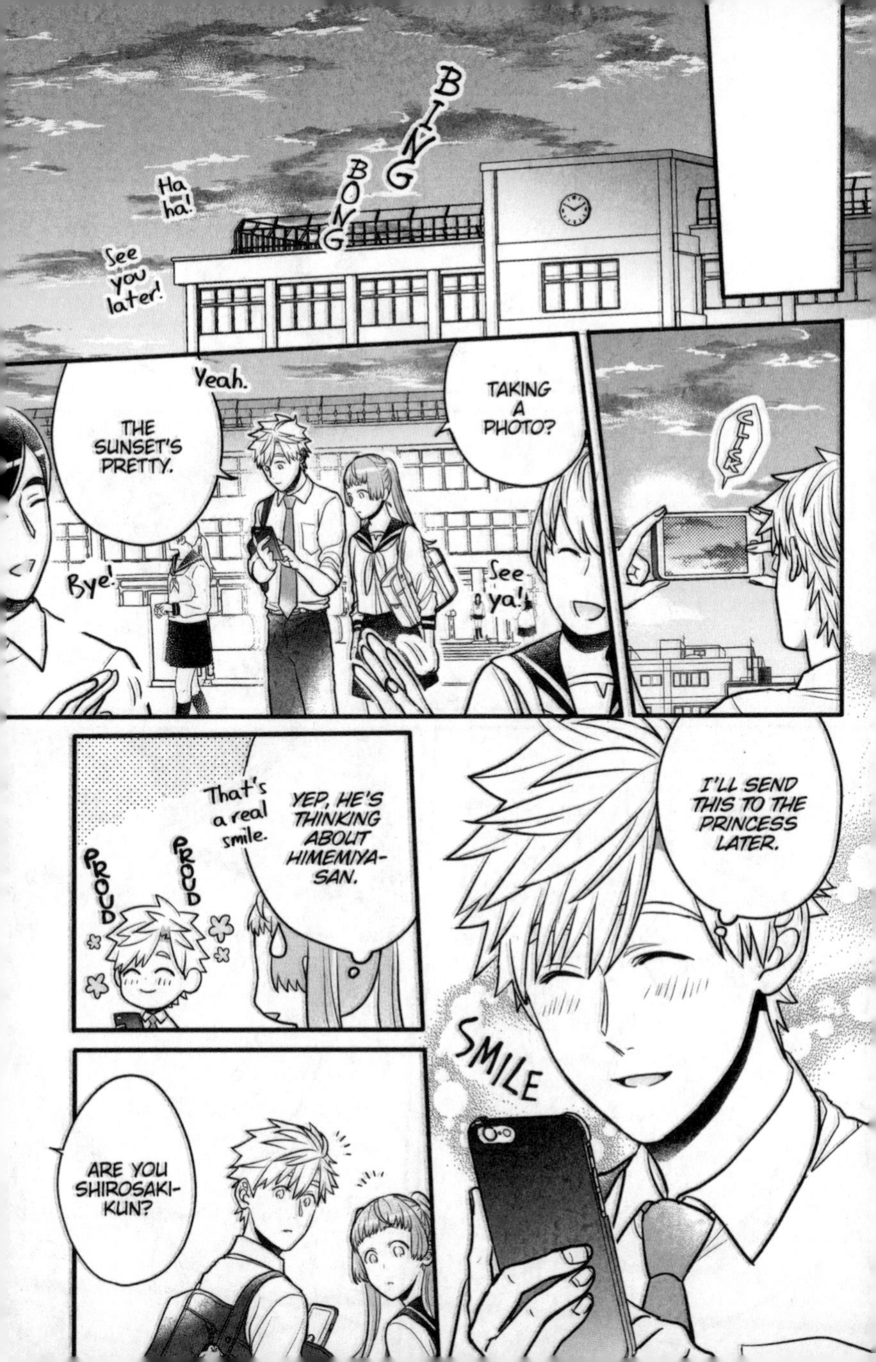
BING
BONG
Ha ha!
See you later!
CLICK
TAKING A PHOTO?
Yeah.
THE SUNSET'S PRETTY.
See ya!
Bye!
I'LL SEND THIS TO THE PRINCESS LATER.
SMILE
YEP, HE'S THINKING ABOUT HIMEMIYA-SAN.
That's a real smile.
PROUD
PROUD
ARE YOU SHIROSAKI-KUN?

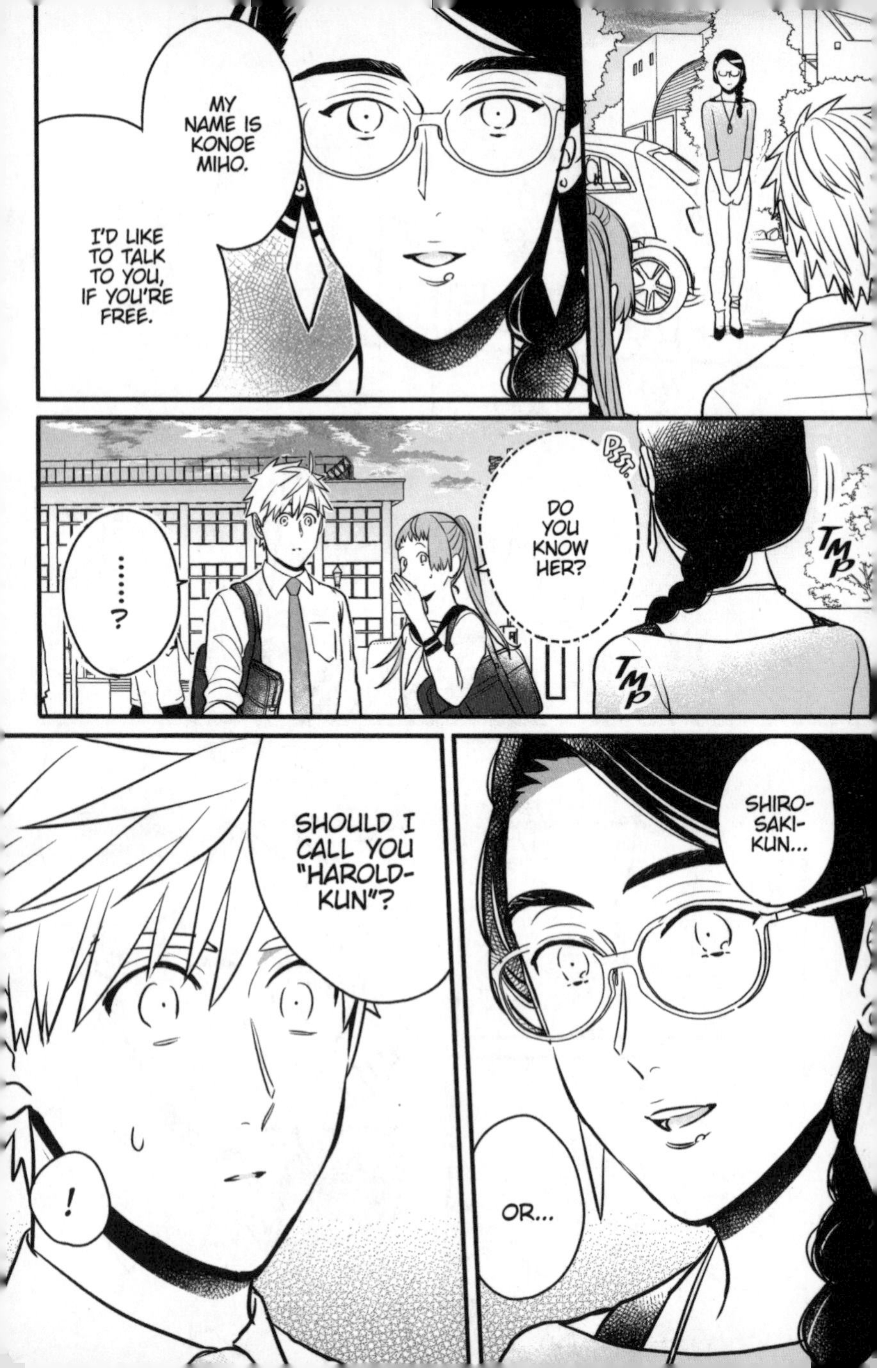
MY NAME IS KONOE MIHO.
I'D LIKE TO TALK TO YOU, IF YOU'RE FREE.
TMP
TMP
PSST.
DO YOU KNOW HER?
......?
SHIRO-SAKI-KUN...
OR...
SHOULD I CALL YOU "HAROLD-KUN"?
!

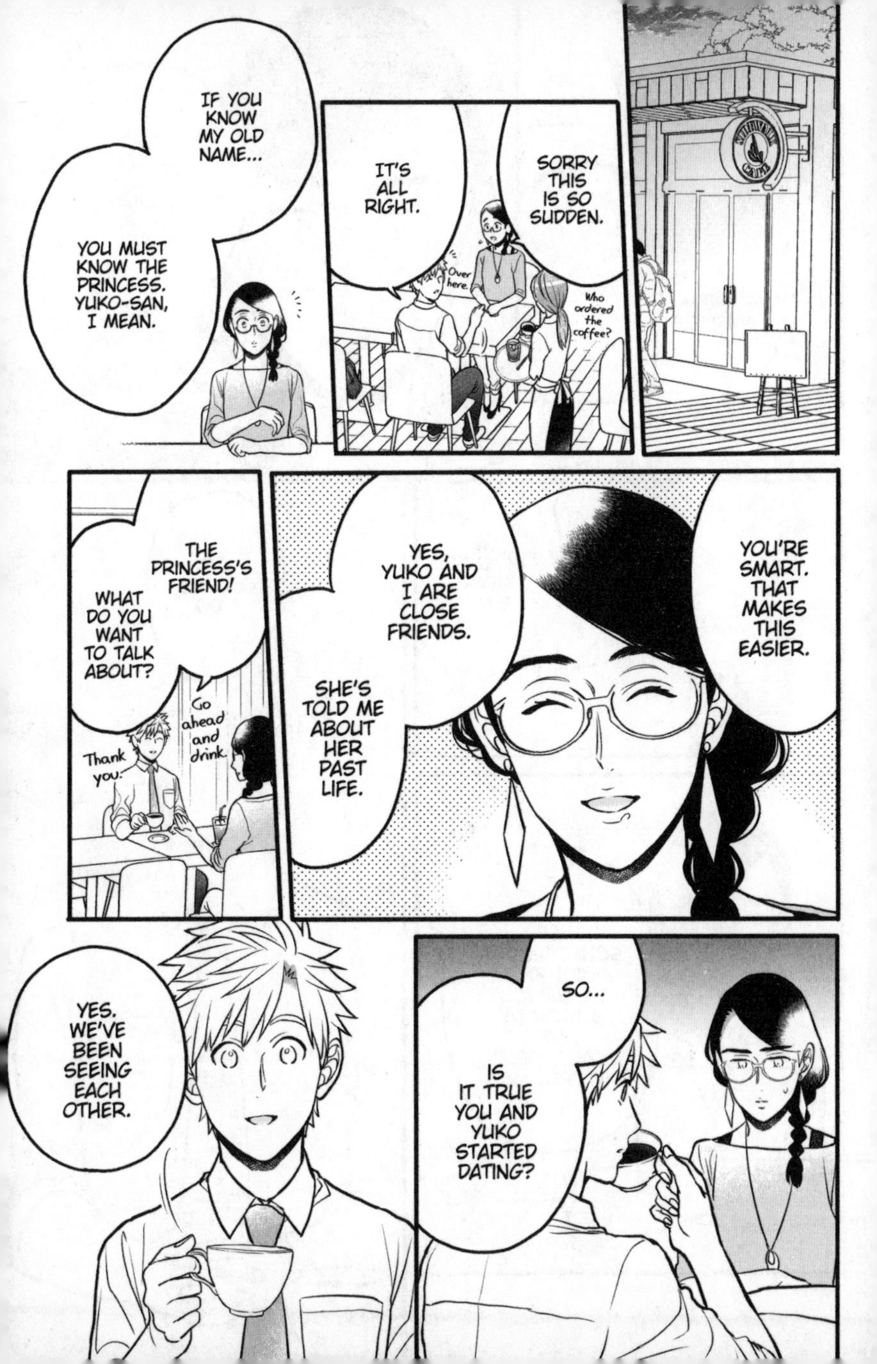
SORRY THIS IS SO SUDDEN.
IT'S ALL RIGHT.
Over here.
Who ordered the coffee?
IF YOU KNOW MY OLD NAME...
YOU MUST KNOW THE PRINCESS. YUKO-SAN, I MEAN.
YOU'RE SMART. THAT MAKES THIS EASIER.
YES, YUKO AND I ARE CLOSE FRIENDS.
SHE'S TOLD ME ABOUT HER PAST LIFE.
THE PRINCESS'S FRIEND!
WHAT DO YOU WANT TO TALK ABOUT?
Go ahead and drink.
Thank you.
SO...
IS IT TRUE YOU AND YUKO STARTED DATING?
YES. WE'VE BEEN SEEING EACH OTHER.

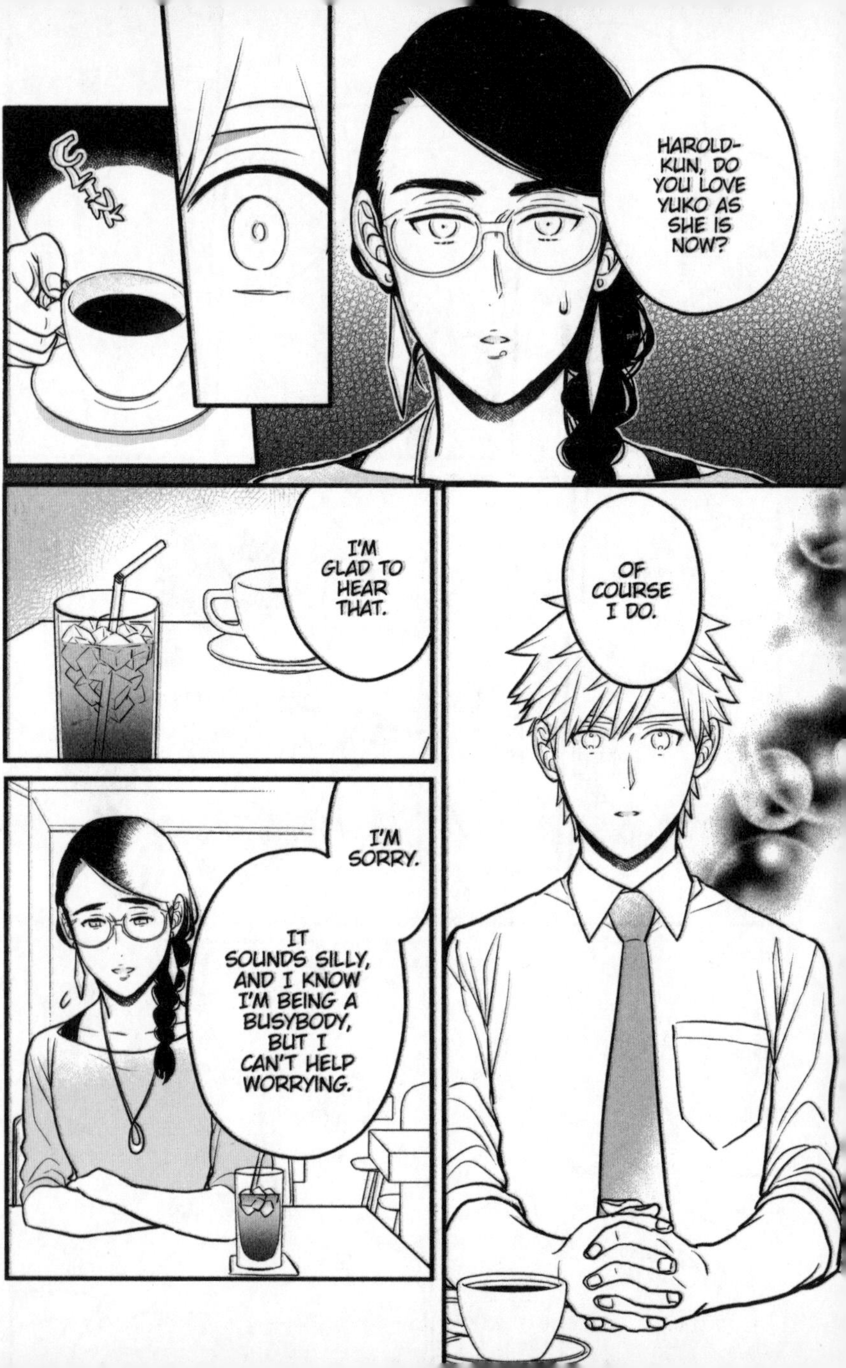
HAROLD-KUN, DO YOU LOVE YUKO AS SHE IS NOW?
CLINK
OF COURSE I DO.
I'M GLAD TO HEAR THAT.
I'M SORRY.
IT SOUNDS SILLY, AND I KNOW I'M BEING A BUSYBODY, BUT I CAN'T HELP WORRYING.

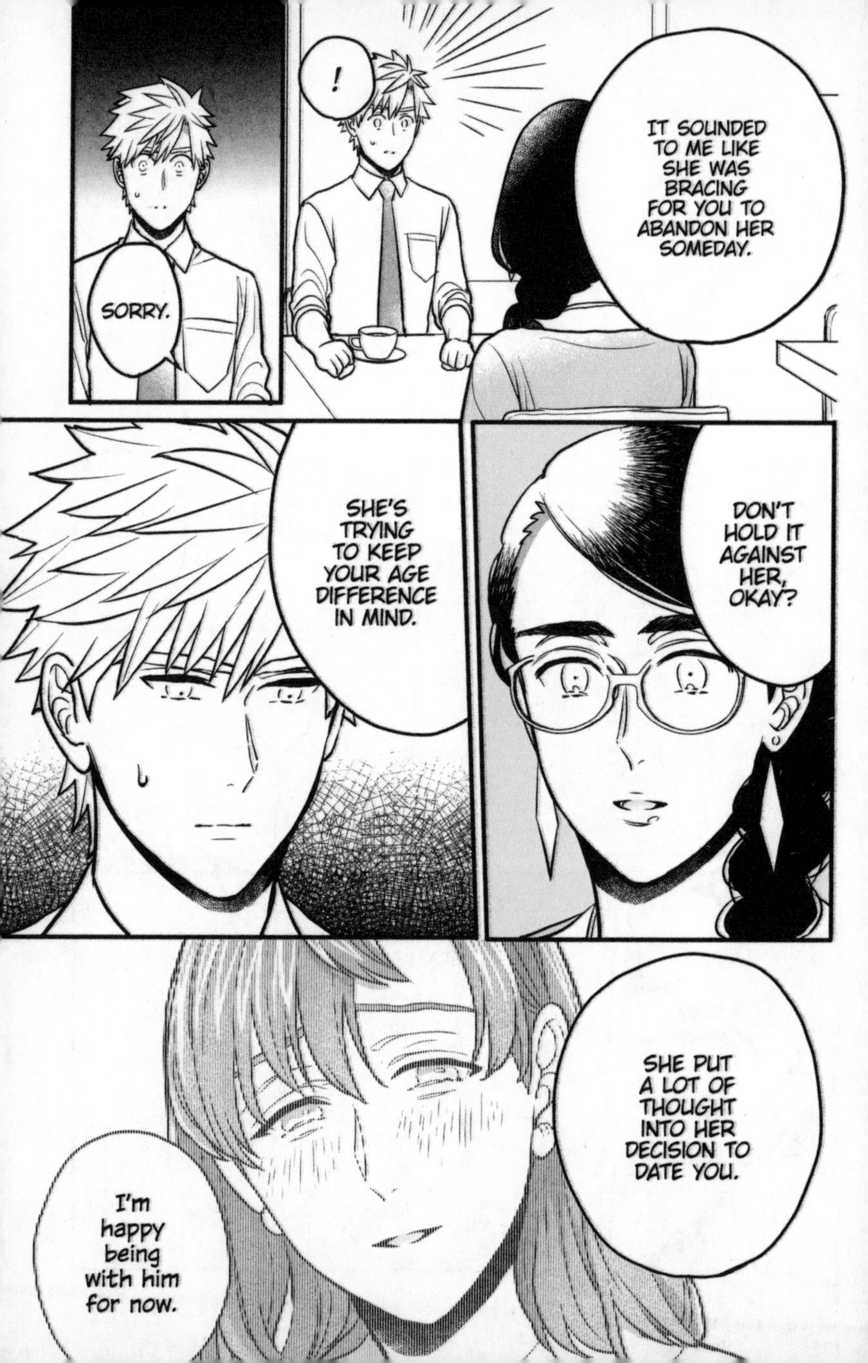
IT SOUNDED TO ME LIKE SHE WAS BRACING FOR YOU TO ABANDON HER SOMEDAY.
!
SORRY.
DON'T HOLD IT AGAINST HER, OKAY?
SHE'S TRYING TO KEEP YOUR AGE DIFFERENCE IN MIND.
SHE PUT A LOT OF THOUGHT INTO HER DECISION TO DATE YOU.
I'm happy being with him for now.

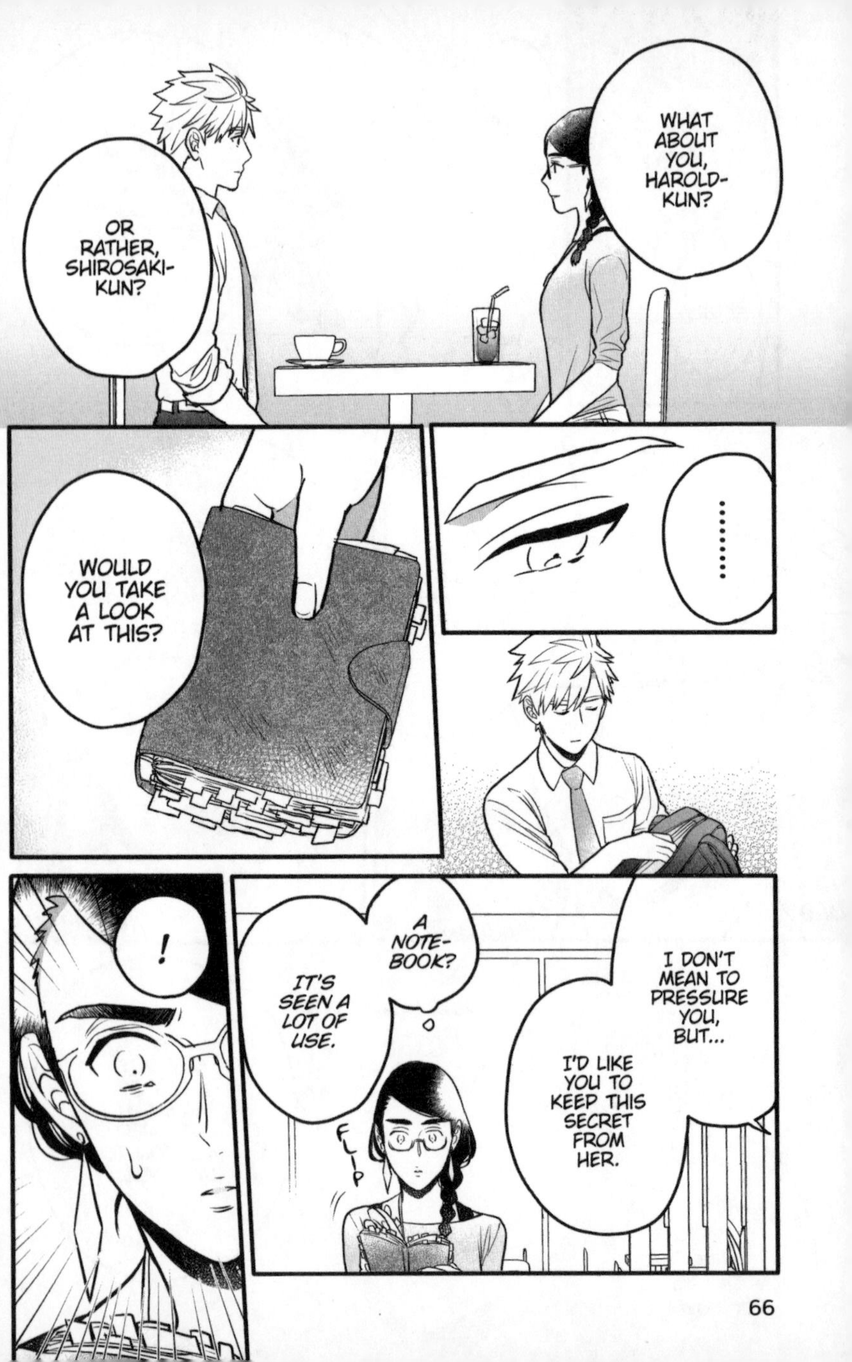
WHAT ABOUT YOU, HAROLD-KUN?
OR RATHER, SHIROSAKI-KUN?
......
WOULD YOU TAKE A LOOK AT THIS?
I DON'T MEAN TO PRESSURE YOU, BUT...
I'D LIKE YOU TO KEEP THIS SECRET FROM HER.
A NOTE-BOOK?
IT'S SEEN A LOT OF USE.
FLIP
!

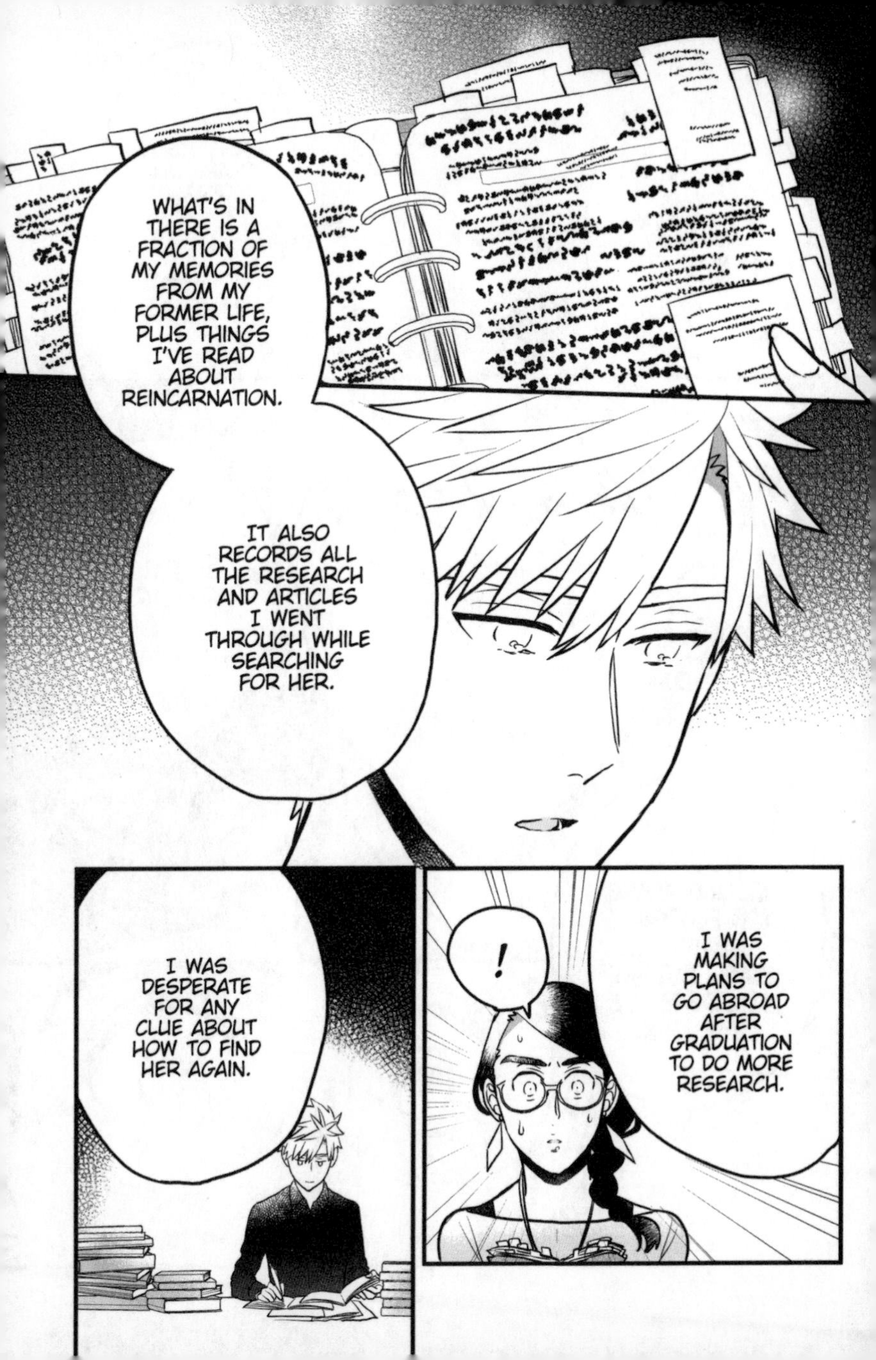
WHAT'S IN THERE IS A FRACTION OF MY MEMORIES FROM MY FORMER LIFE, PLUS THINGS I'VE READ ABOUT REINCARNATION.
IT ALSO RECORDS ALL THE RESEARCH AND ARTICLES I WENT THROUGH WHILE SEARCHING FOR HER.
I WAS MAKING PLANS TO GO ABROAD AFTER GRADUATION TO DO MORE RESEARCH.
!
I WAS DESPERATE FOR ANY CLUE ABOUT HOW TO FIND HER AGAIN.

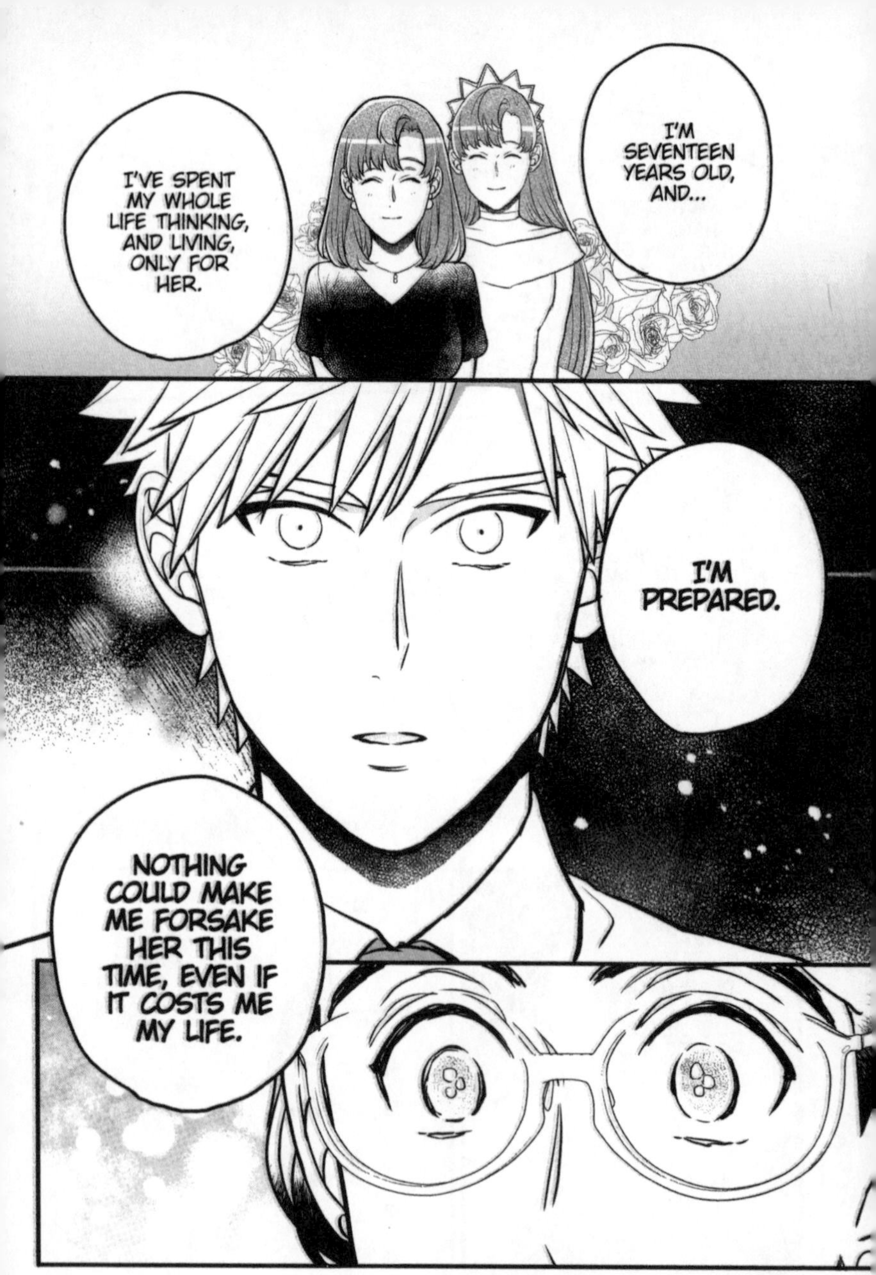
I'M SEVENTEEN YEARS OLD, AND...
I'VE SPENT MY WHOLE LIFE THINKING, AND LIVING, ONLY FOR HER.
I'M PREPARED.
NOTHING COULD MAKE ME FORSAKE HER THIS TIME, EVEN IF IT COSTS ME MY LIFE.

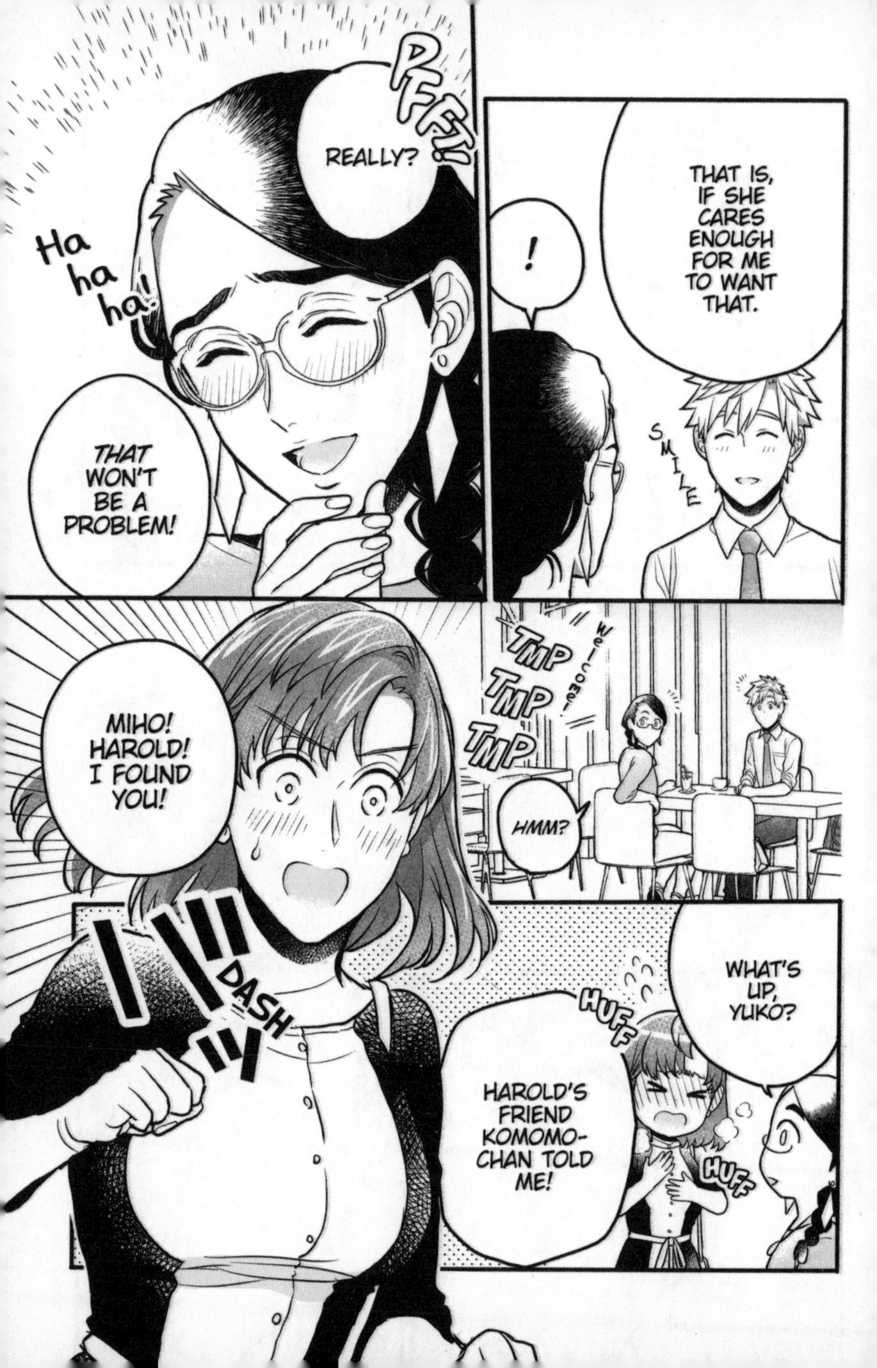
THAT IS, IF SHE CARES ENOUGH FOR ME TO WANT THAT.
!
SMILE
PFFT!
REALLY?
Ha ha ha!
THAT WON'T BE A PROBLEM!
TMP TMP TMP
Welcome!
HMM?
WHAT'S UP, YUKO?
HUFF HUFF
HAROLD'S FRIEND KOMOMO-CHAN TOLD ME!
MIHO! HAROLD! I FOUND YOU!
DASH

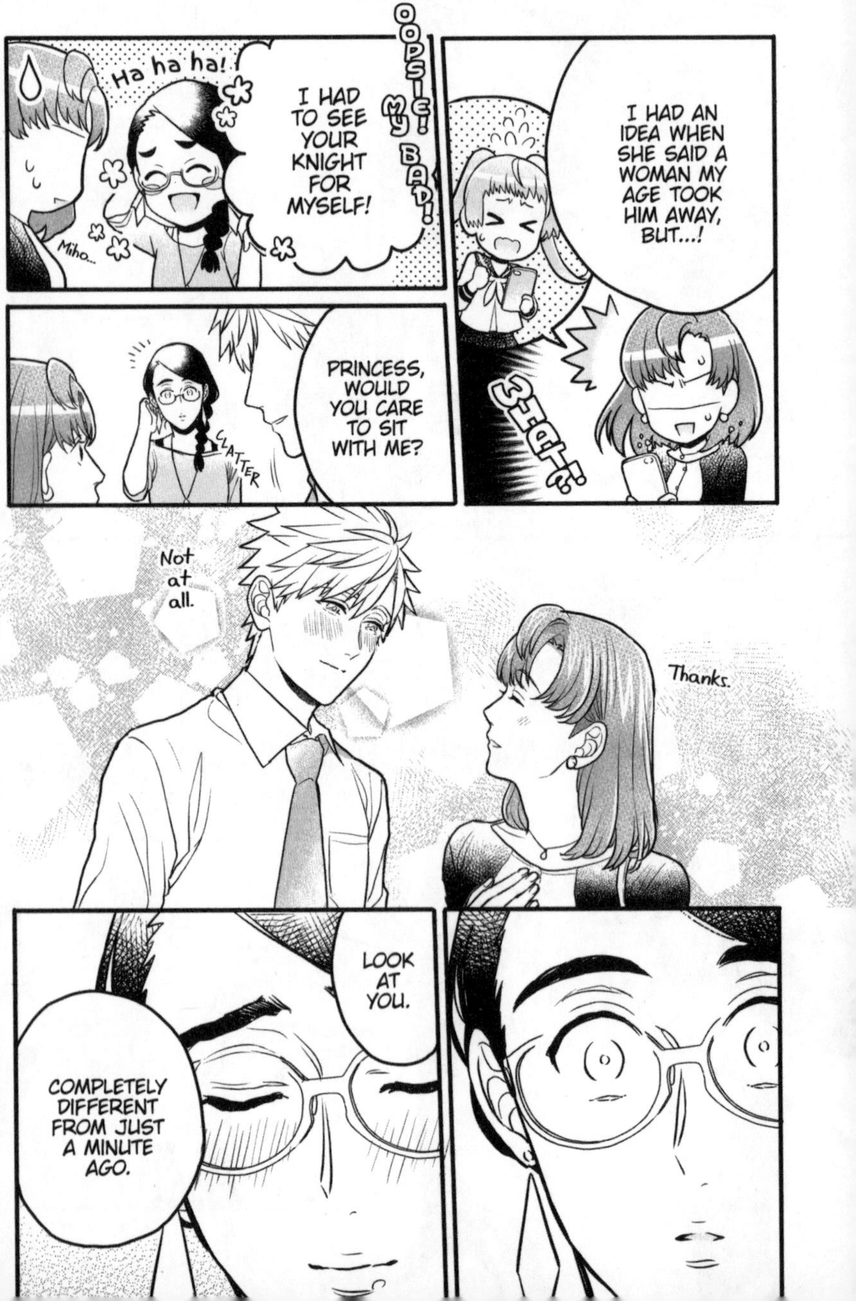
I HAD AN IDEA WHEN SHE SAID A WOMAN MY AGE TOOK HIM AWAY, BUT...!
WHAT!?
OOPSIE! MY BAD!
I HAD TO SEE YOUR KNIGHT FOR MYSELF!
Ha ha ha!
Miho...
PRINCESS, WOULD YOU CARE TO SIT WITH ME?
CLATTER
Thanks.
Not at all.
LOOK AT YOU.
COMPLETELY DIFFERENT FROM JUST A MINUTE AGO.

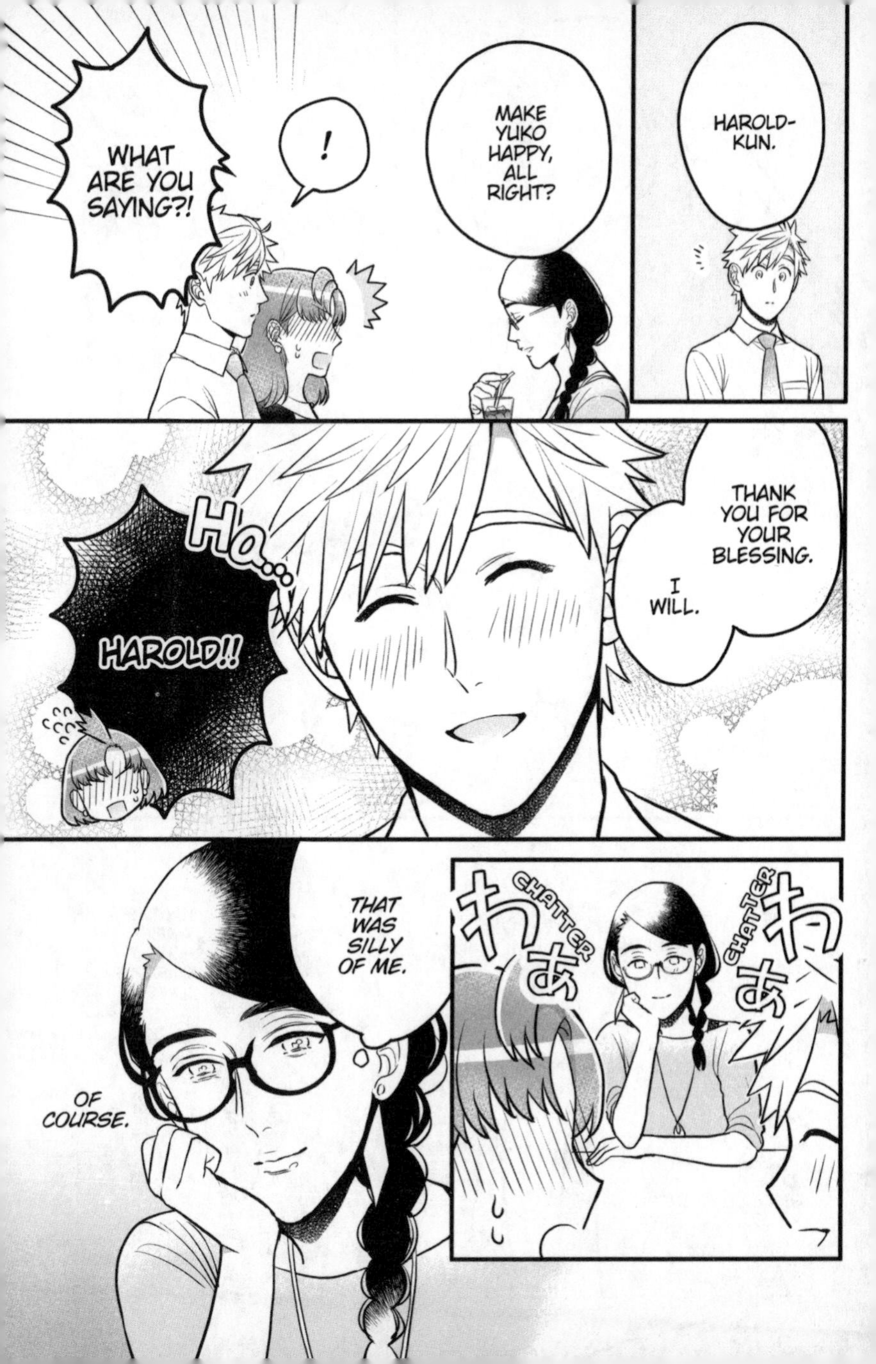
HAROLD-KUN.
MAKE YUKO HAPPY, ALL RIGHT?
!
WHAT ARE YOU SAYING?!
THANK YOU FOR YOUR BLESSING.
I WILL.
Ha...
HAROLD!!
わあ CHATTER
わあ CHATTER
THAT WAS SILLY OF ME.
OF COURSE.

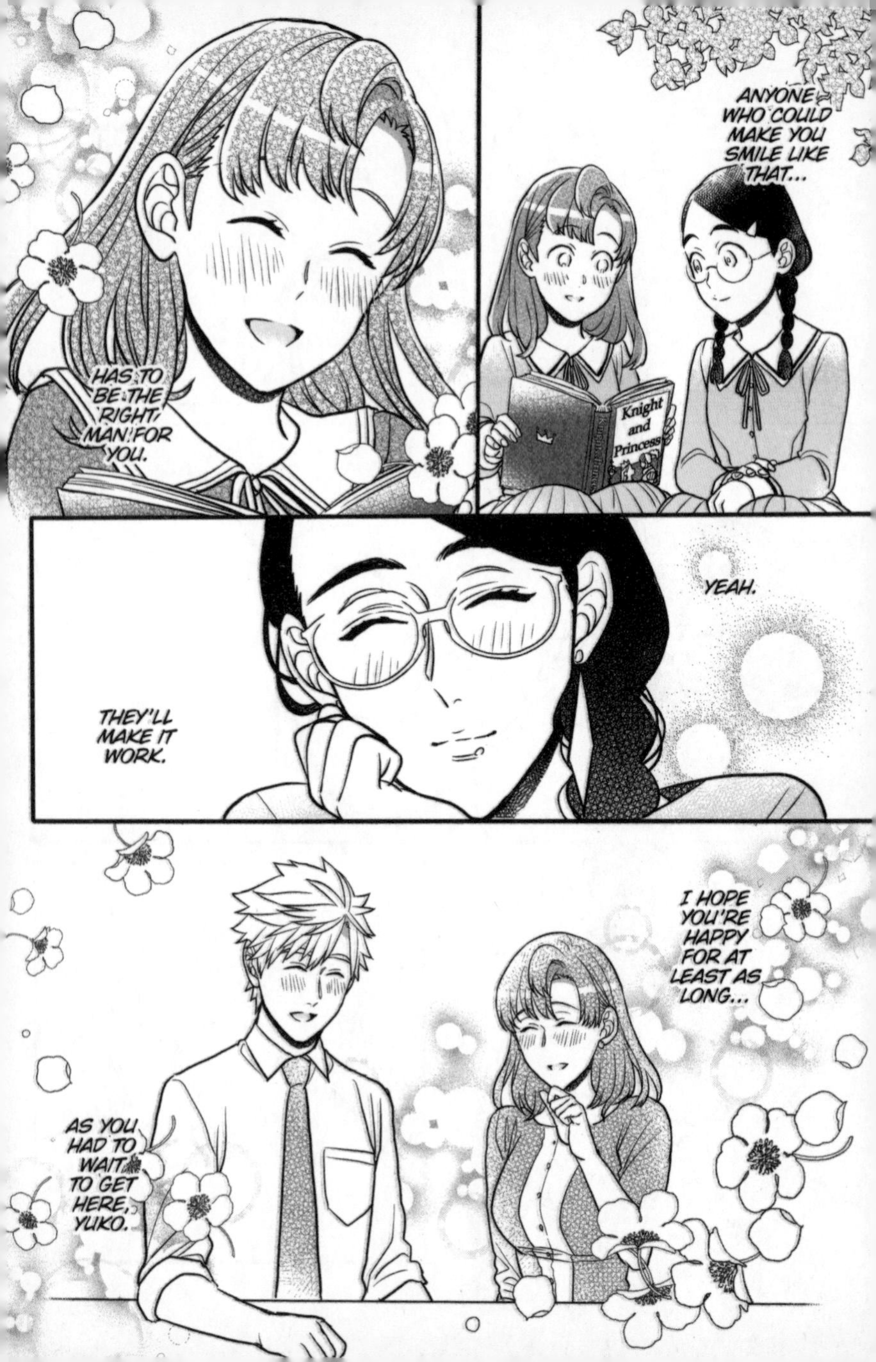
ANYONE WHO COULD MAKE YOU SMILE LIKE THAT...
Knight and Princess
HAS TO BE THE RIGHT MAN FOR YOU.
YEAH.
THEY'LL MAKE IT WORK.
I HOPE YOU'RE HAPPY FOR AT LEAST AS LONG...
AS YOU HAD TO WAIT TO GET HERE, YUKO.

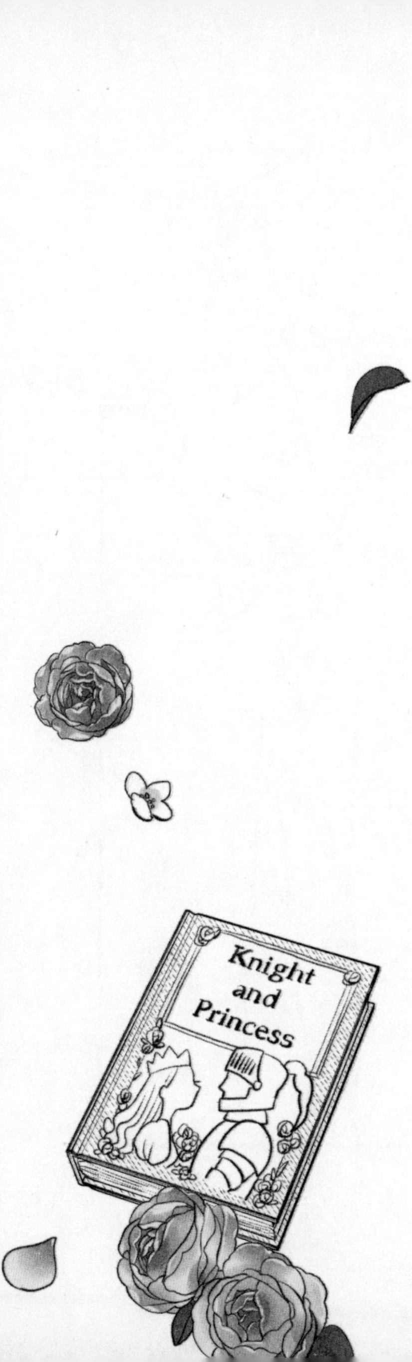
Knight and Princess

Konoe Miho (39)

Yuko's best friend, who's heard all about Yuko's past life. A best-selling author. They were in the same class in middle school, where they became friends.

It means a lot to Yuko that Miho never made fun of her past life stories.

As it happens, because age is one of the themes of this manga, I tried to choose everyone's given names to reflect the year they were born. For example, both Yuko and Miho's names topped the baby name charts from around forty years ago.

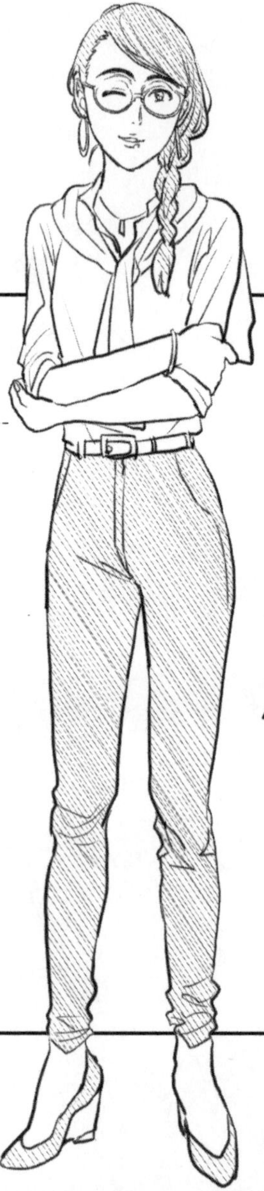

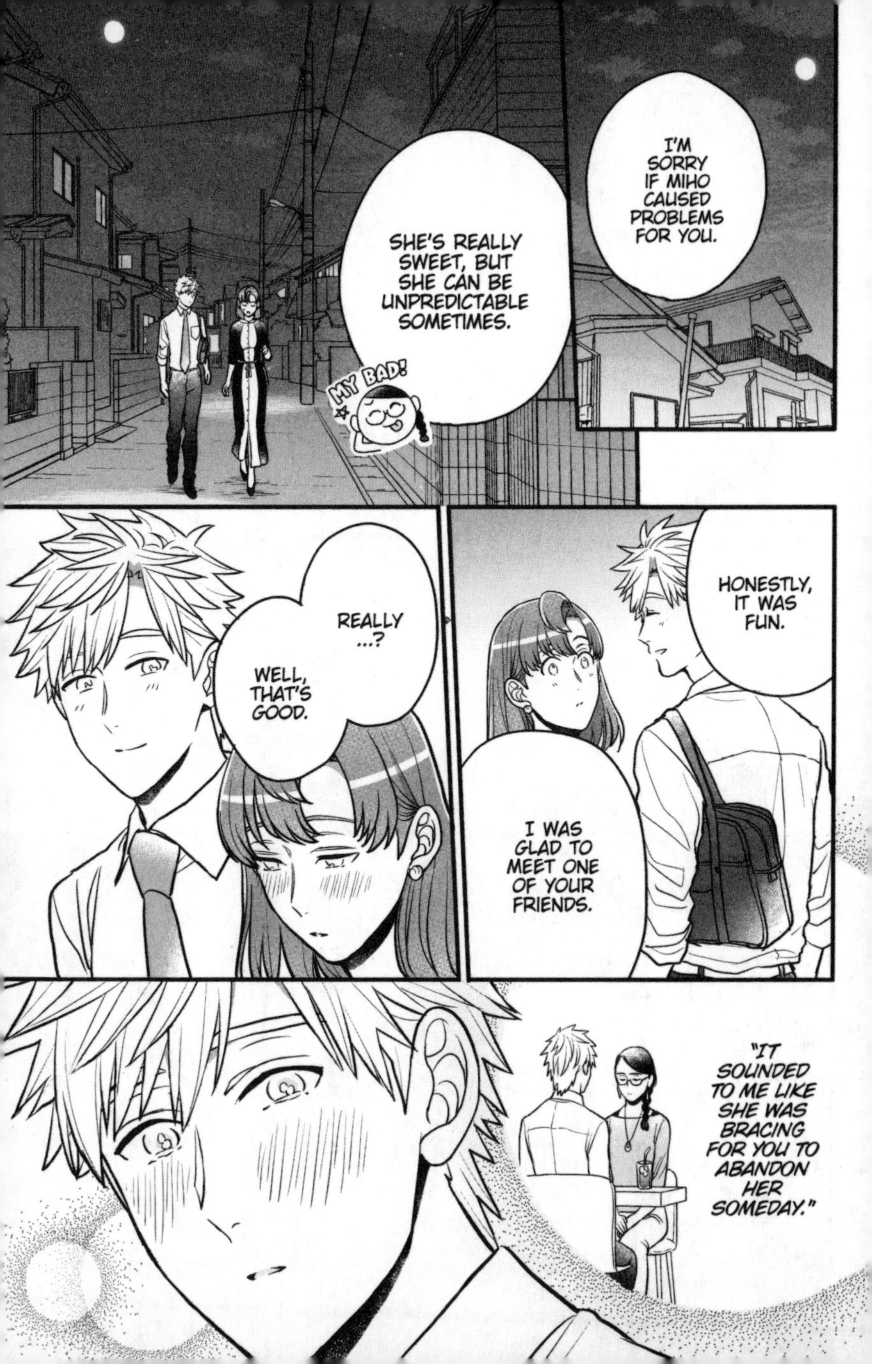
I'M SORRY IF MIHO CAUSED PROBLEMS FOR YOU.
SHE'S REALLY SWEET, BUT SHE CAN BE UNPREDICTABLE SOMETIMES.
MY BAD!
HONESTLY, IT WAS FUN.
I WAS GLAD TO MEET ONE OF YOUR FRIENDS.
REALLY ...?
WELL, THAT'S GOOD.
"IT SOUNDED TO ME LIKE SHE WAS BRACING FOR YOU TO ABANDON HER SOMEDAY."

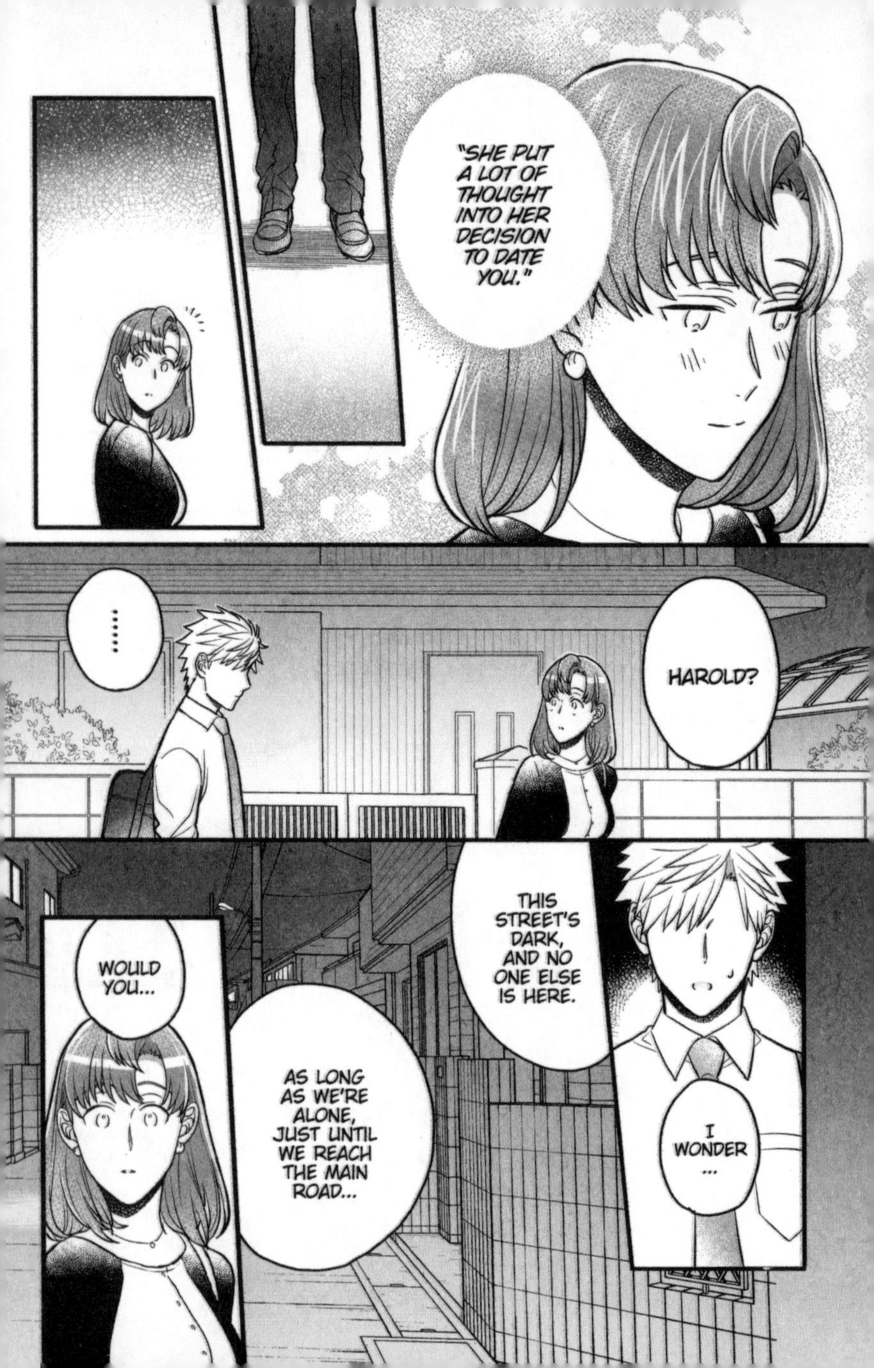
"SHE PUT A LOT OF THOUGHT INTO HER DECISION TO DATE YOU."
HAROLD?
......
THIS STREET'S DARK, AND NO ONE ELSE IS HERE.
I WONDER ...
WOULD YOU...
AS LONG AS WE'RE ALONE, JUST UNTIL WE REACH THE MAIN ROAD...

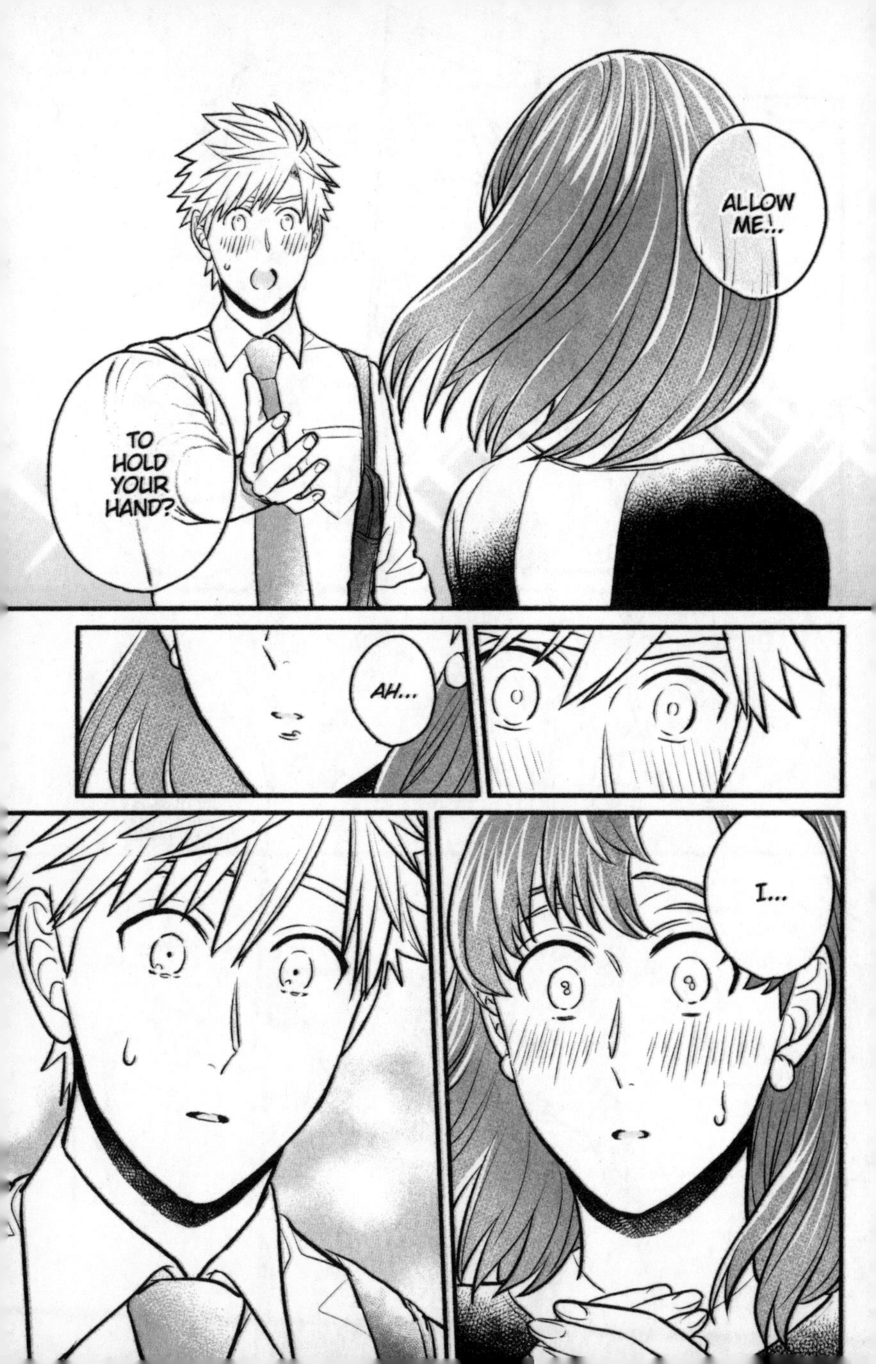
ALLOW ME!...
TO HOLD YOUR HAND?
AH...
I...

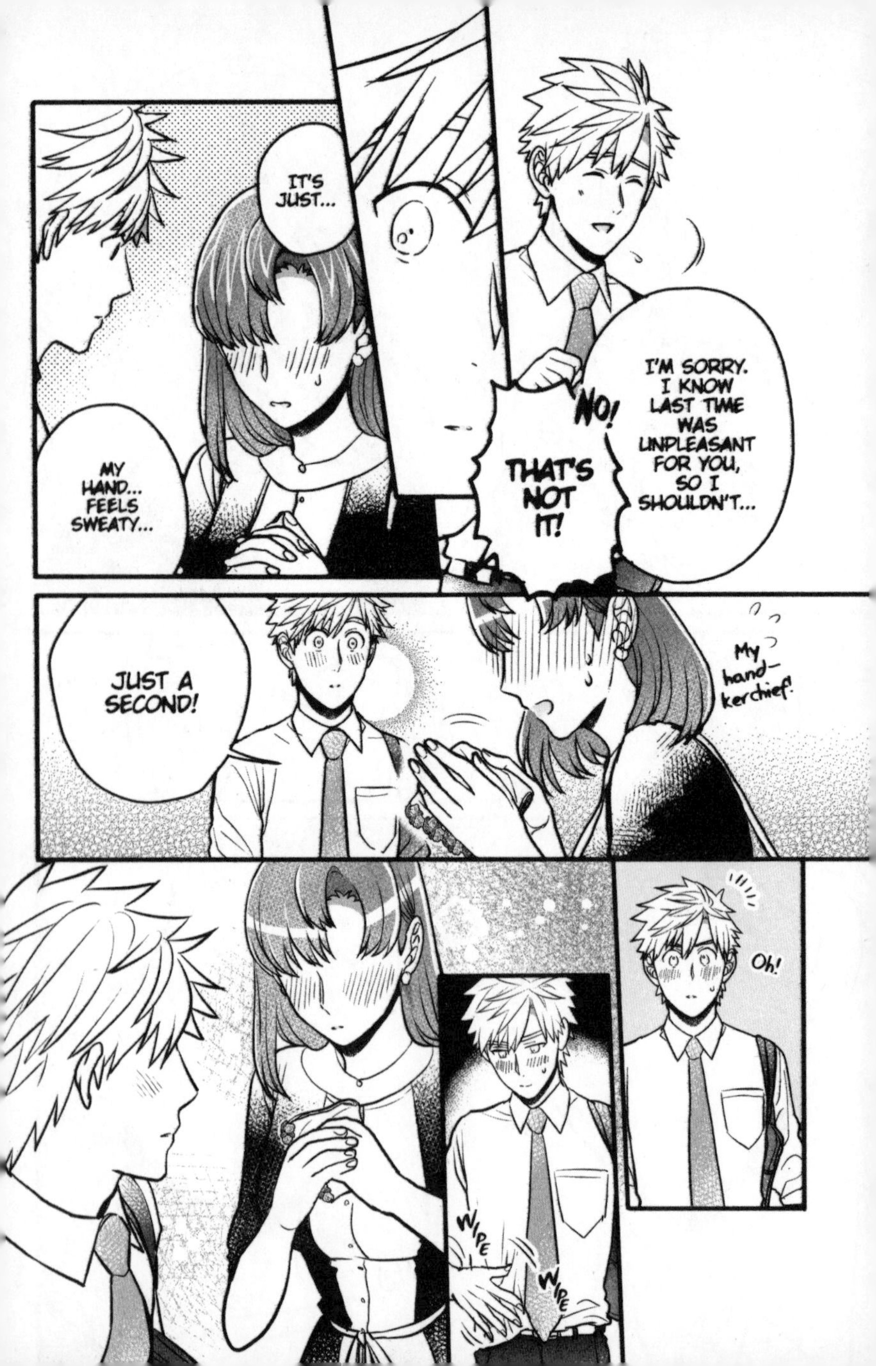
I'M SORRY. I KNOW LAST TIME WAS UNPLEASANT FOR YOU, SO I SHOULDN'T...
NO! THAT'S NOT IT!
IT'S JUST...
MY HAND... FEELS SWEATY...
My hand-kerchief!
JUST A SECOND!
Oh!
WIPE
WIPE

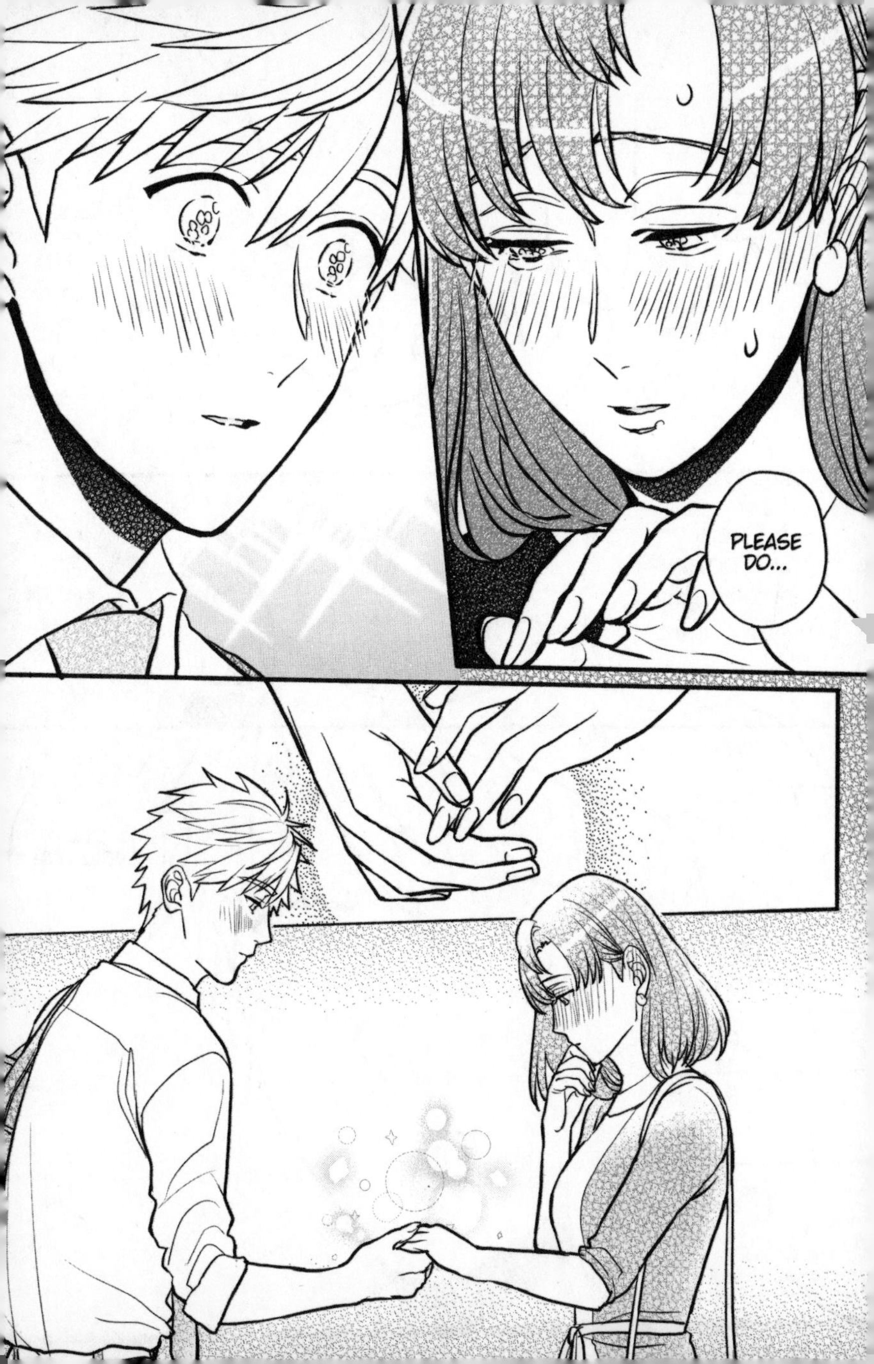
PLEASE DO...

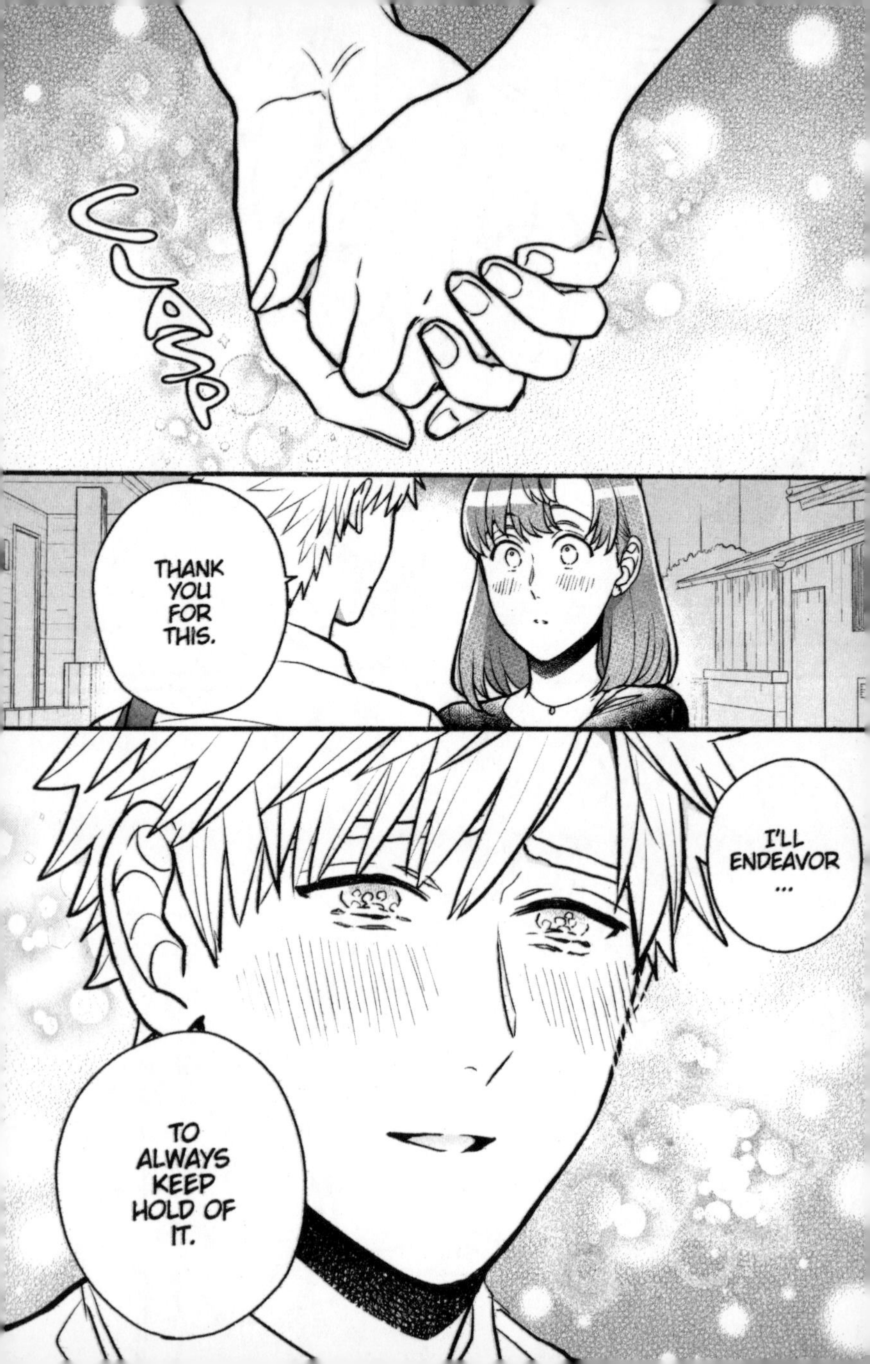
CLASP
THANK YOU FOR THIS.
I'LL ENDEAVOR ...
TO ALWAYS KEEP HOLD OF IT.

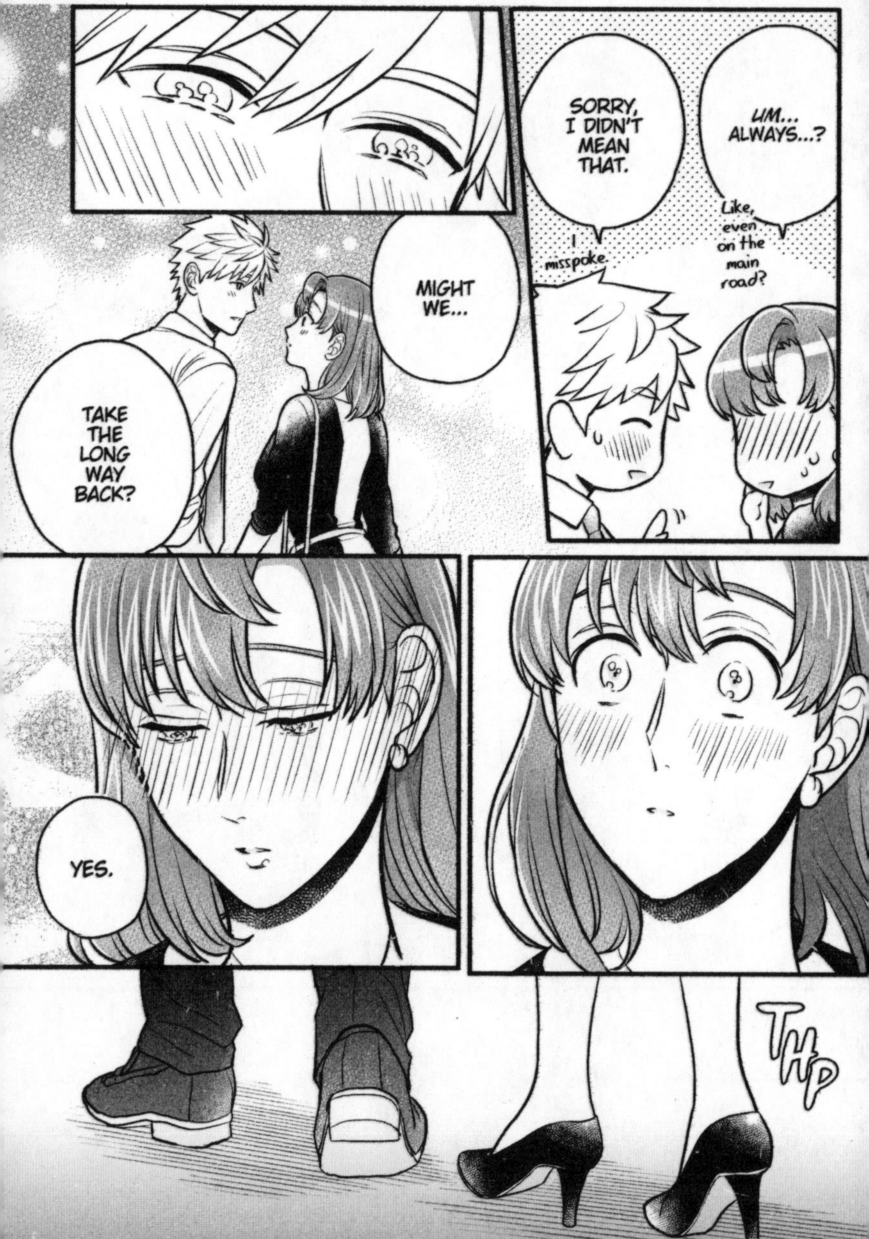
UM... ALWAYS...?
Like, even on the main road?
SORRY, I DIDN'T MEAN THAT.
I misspoke.
MIGHT WE...
TAKE THE LONG WAY BACK?
YES.
THP

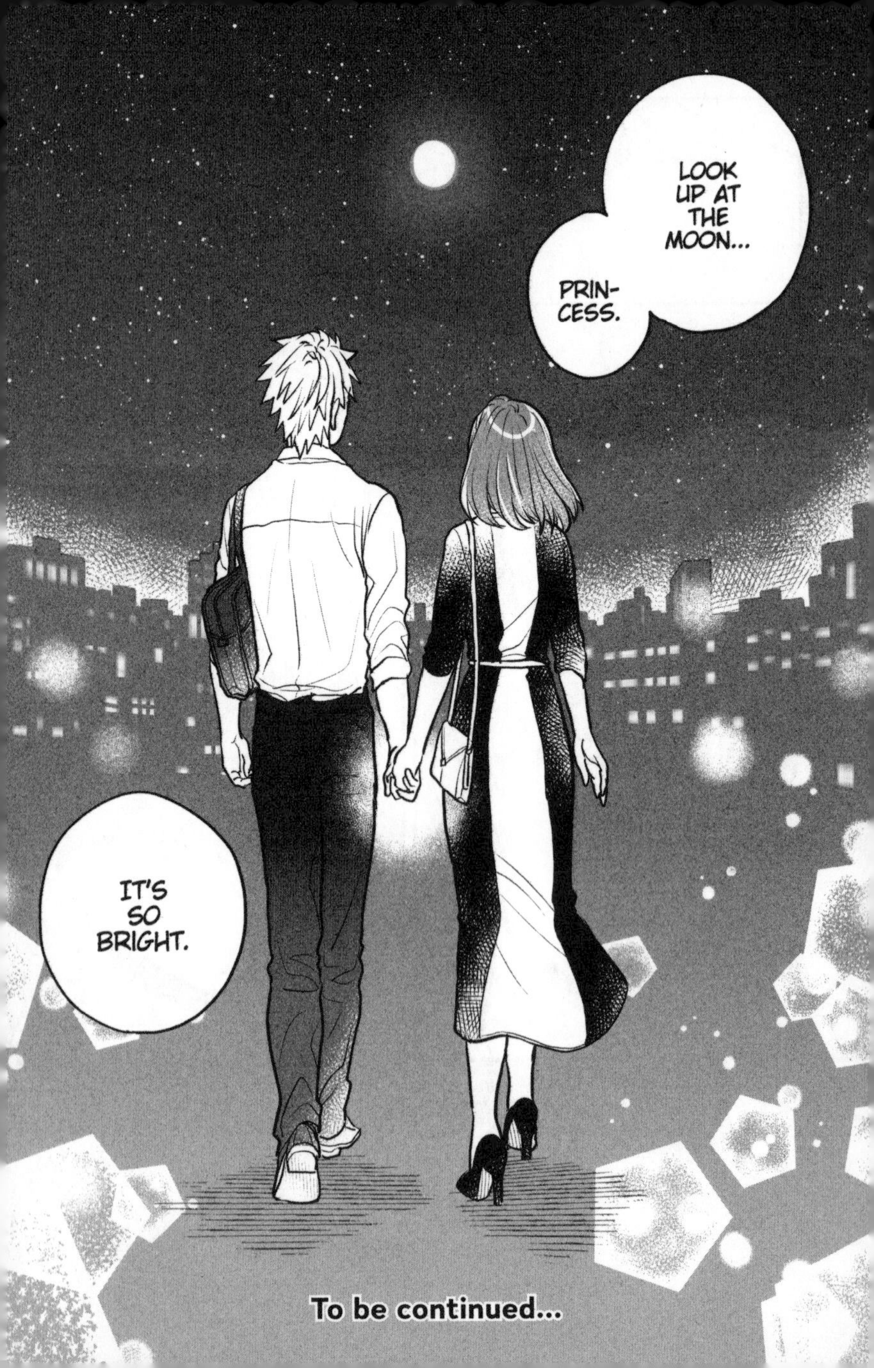
LOOK UP AT THE MOON...
PRIN-CESS.
IT'S SO BRIGHT.
To be continued...

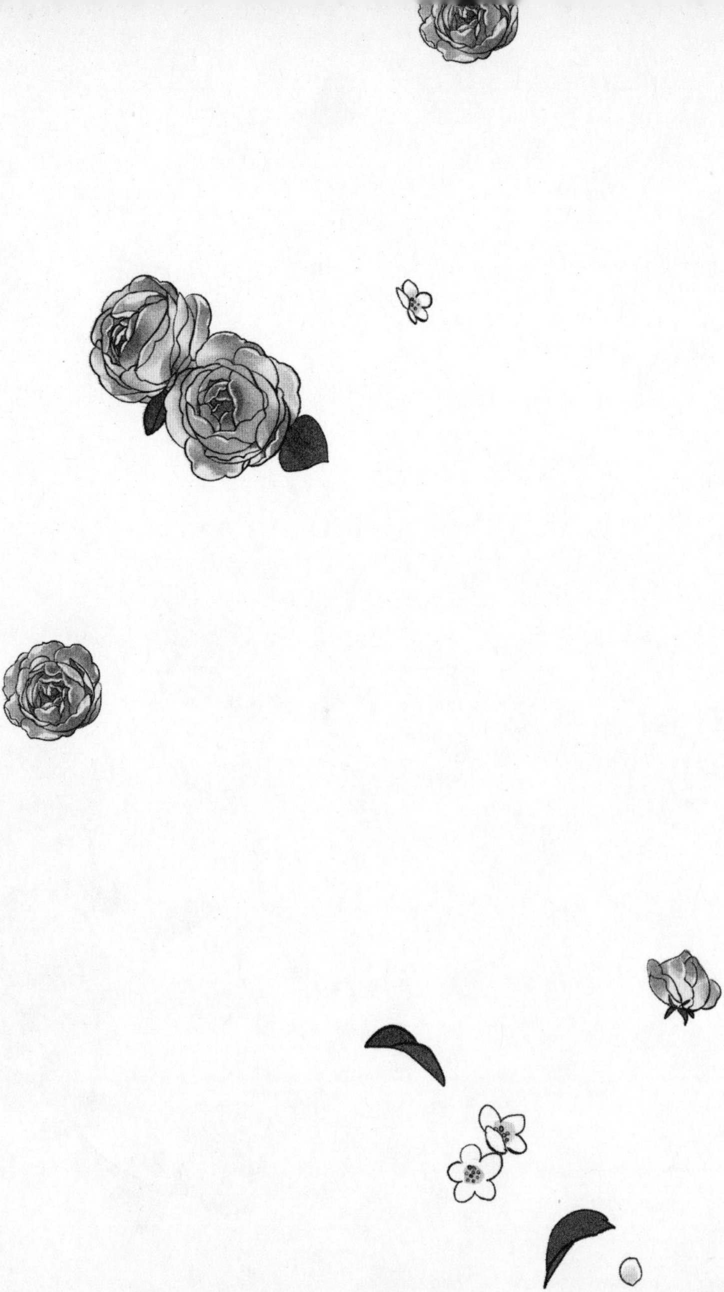

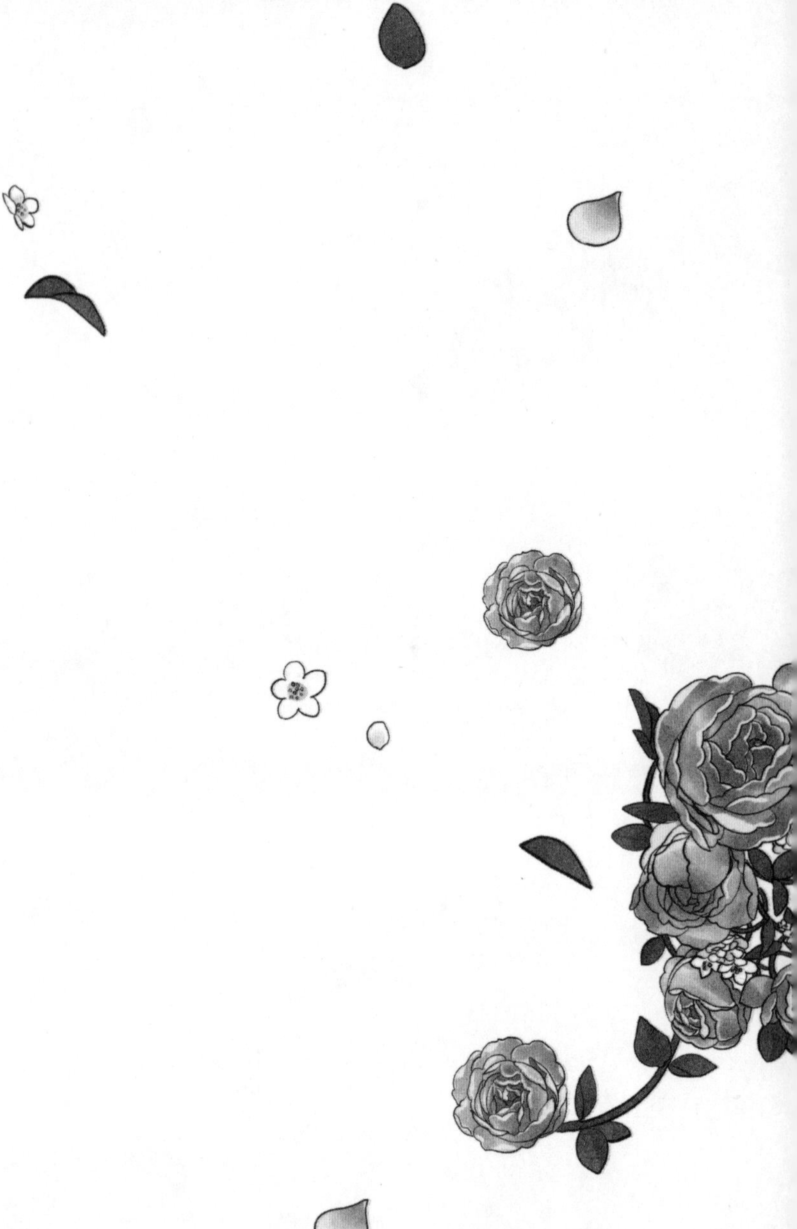

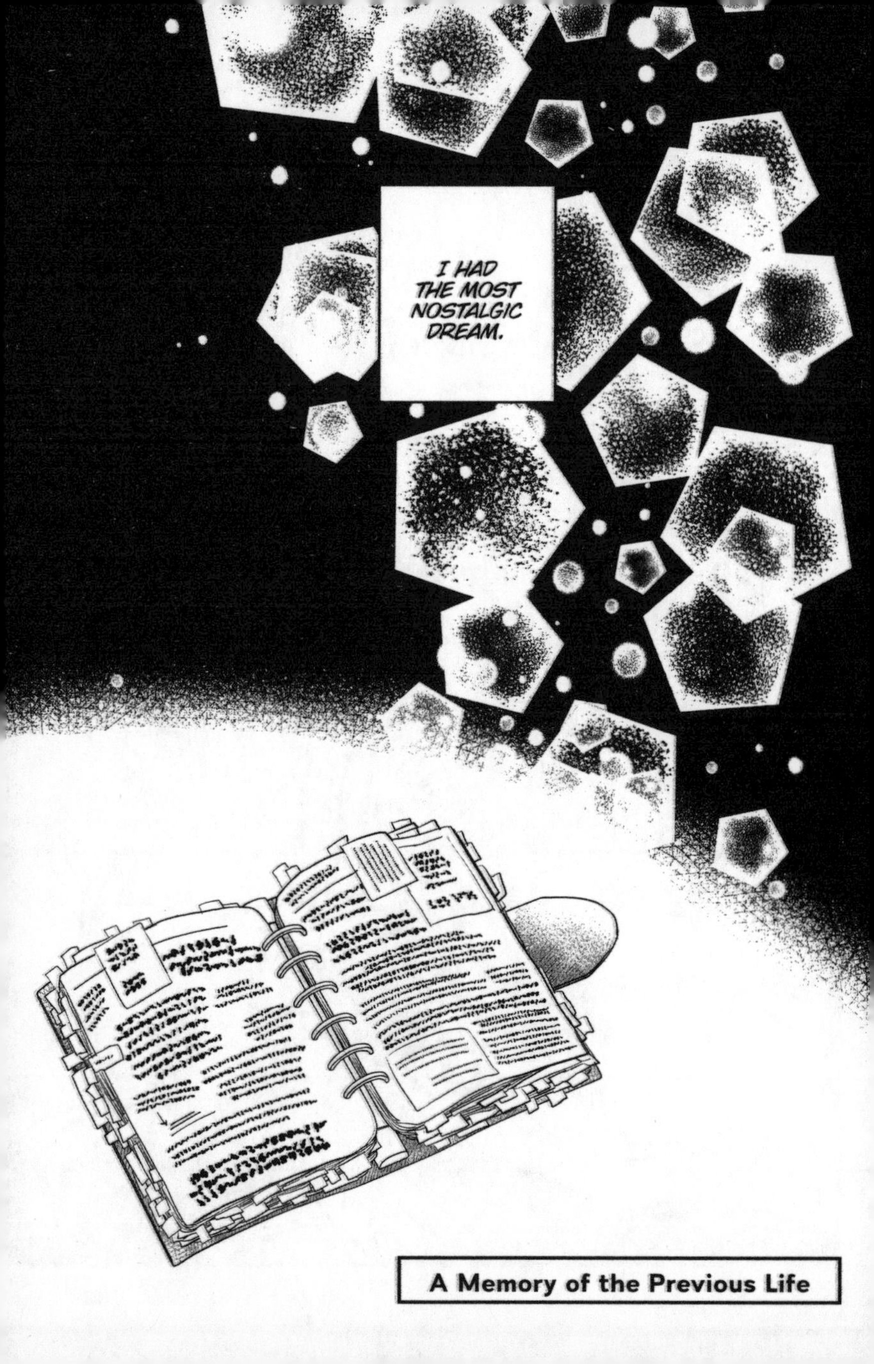
I HAD THE MOST NOSTALGIC DREAM.
A Memory of the Previous Life

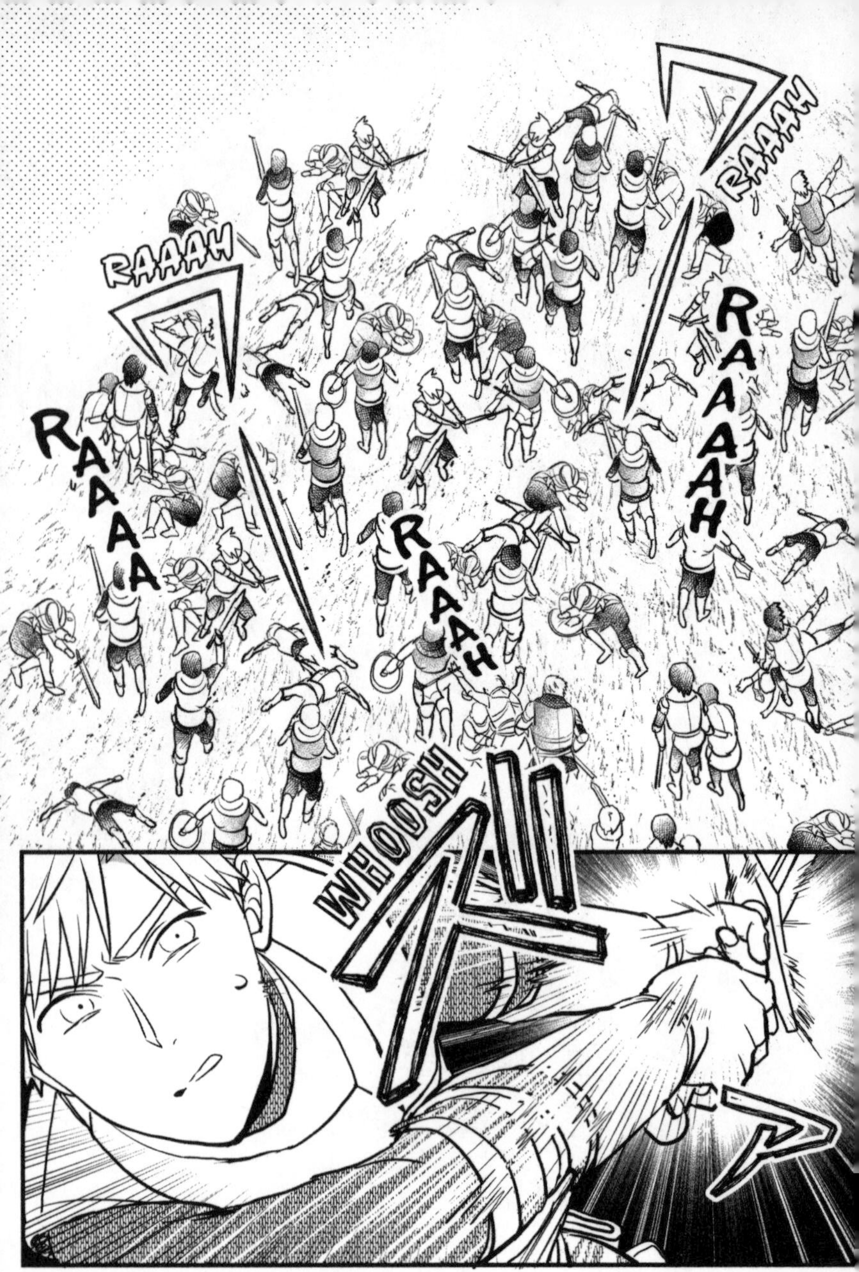
RAAAH
RAAAAAH
RAAAH
RAAAH
RAAAAA
WHOOSH

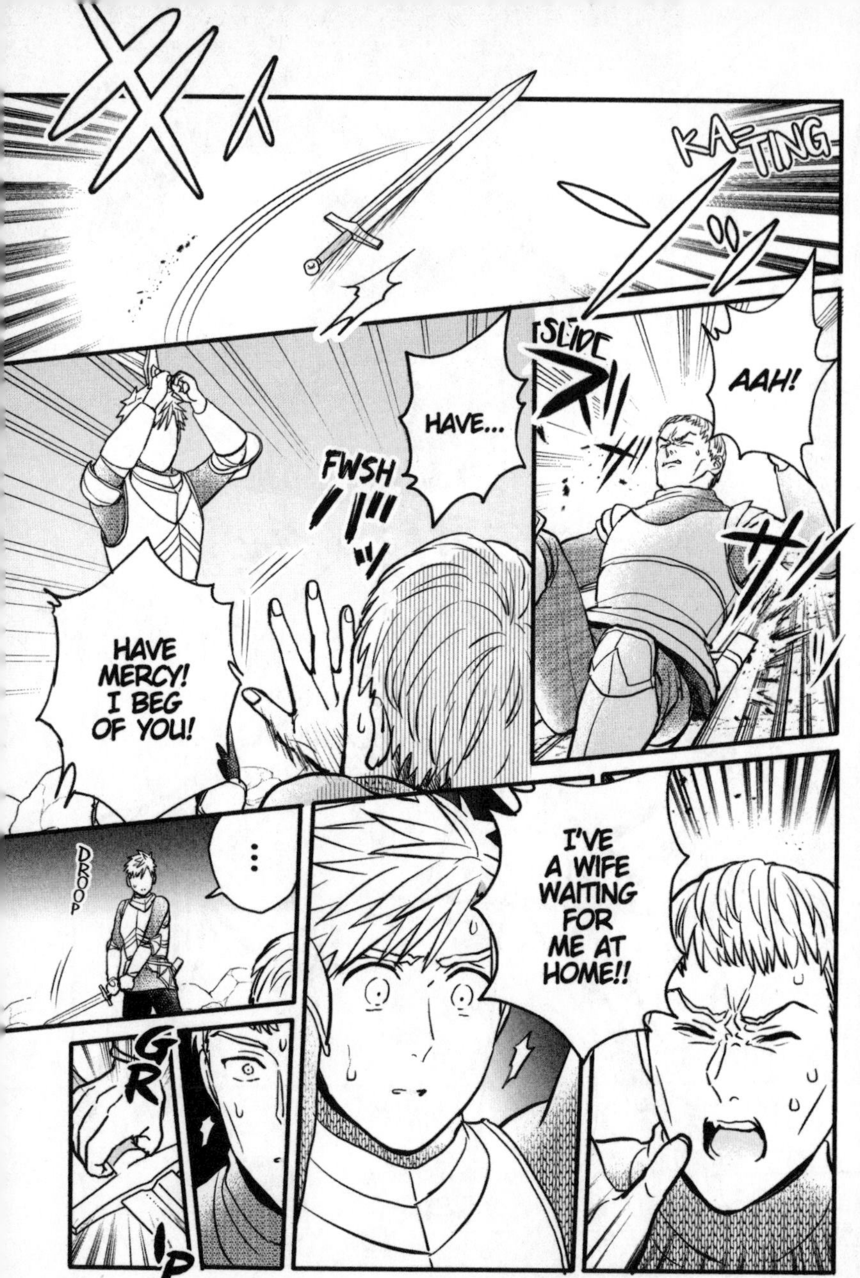
KA-TING
SLIDE
AAH!
HAVE...
FWSH
HAVE MERCY! I BEG OF YOU!
I'VE A WIFE WAITING FOR ME AT HOME!!
...
DROOP
GRIP

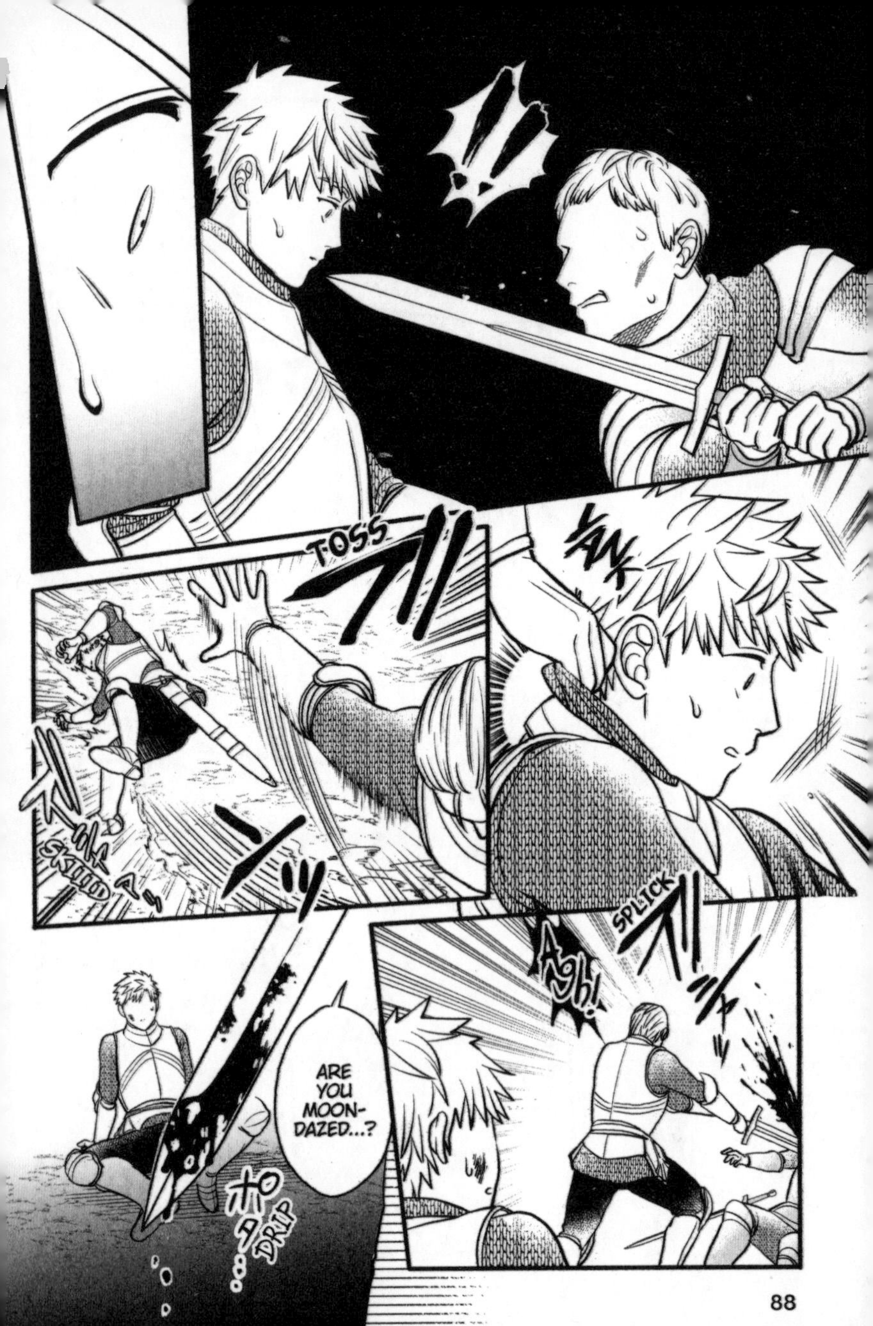
!!
YANK
TOSS
SKIDDD
SPLICK
Agh!
ARE YOU MOON-DAZED...?
DRIP

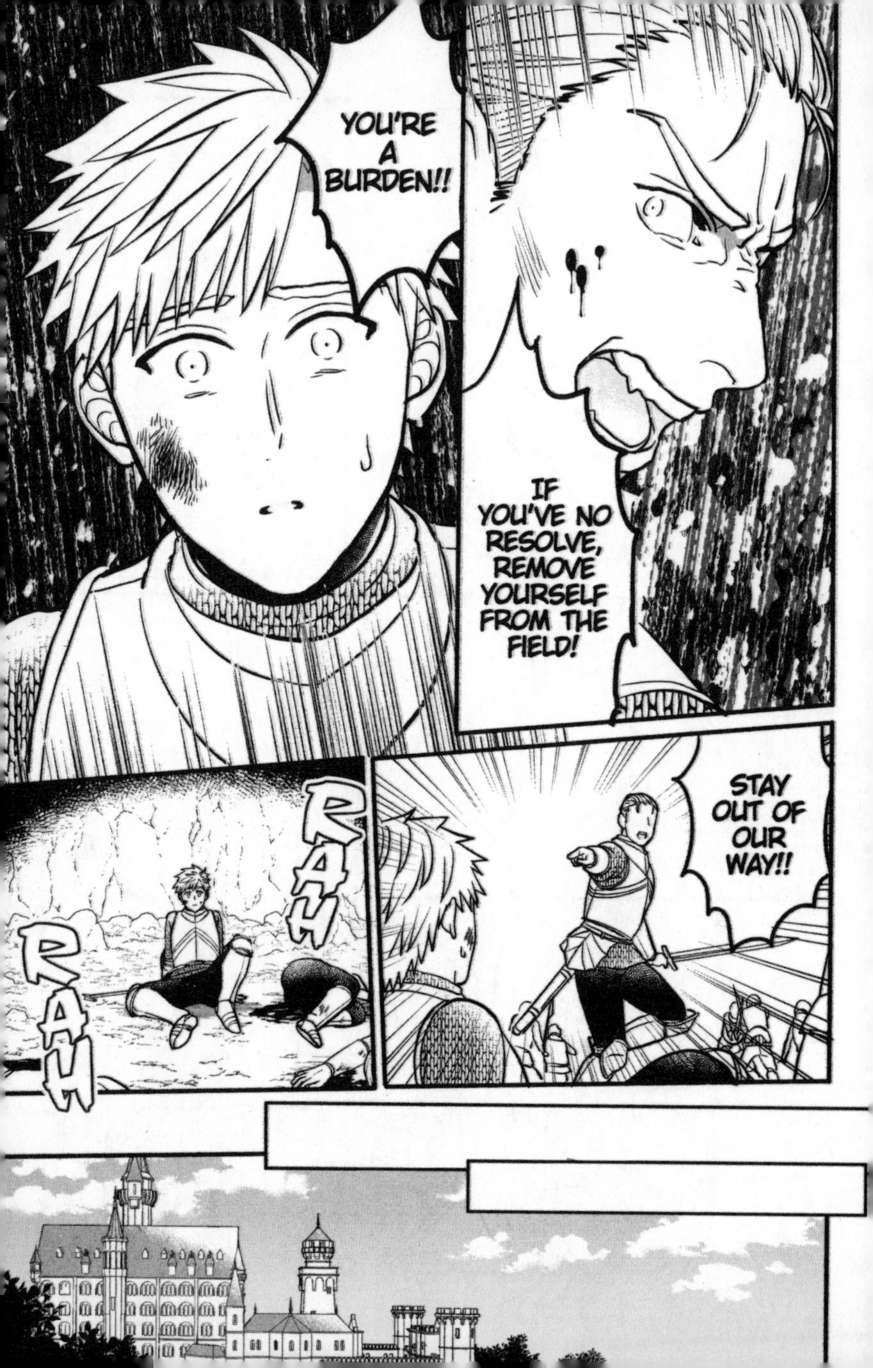
YOU'RE A BURDEN!!
IF YOU'VE NO RESOLVE, REMOVE YOURSELF FROM THE FIELD!
STAY OUT OF OUR WAY!!
RAH
RAH

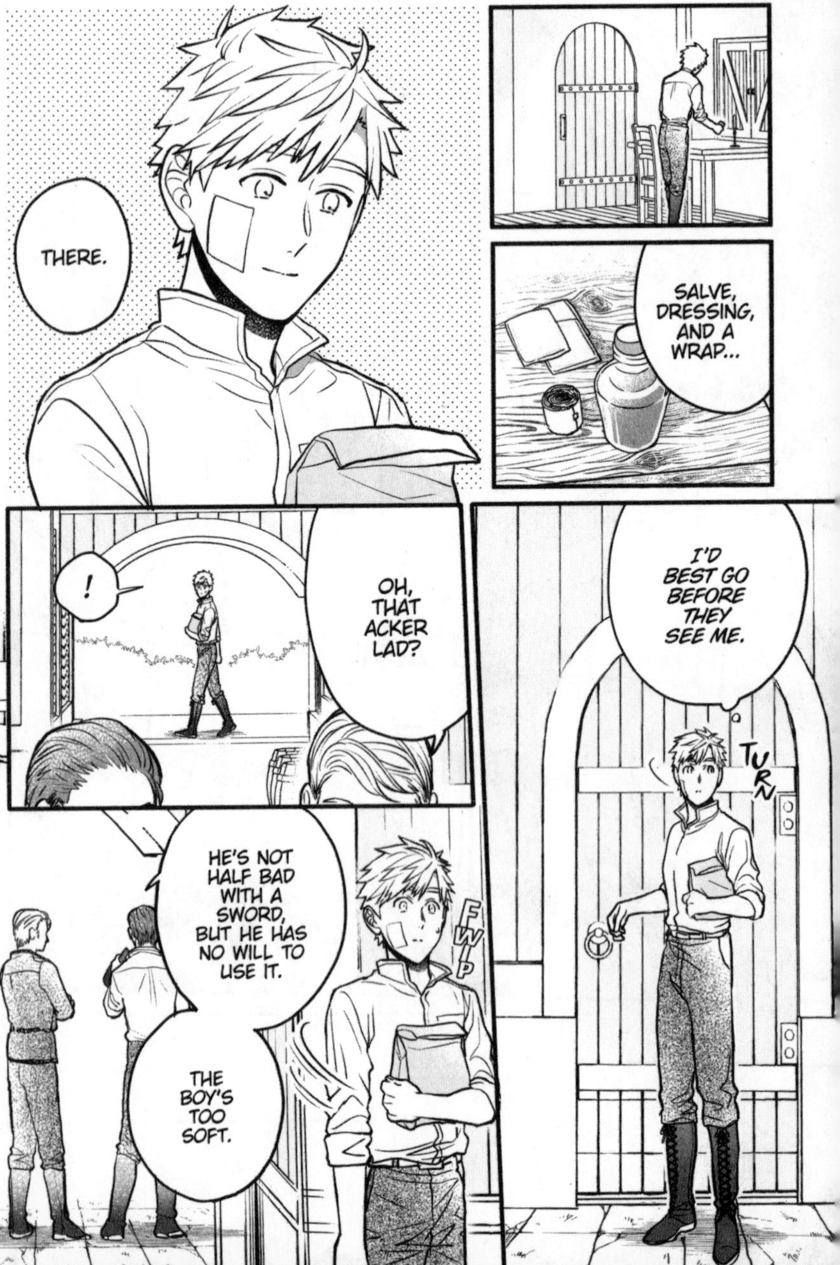
SALVE, DRESSING, AND A WRAP...
THERE.
I'D BEST GO BEFORE THEY SEE ME.
TURN
!
OH, THAT ACKER LAD?
HE'S NOT HALF BAD WITH A SWORD, BUT HE HAS NO WILL TO USE IT.
THE BOY'S TOO SOFT.
FWIP

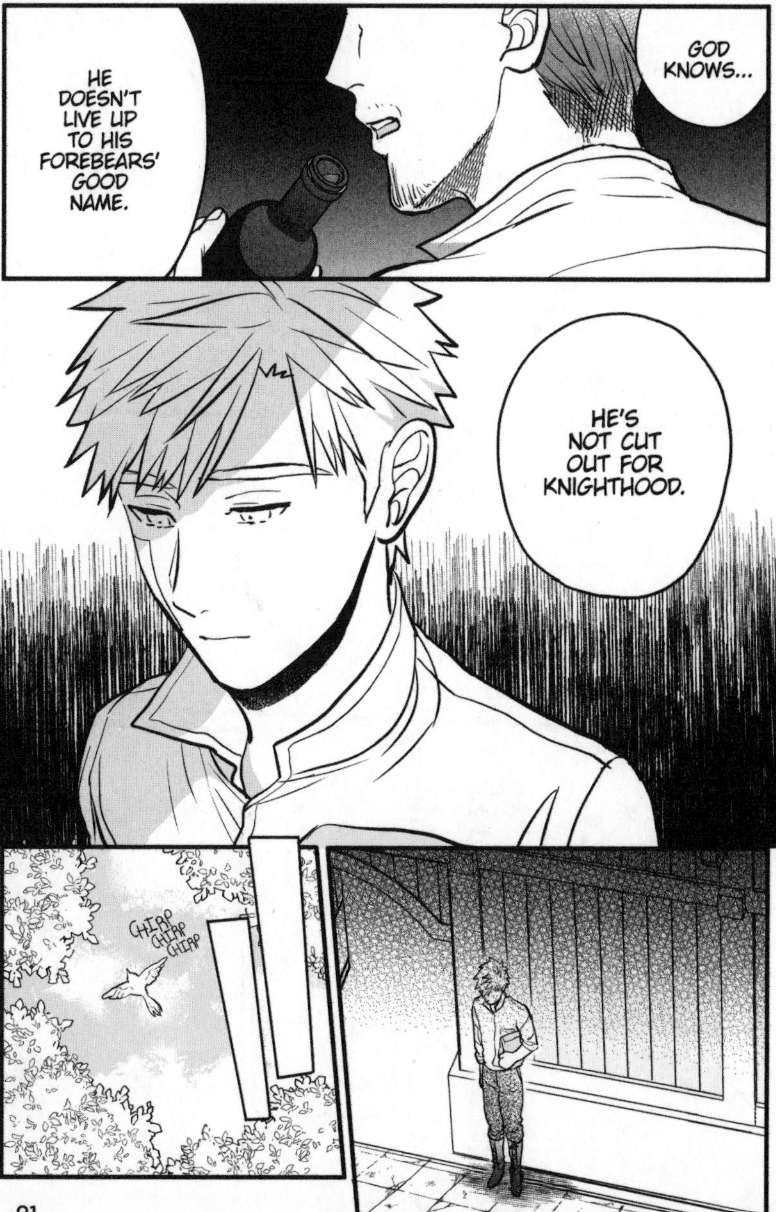
GOD KNOWS...
HE DOESN'T LIVE UP TO HIS FOREBEARS' GOOD NAME.
HE'S NOT CUT OUT FOR KNIGHTHOOD.
CHIRP CHIRP CHIRP

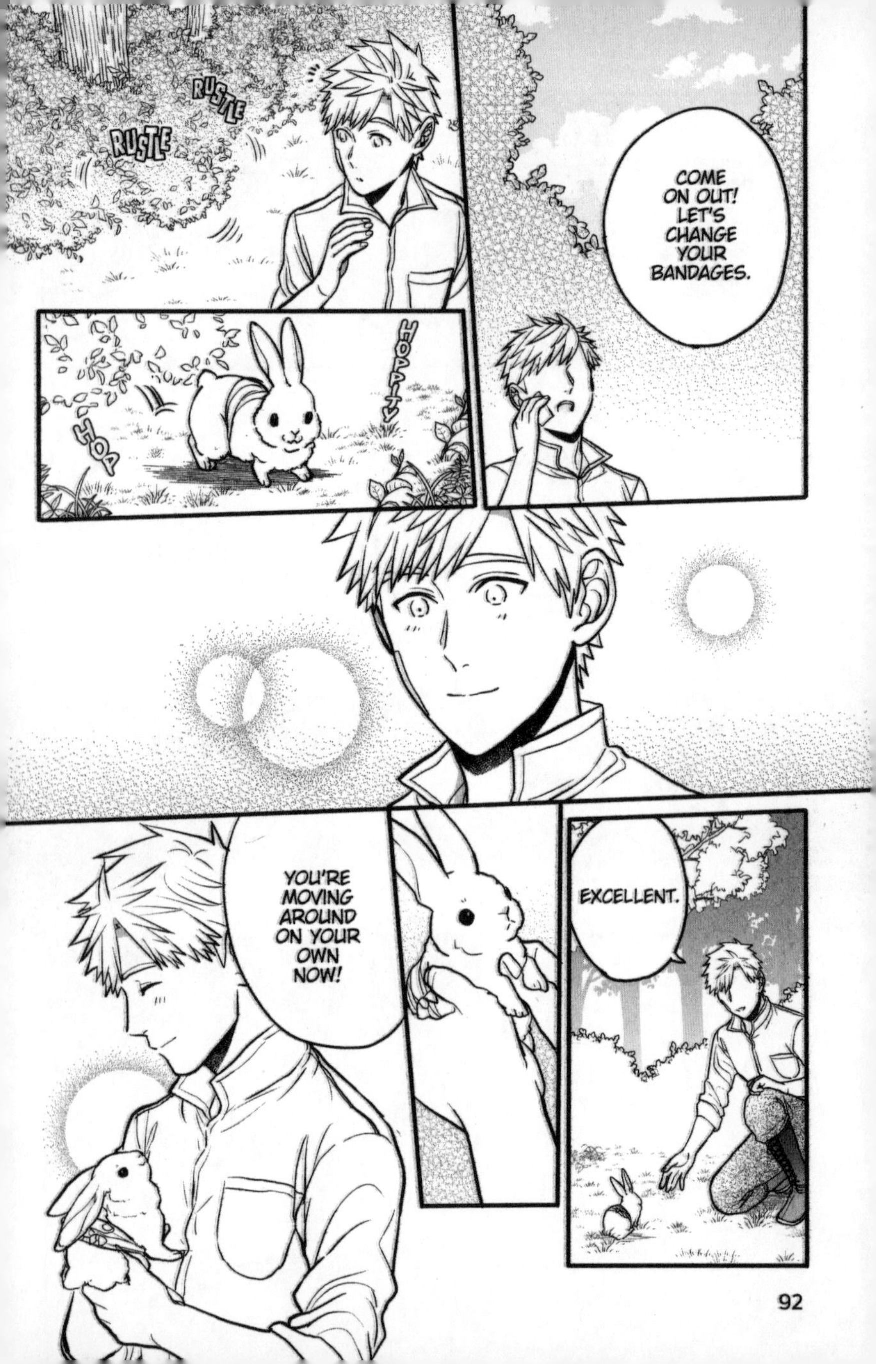
COME ON OUT! LET'S CHANGE YOUR BANDAGES.
RUSTLE
RUSTLE
HOPPITY
HOP
EXCELLENT.
YOU'RE MOVING AROUND ON YOUR OWN NOW!

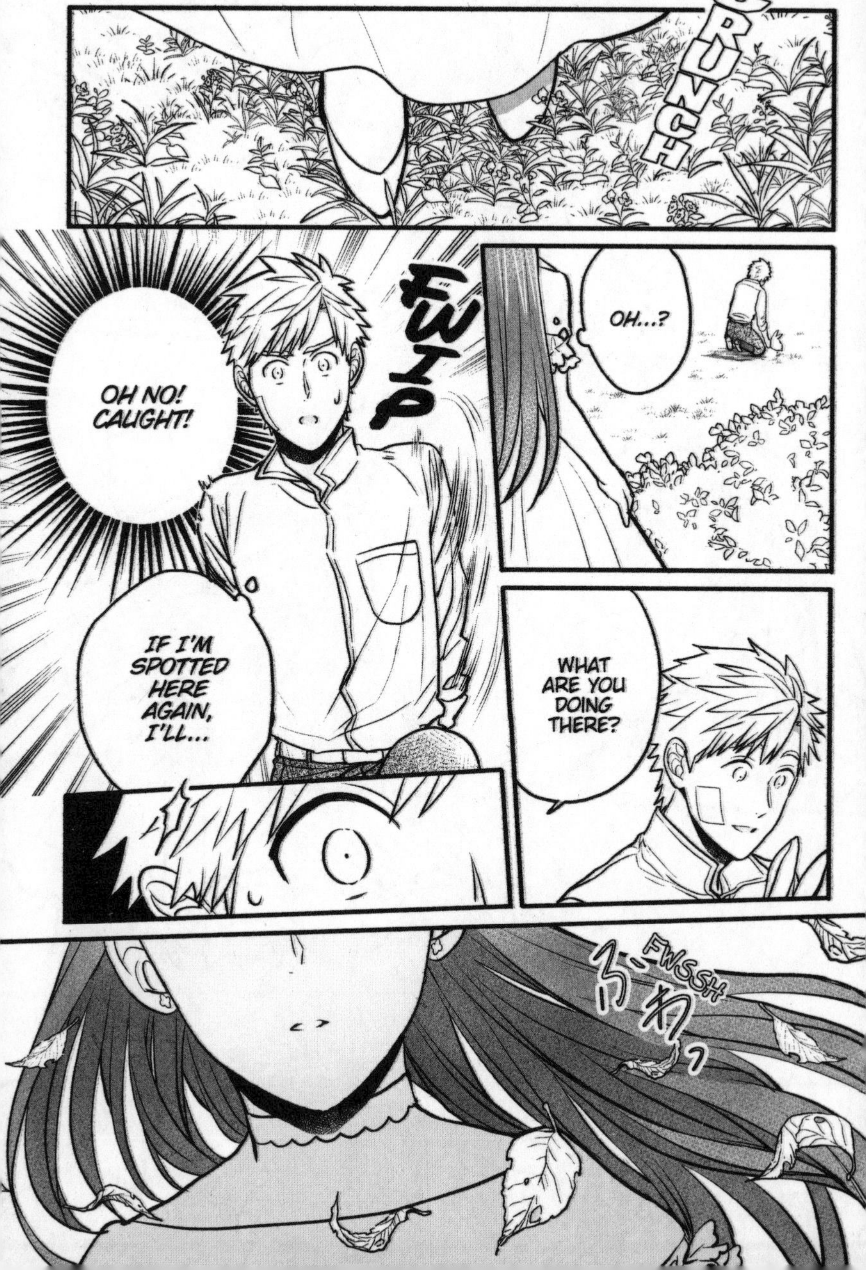
CRUNCH
OH...?
WHAT ARE YOU DOING THERE?
FWIP
OH NO! CAUGHT!
IF I'M SPOTTED HERE AGAIN, I'LL...
FWSSH

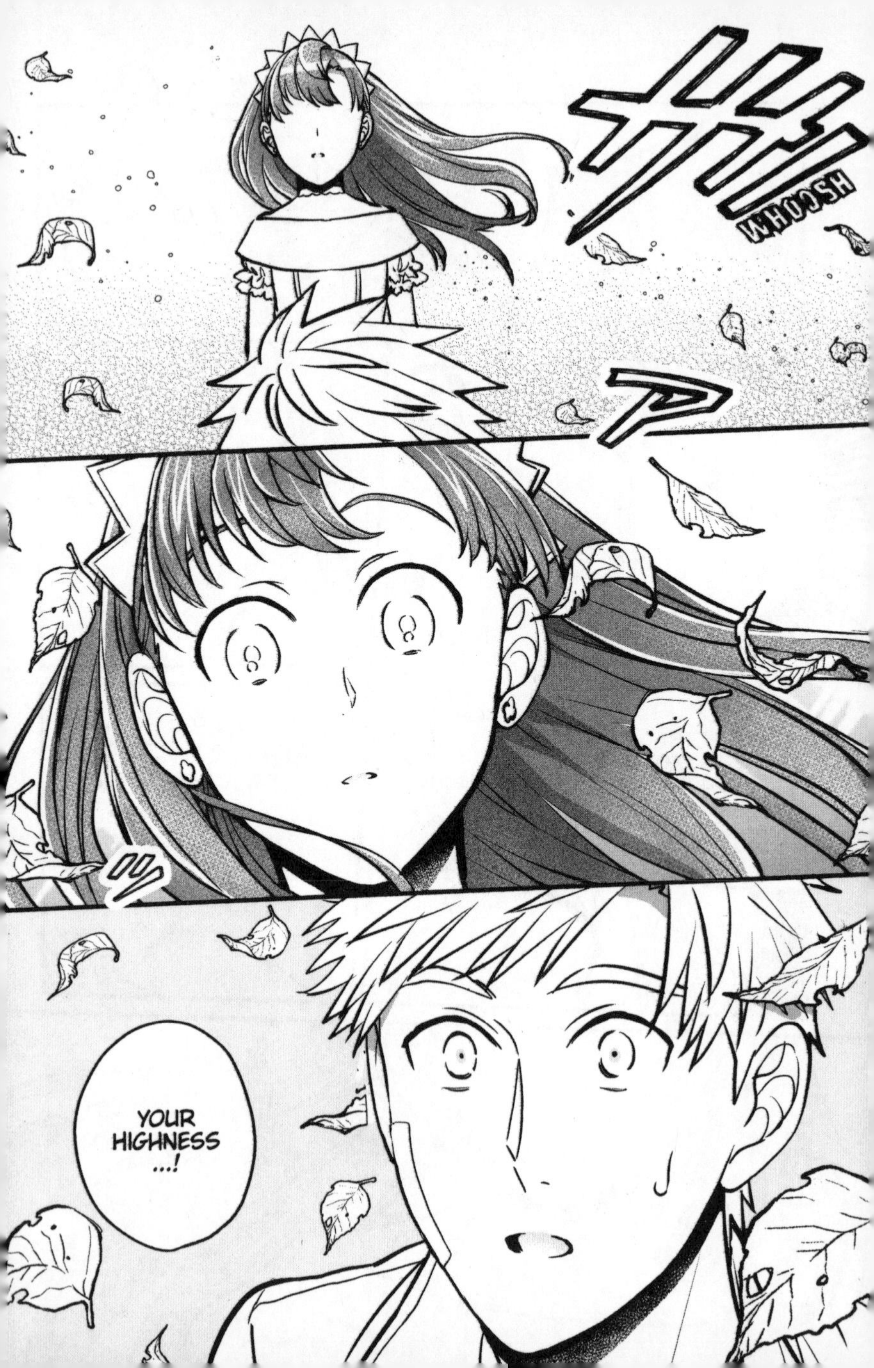
WHOOSH
YOUR HIGHNESS ...!

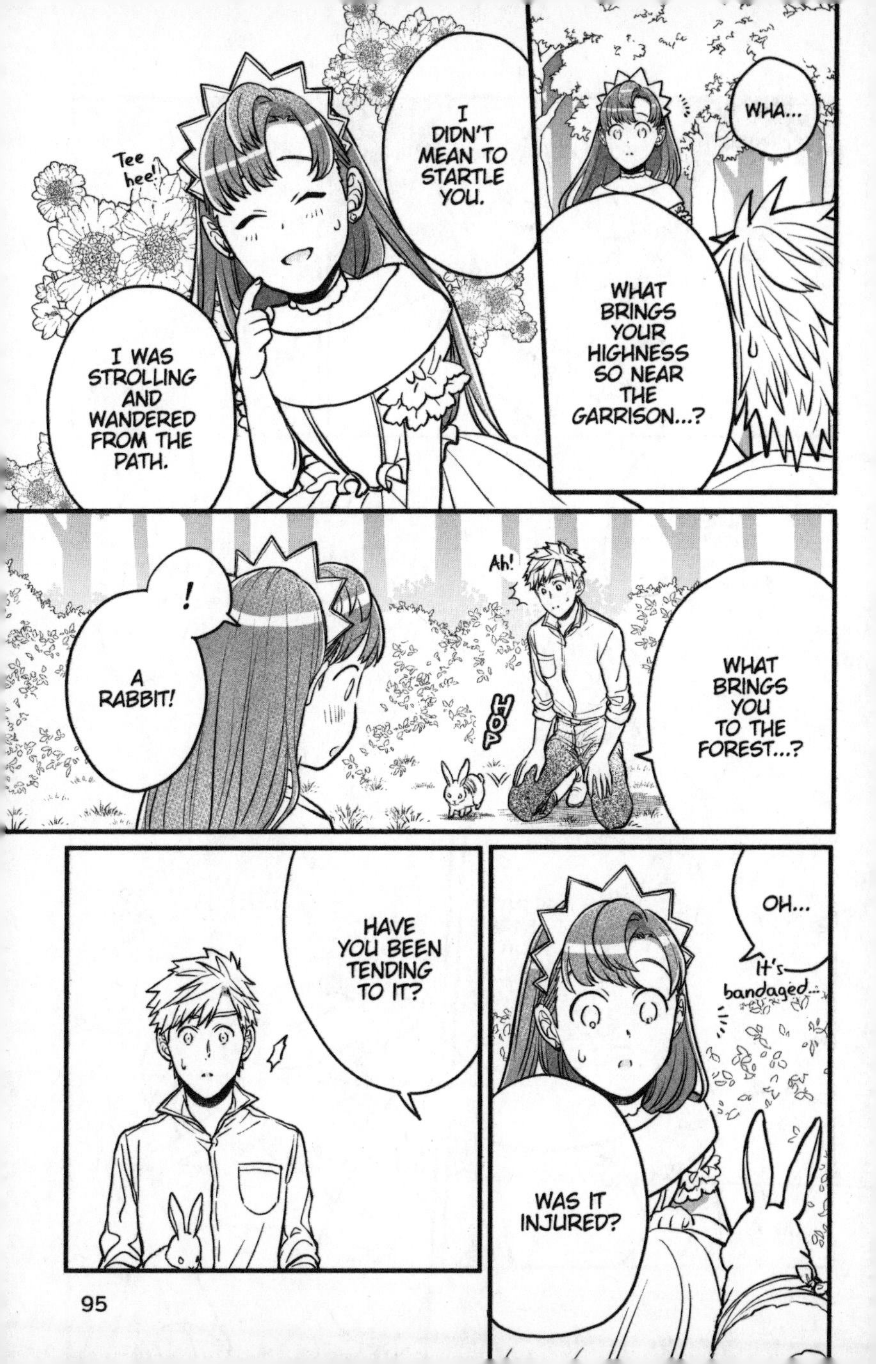
WHA...
WHAT BRINGS YOUR HIGHNESS SO NEAR THE GARRISON...?
I DIDN'T MEAN TO STARTLE YOU.
Tee hee!
I WAS STROLLING AND WANDERED FROM THE PATH.
WHAT BRINGS YOU TO THE FOREST...?
Ah!
HOP
!
A RABBIT!
OH...
It's bandaged...
WAS IT INJURED?
HAVE YOU BEEN TENDING TO IT?

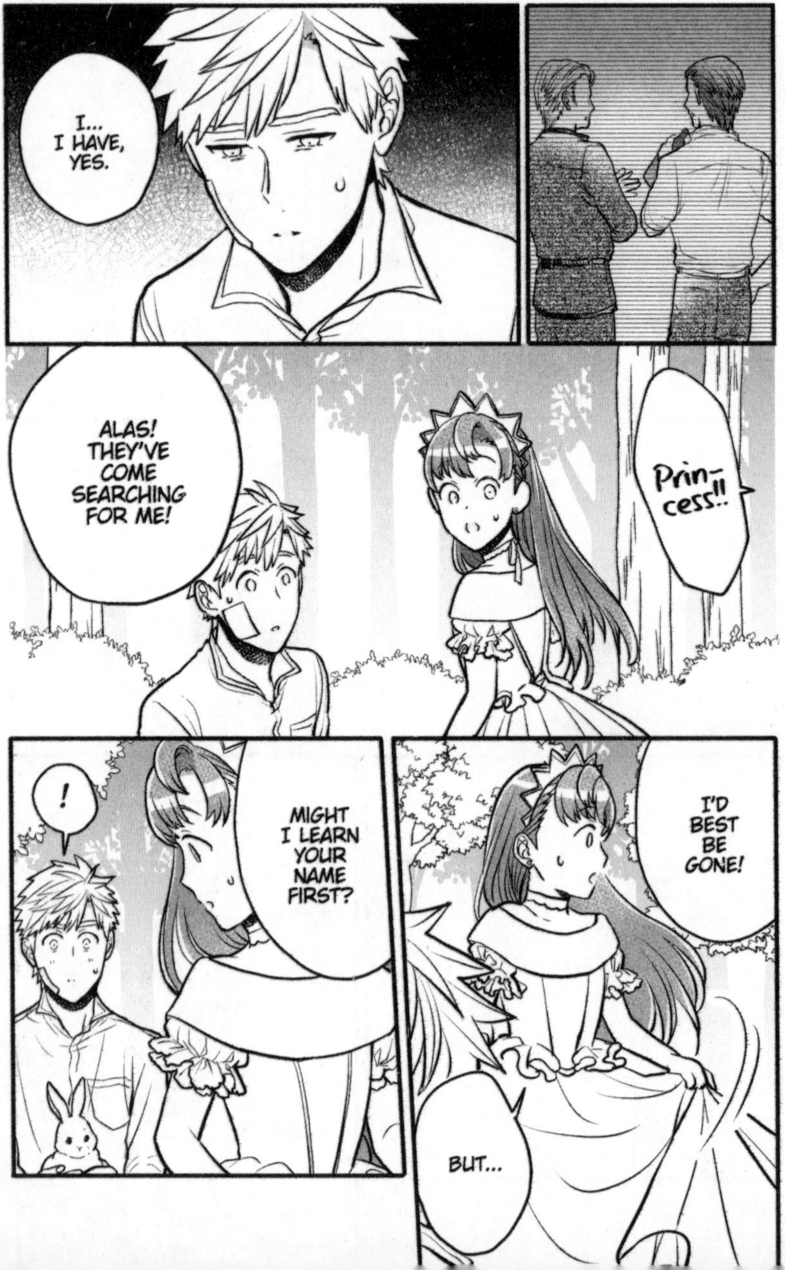
I... I HAVE, YES.
Prin-cess!!
ALAS! THEY'VE COME SEARCHING FOR ME!
I'D BEST BE GONE!
BUT...
MIGHT I LEARN YOUR NAME FIRST?
!

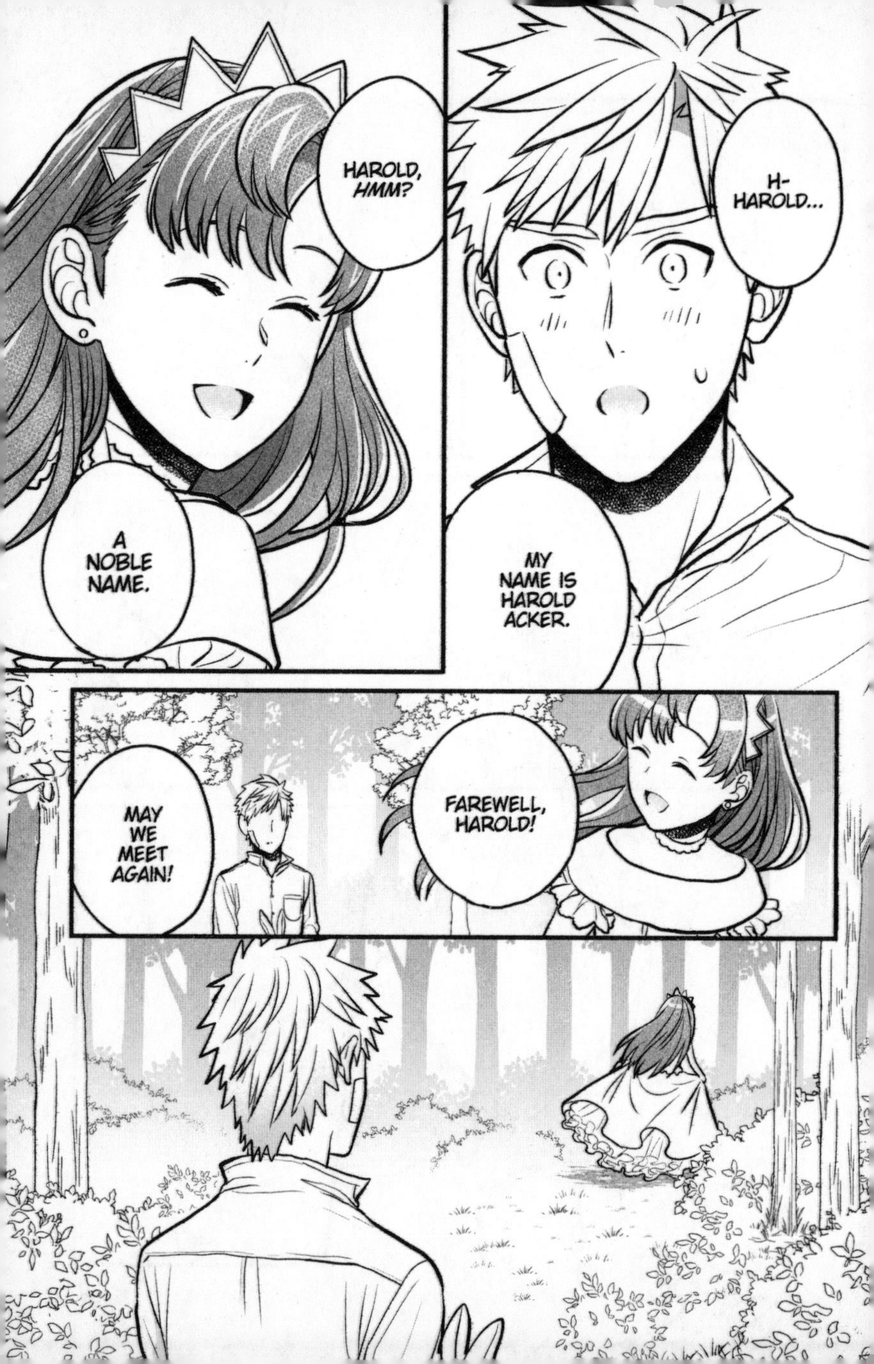
H-HAROLD...
MY NAME IS HAROLD ACKER.
HAROLD, HMM?
A NOBLE NAME.
FAREWELL, HAROLD!
MAY WE MEET AGAIN!

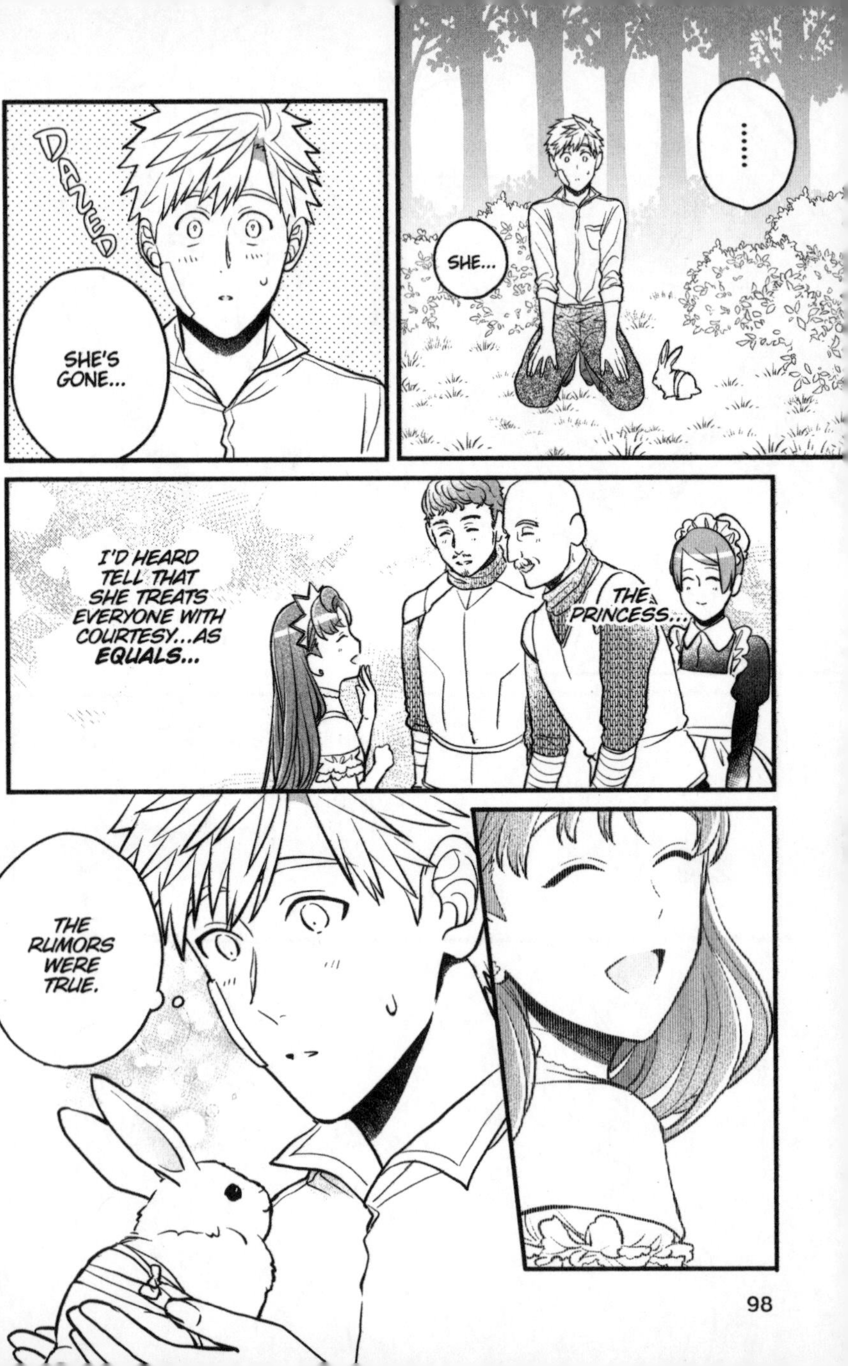
......
SHE...
DAZED
SHE'S GONE...
THE PRINCESS...
I'D HEARD TELL THAT SHE TREATS EVERYONE WITH COURTESY...AS EQUALS...
THE RUMORS WERE TRUE.

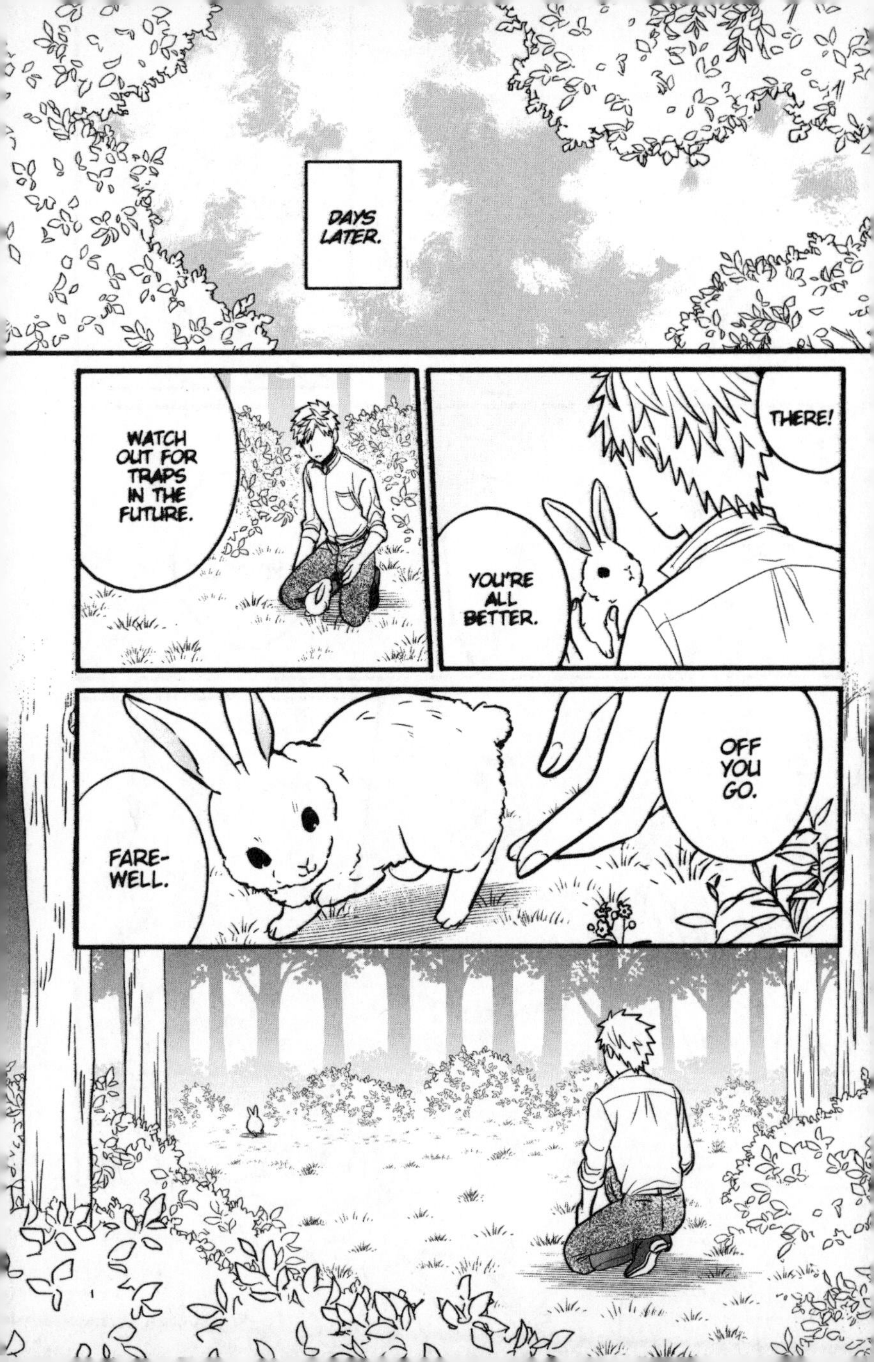
DAYS LATER.
THERE!
YOU'RE ALL BETTER.
WATCH OUT FOR TRAPS IN THE FUTURE.
OFF YOU GO.
FARE-WELL.

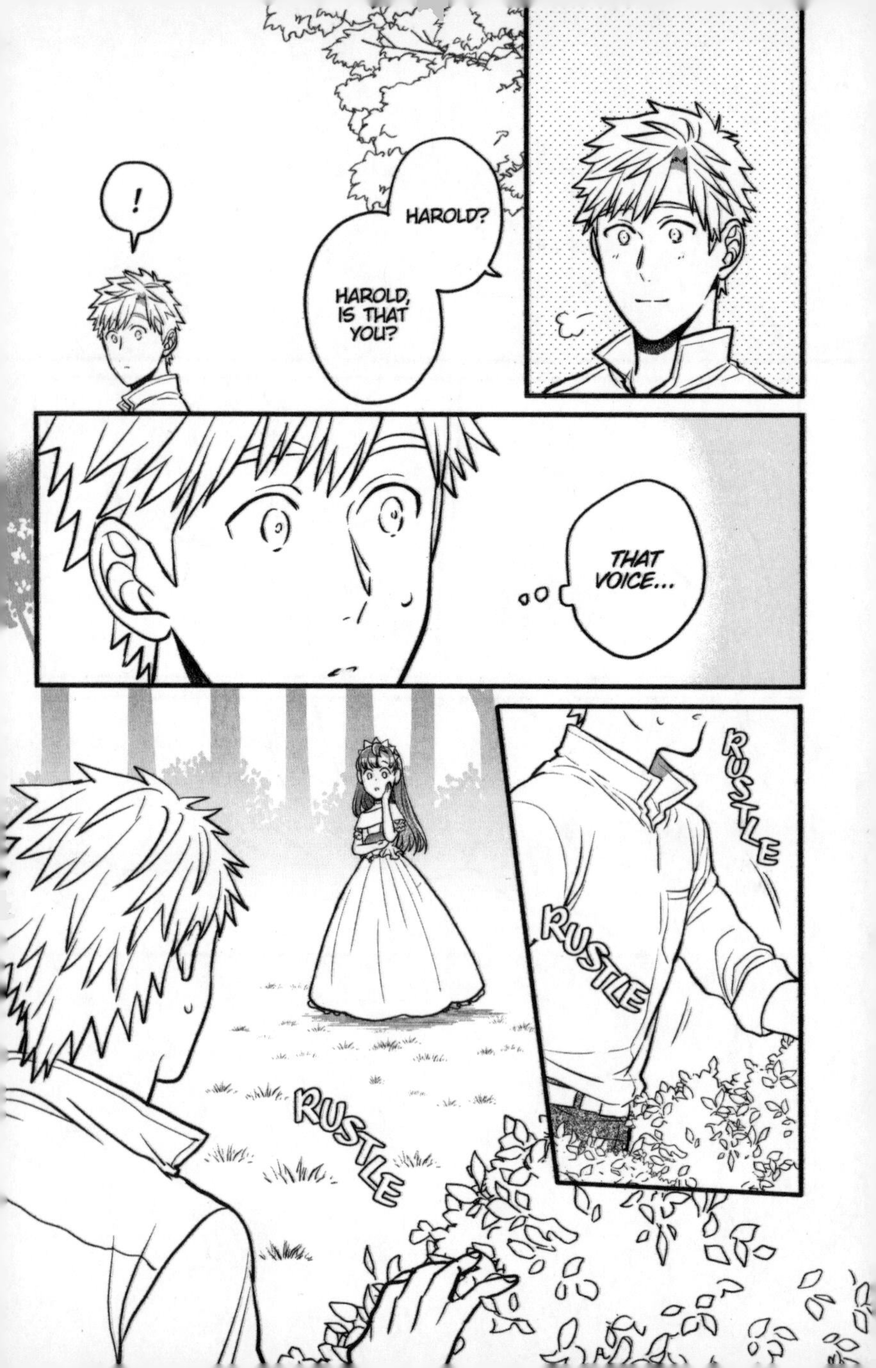
HAROLD?
HAROLD, IS THAT YOU?
!
THAT VOICE...
RUSTLE
RUSTLE
RUSTLE

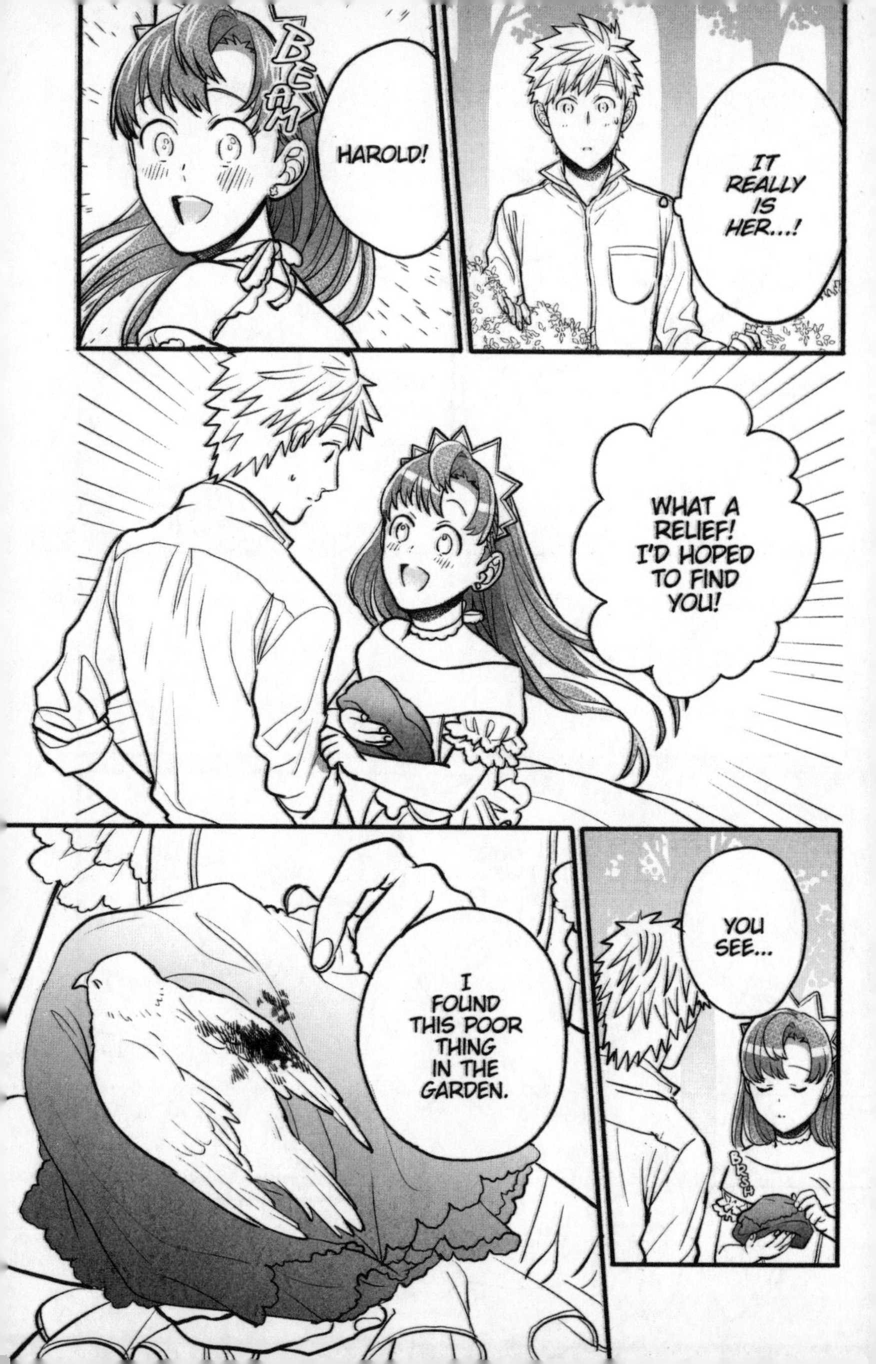
IT REALLY IS HER...!
BEAM
HAROLD!
WHAT A RELIEF! I'D HOPED TO FIND YOU!
YOU SEE...
BRSH
I FOUND THIS POOR THING IN THE GARDEN.

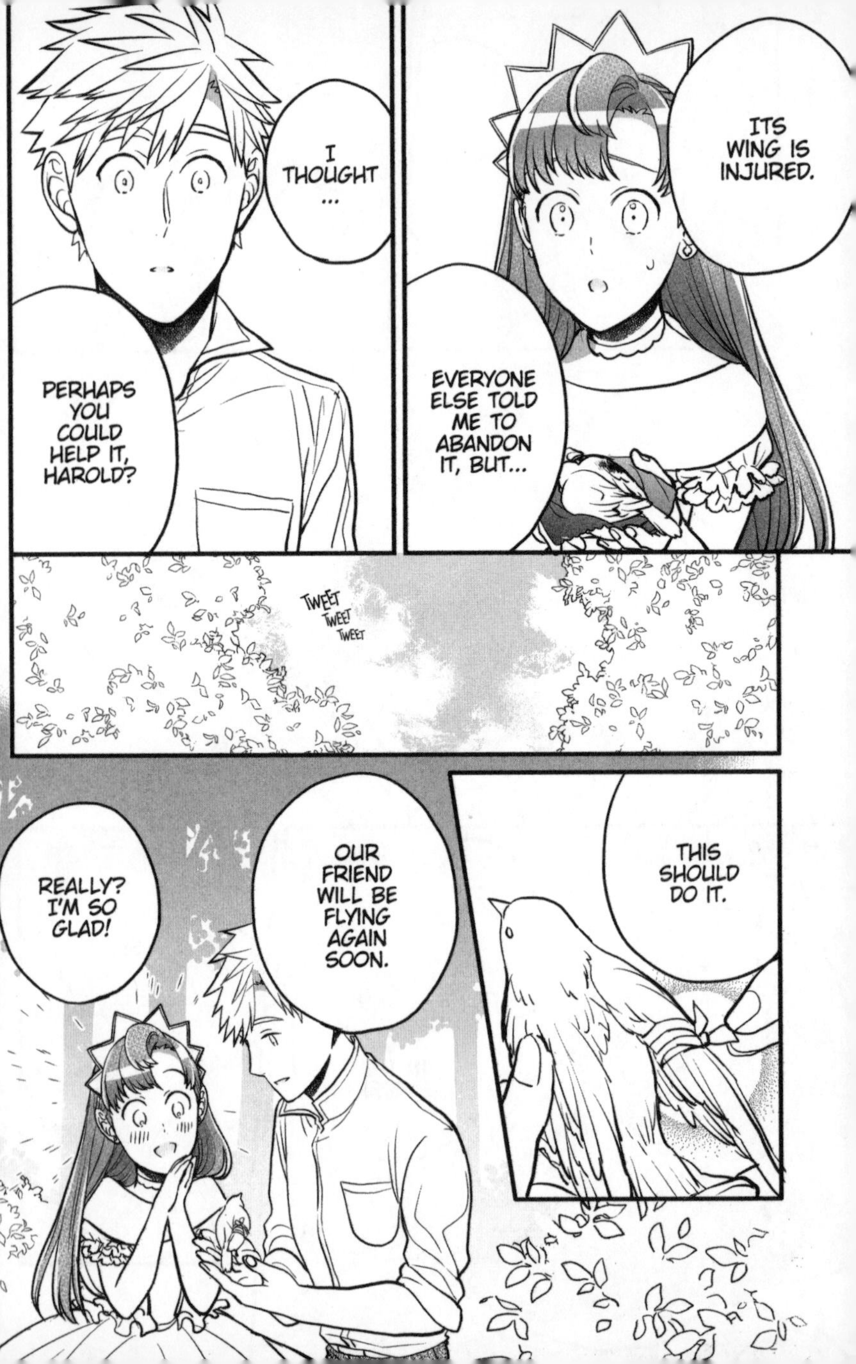
ITS WING IS INJURED.
EVERYONE ELSE TOLD ME TO ABANDON IT, BUT...
I THOUGHT ...
PERHAPS YOU COULD HELP IT, HAROLD?
TWEET TWEET TWEET
THIS SHOULD DO IT.
OUR FRIEND WILL BE FLYING AGAIN SOON.
REALLY? I'M SO GLAD!

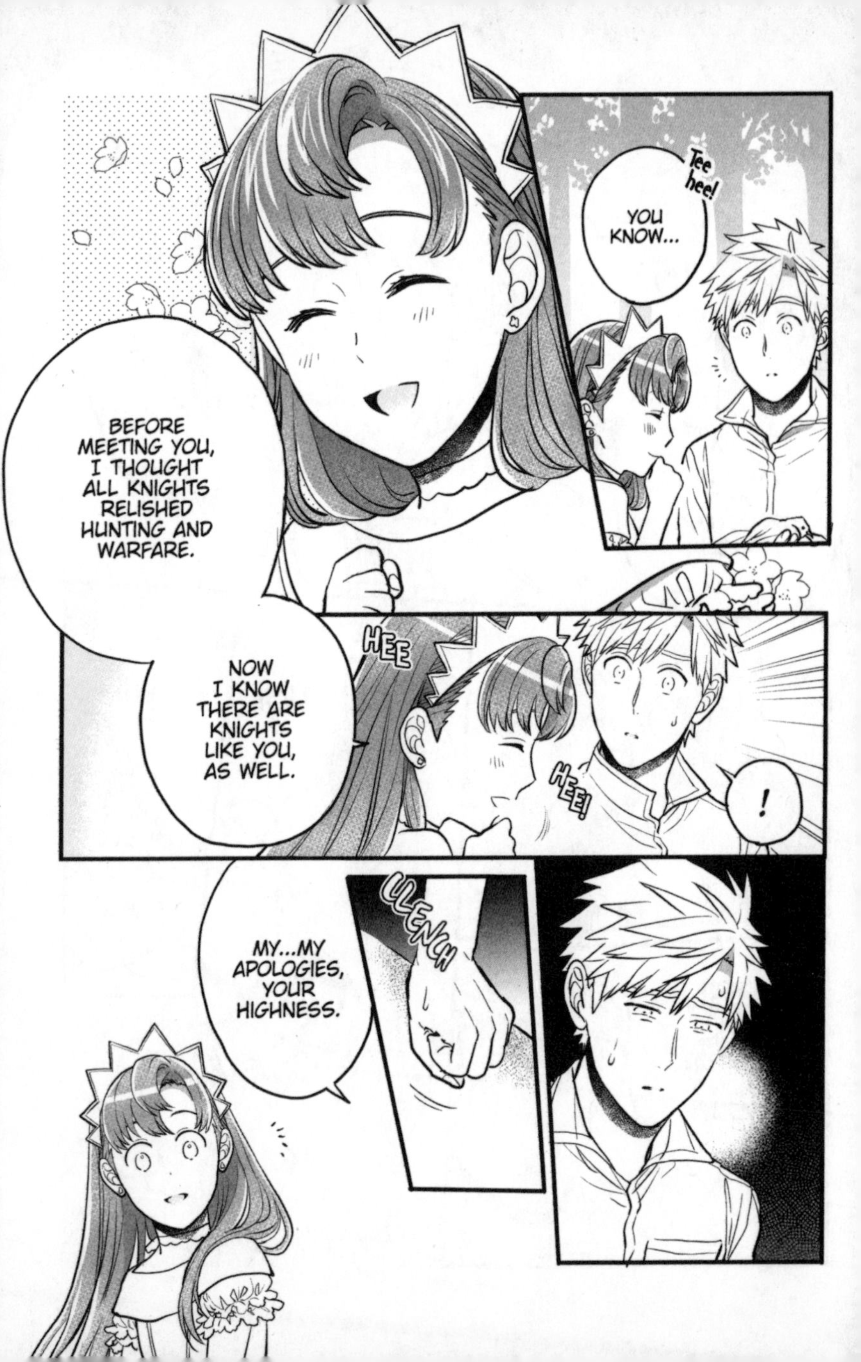
Tee hee!
YOU KNOW...
BEFORE MEETING YOU, I THOUGHT ALL KNIGHTS RELISHED HUNTING AND WARFARE.
HEE
NOW I KNOW THERE ARE KNIGHTS LIKE YOU, AS WELL.
HEE!
!
CLENCH
MY...MY APOLOGIES, YOUR HIGHNESS.

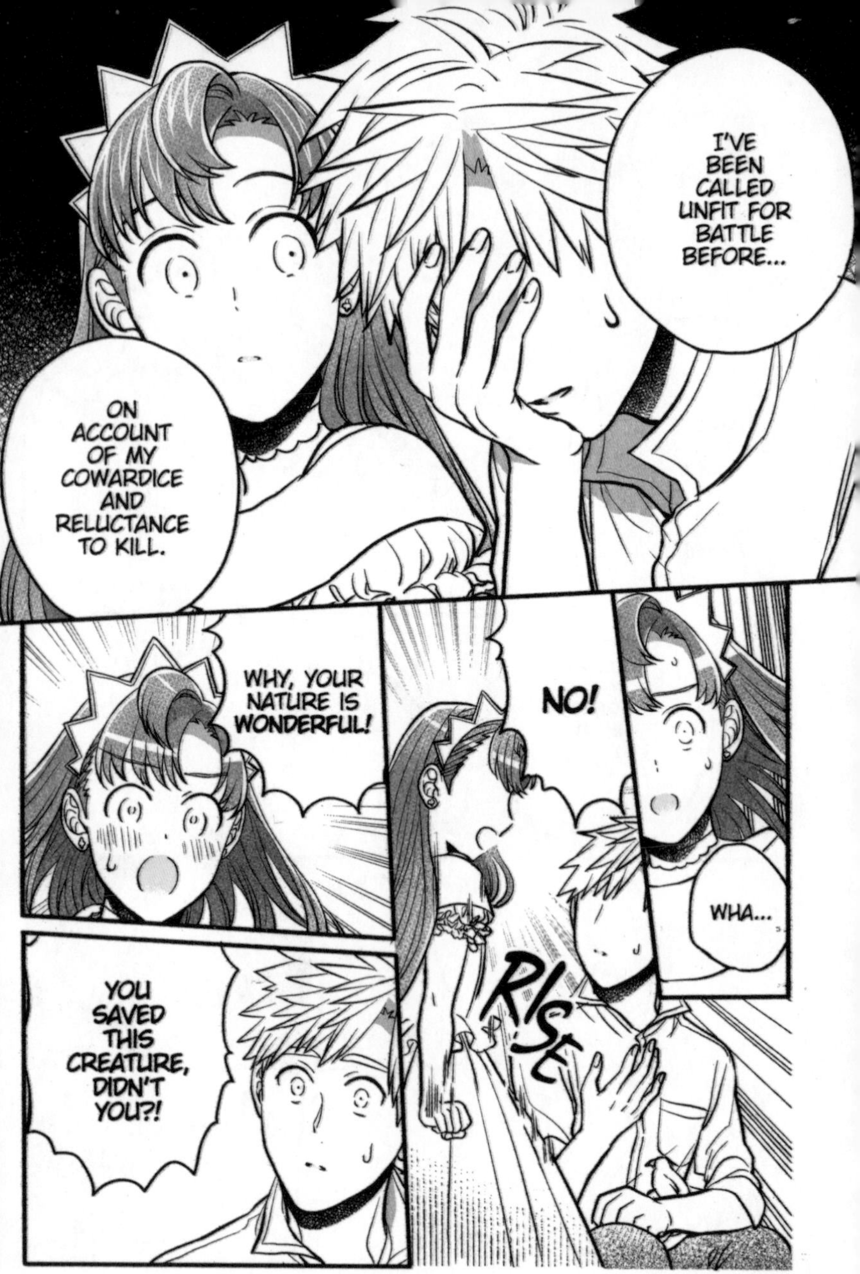
I'VE BEEN CALLED UNFIT FOR BATTLE BEFORE...
ON ACCOUNT OF MY COWARDICE AND RELUCTANCE TO KILL.
WHA...
NO!
RISE
WHY, YOUR NATURE IS WONDERFUL!
YOU SAVED THIS CREATURE, DIDN'T YOU?!

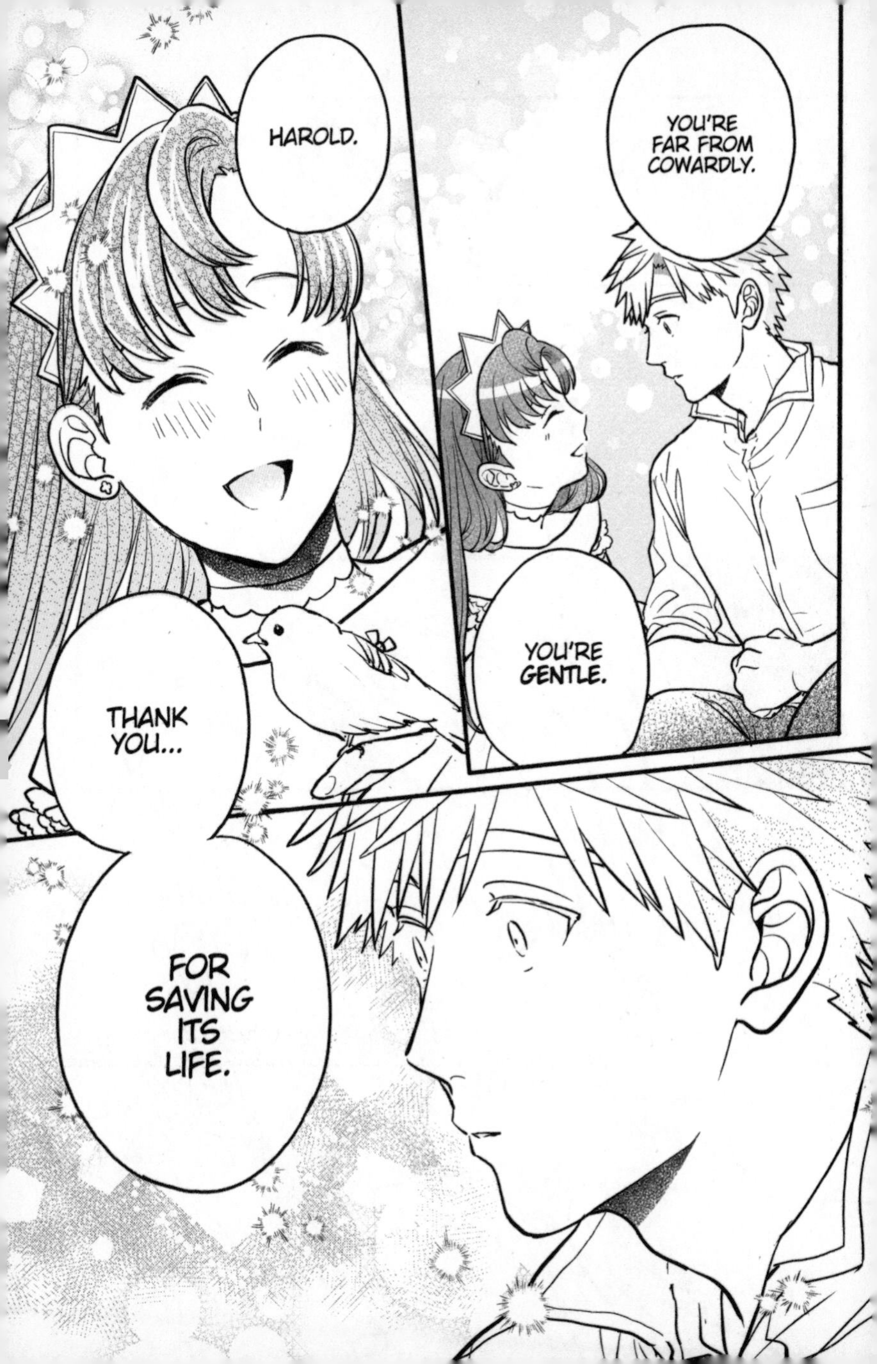
YOU'RE FAR FROM COWARDLY.
YOU'RE GENTLE.
HAROLD.
THANK YOU...
FOR SAVING ITS LIFE.

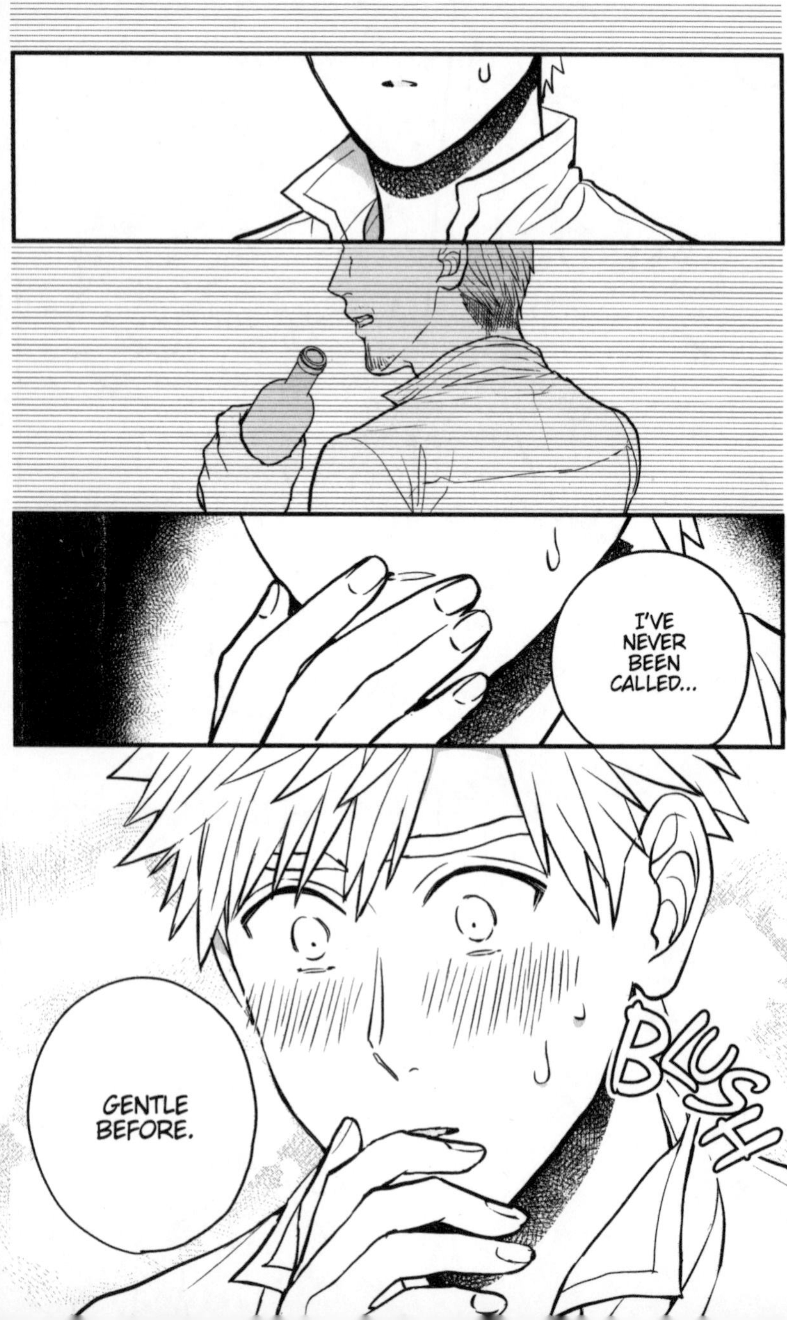
I'VE NEVER BEEN CALLED...
BLUSH
GENTLE BEFORE.

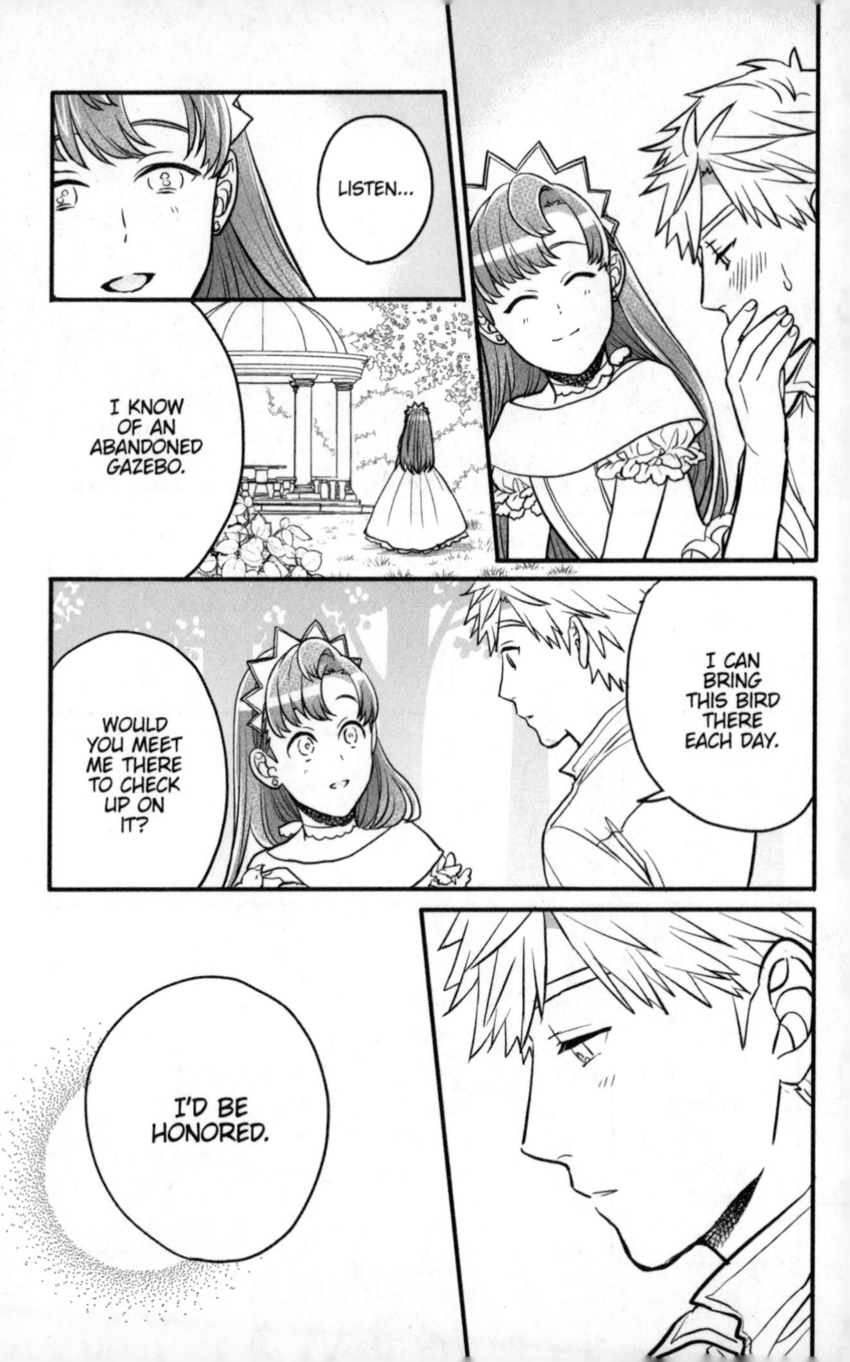
LISTEN...
I KNOW OF AN ABANDONED GAZEBO.
I CAN BRING THIS BIRD THERE EACH DAY.
WOULD YOU MEET ME THERE TO CHECK UP ON IT?
I'D BE HONORED.

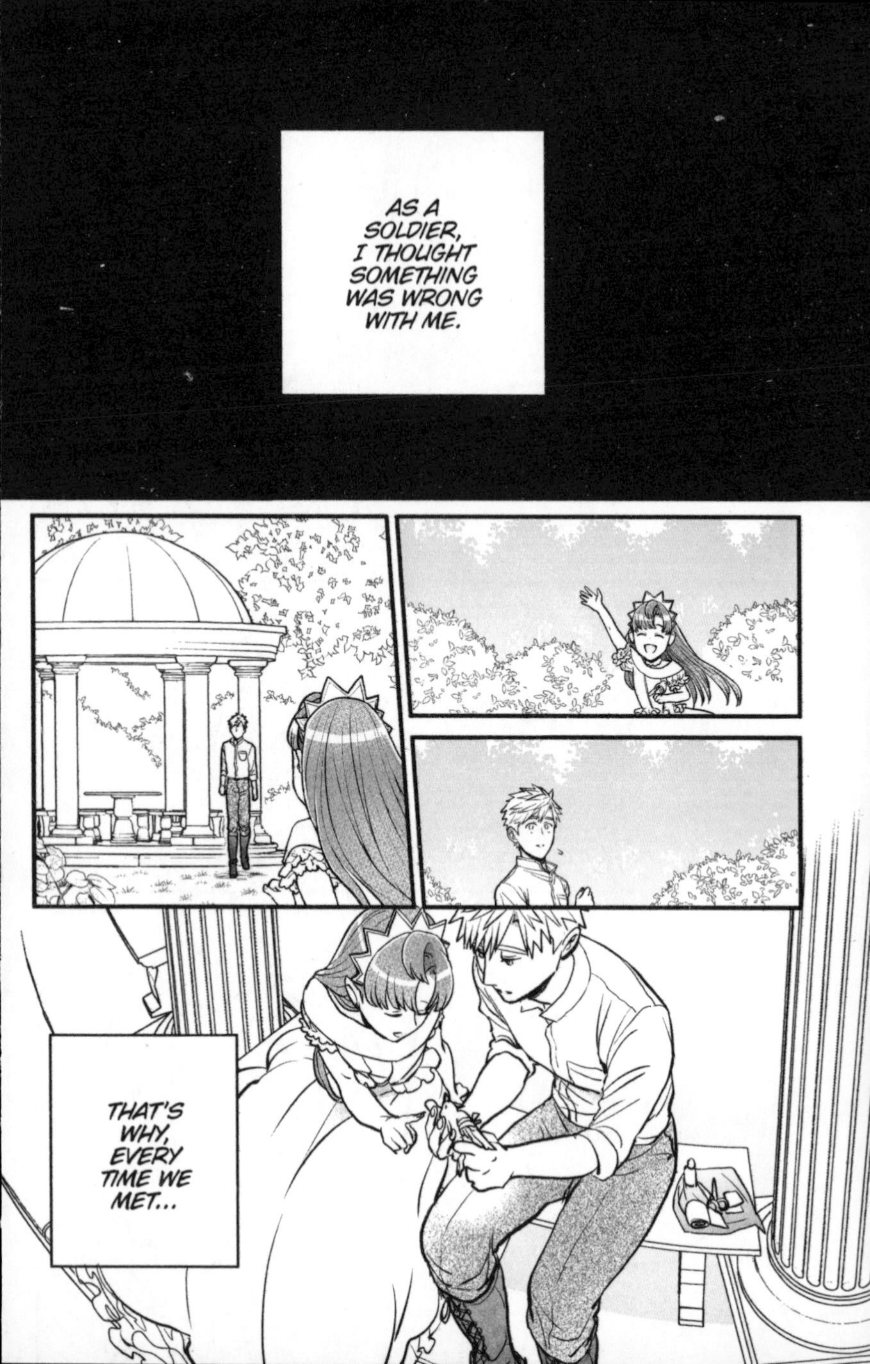
AS A SOLDIER, I THOUGHT SOMETHING WAS WRONG WITH ME.
THAT'S WHY, EVERY TIME WE MET...

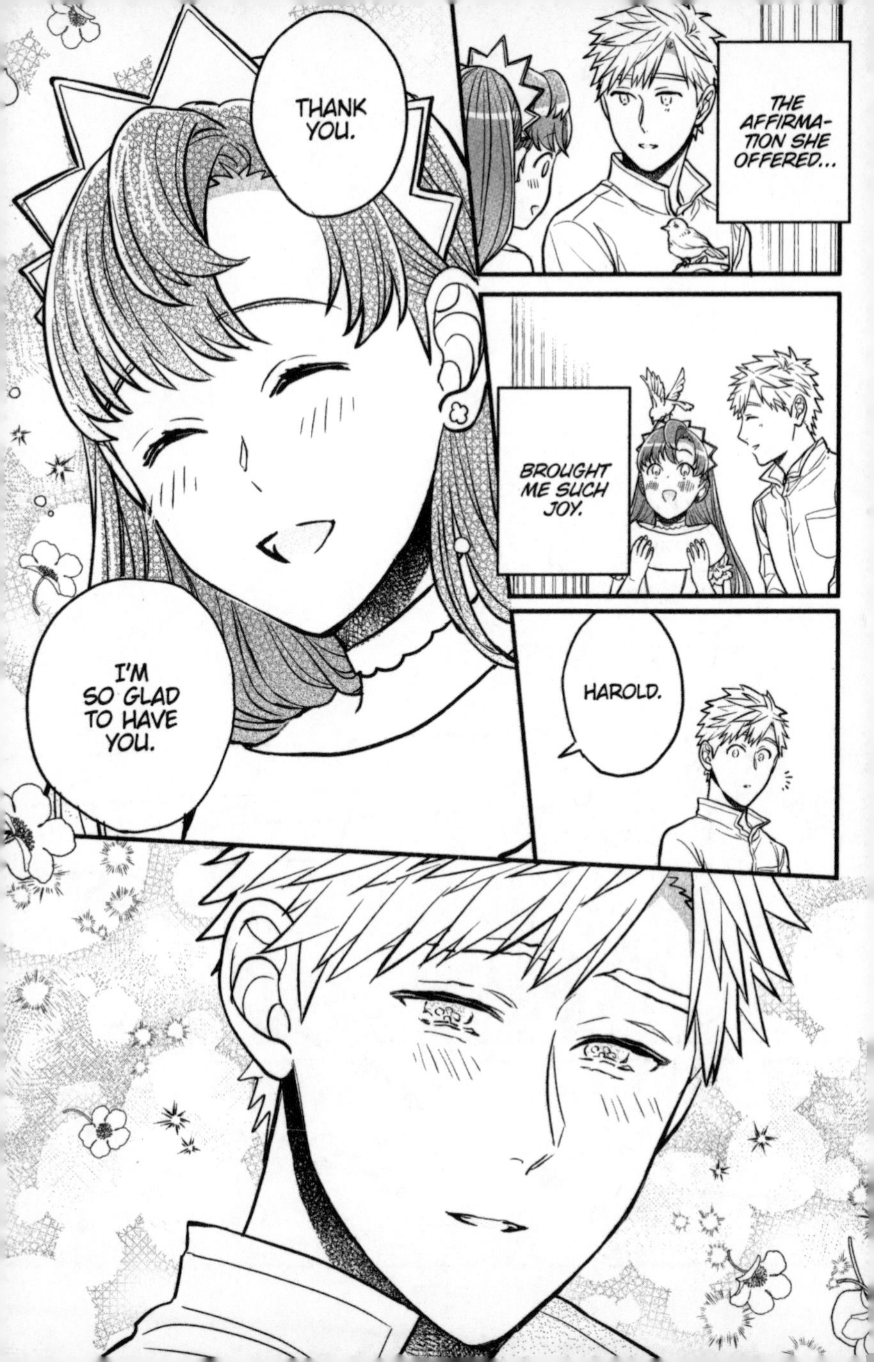
THE AFFIRMATION SHE OFFERED...
BROUGHT ME SUCH JOY.
HAROLD.
THANK YOU.
I'M SO GLAD TO HAVE YOU.

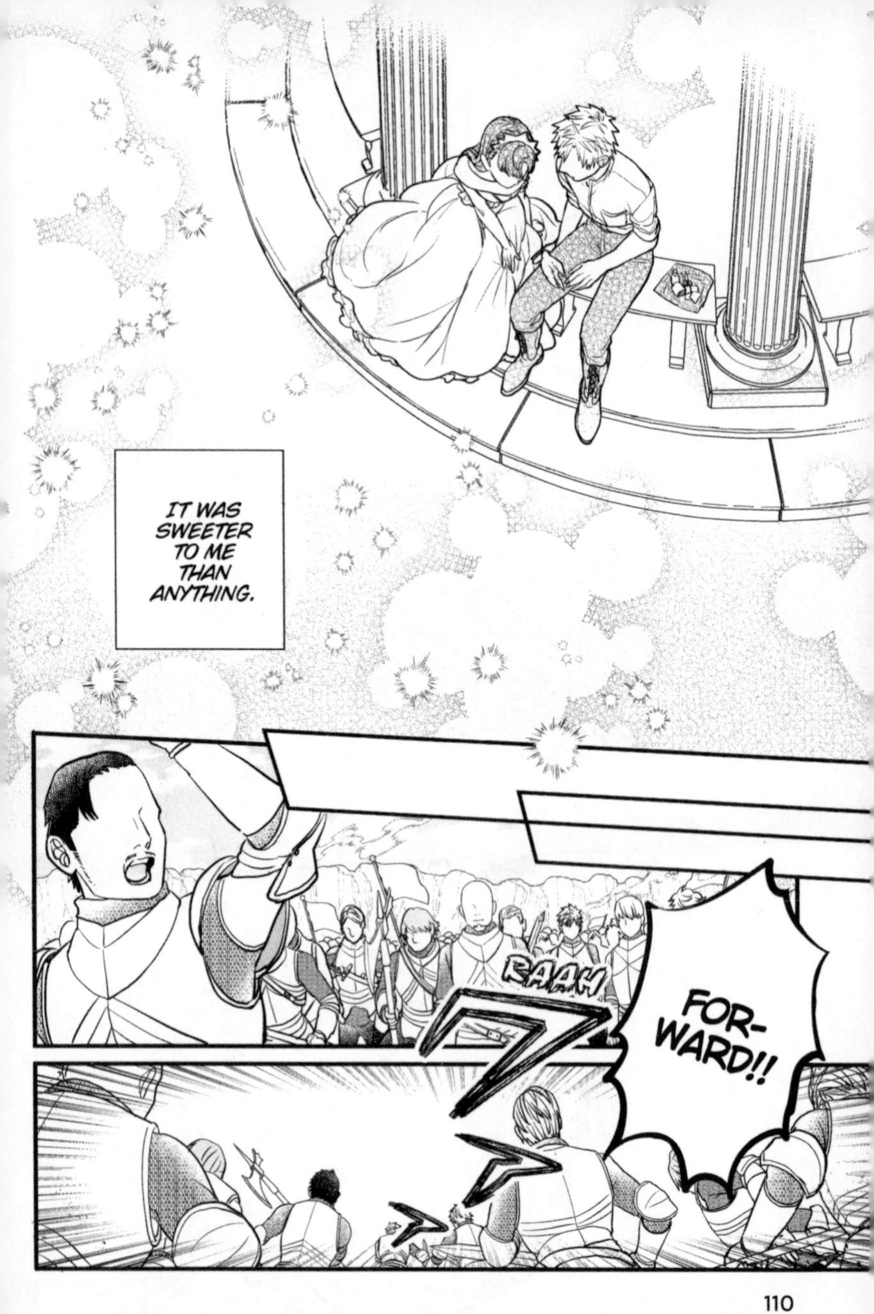
IT WAS SWEETER TO ME THAN ANYTHING.
FOR-WARD!!
RAAH

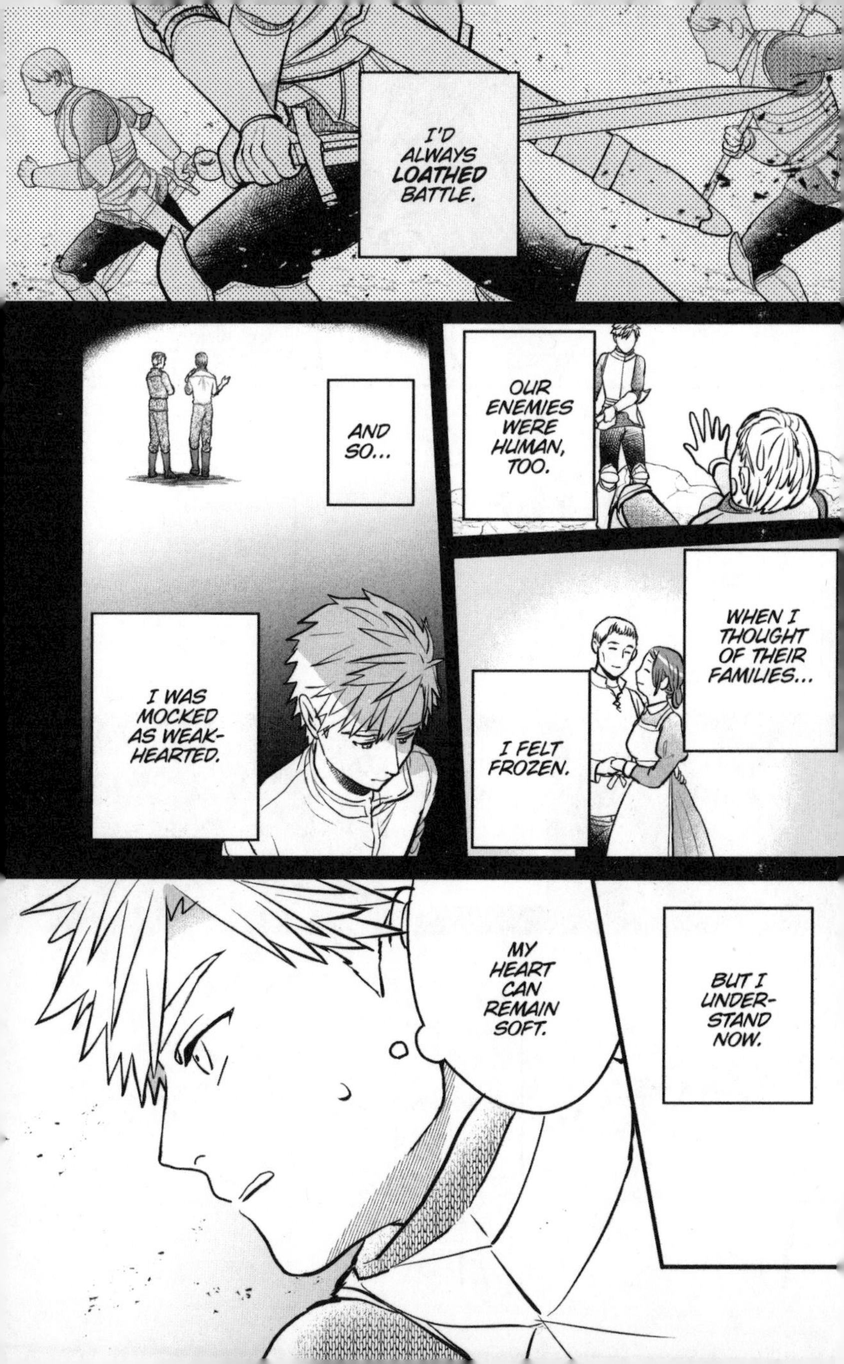
I'D ALWAYS LOATHED BATTLE.
OUR ENEMIES WERE HUMAN, TOO.
WHEN I THOUGHT OF THEIR FAMILIES...
I FELT FROZEN.
AND SO...
I WAS MOCKED AS WEAK-HEARTED.
BUT I UNDER-STAND NOW.
MY HEART CAN REMAIN SOFT.

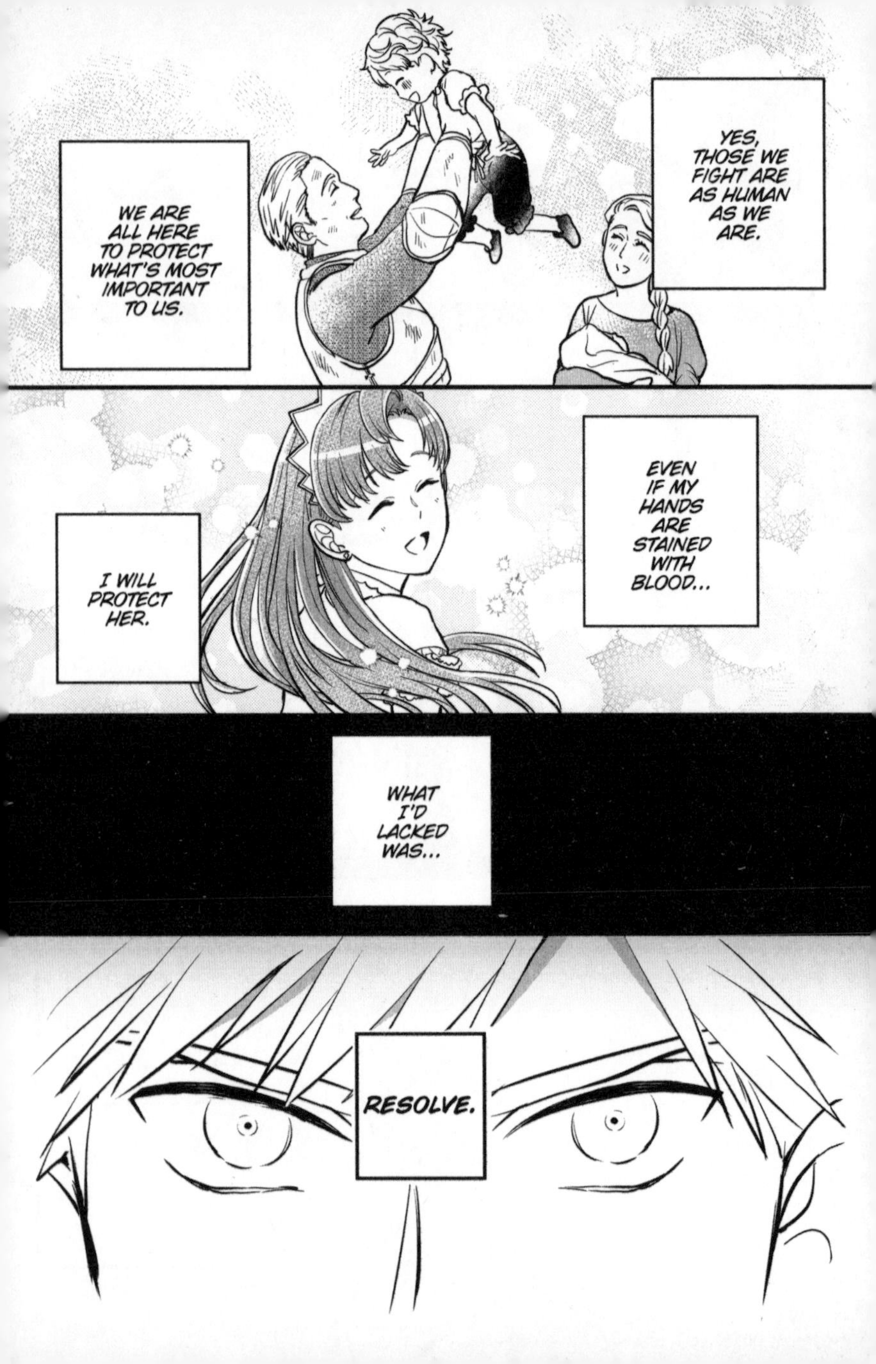
YES, THOSE WE FIGHT ARE AS HUMAN AS WE ARE.
WE ARE ALL HERE TO PROTECT WHAT'S MOST IMPORTANT TO US.
EVEN IF MY HANDS ARE STAINED WITH BLOOD...
I WILL PROTECT HER.
WHAT I'D LACKED WAS...
RESOLVE.

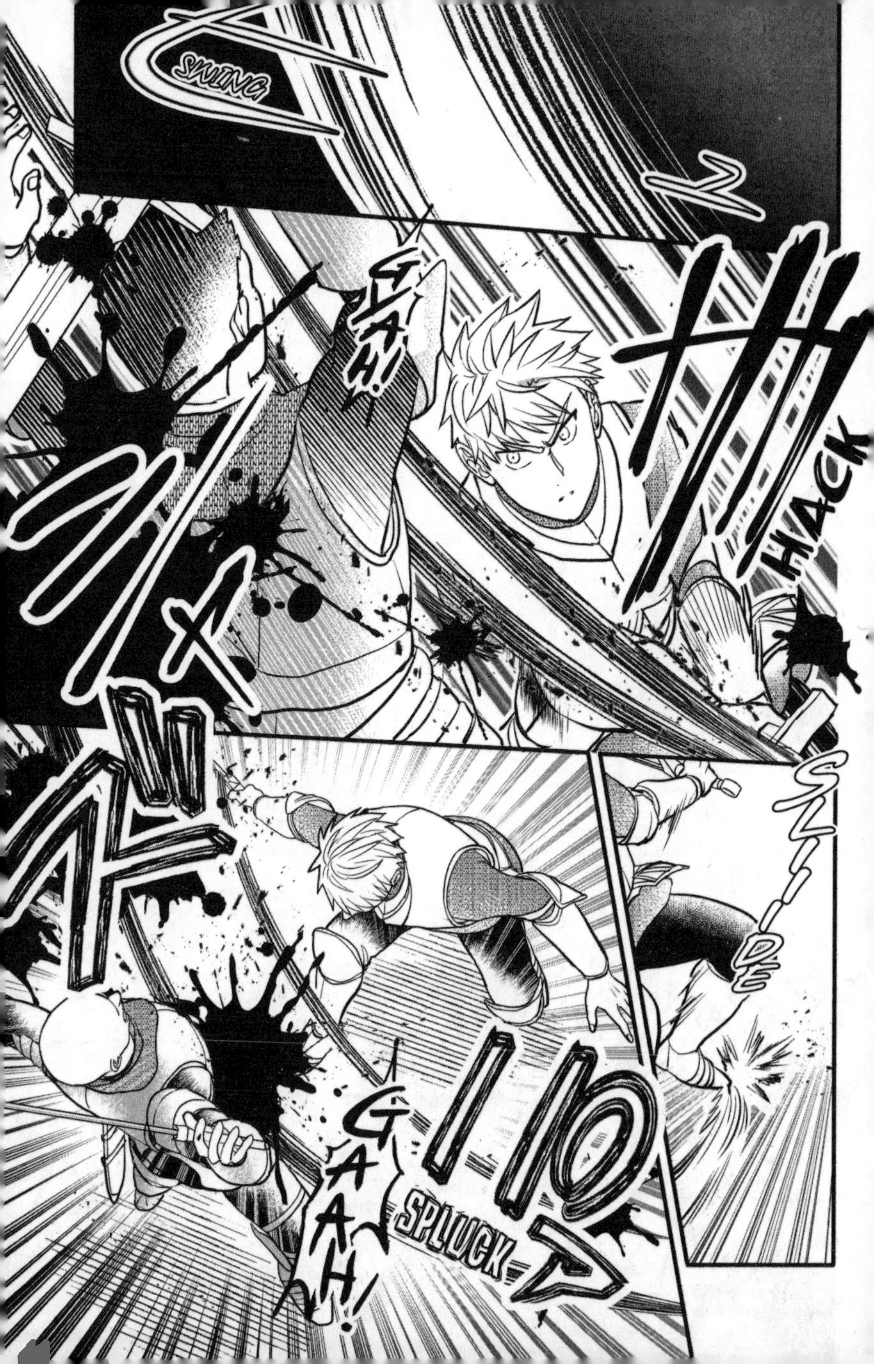
SWING
GYAAH!
HACK
SLI—DE
SPLUCK
GAAAH!

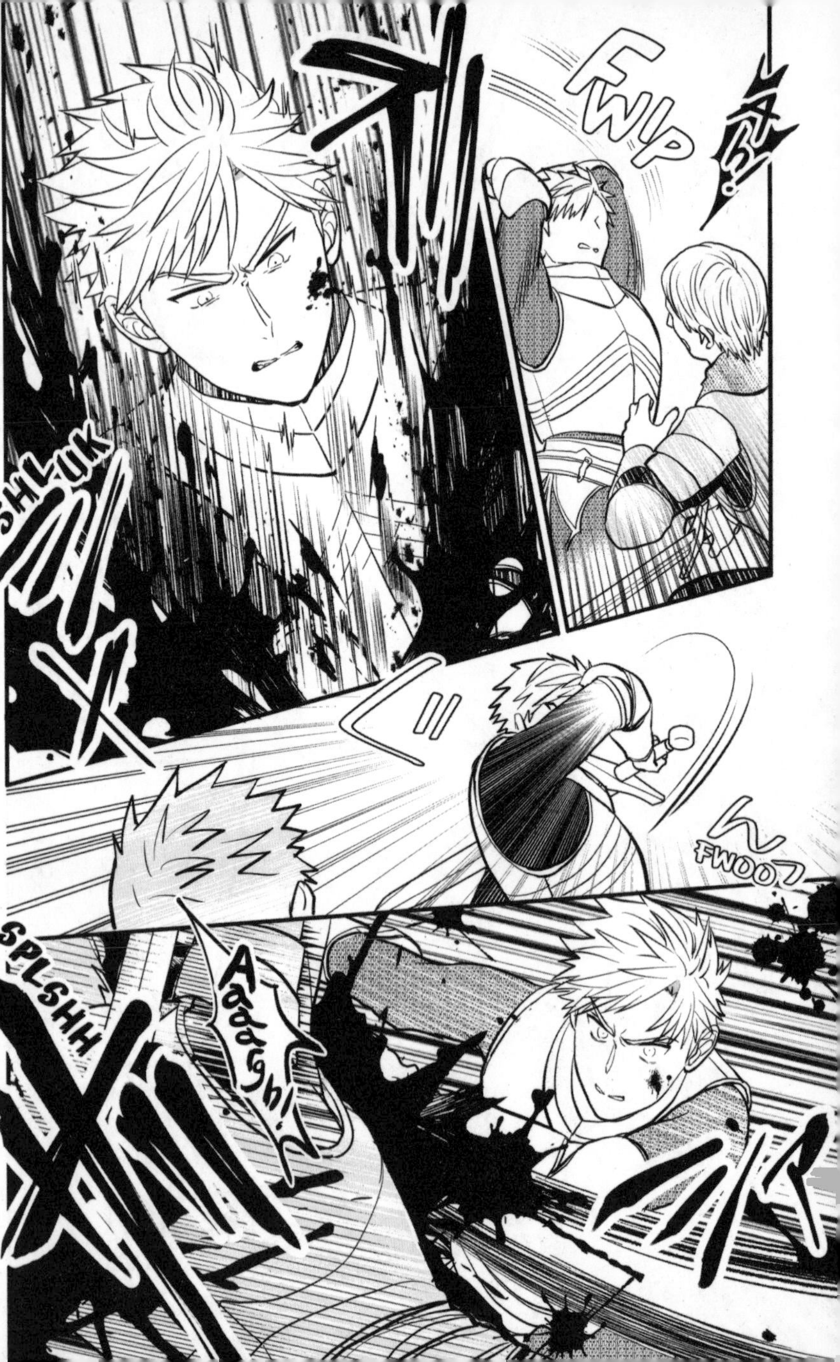FWIP
SHLUK
FWOOT
SPLSHH
Aaaagh!

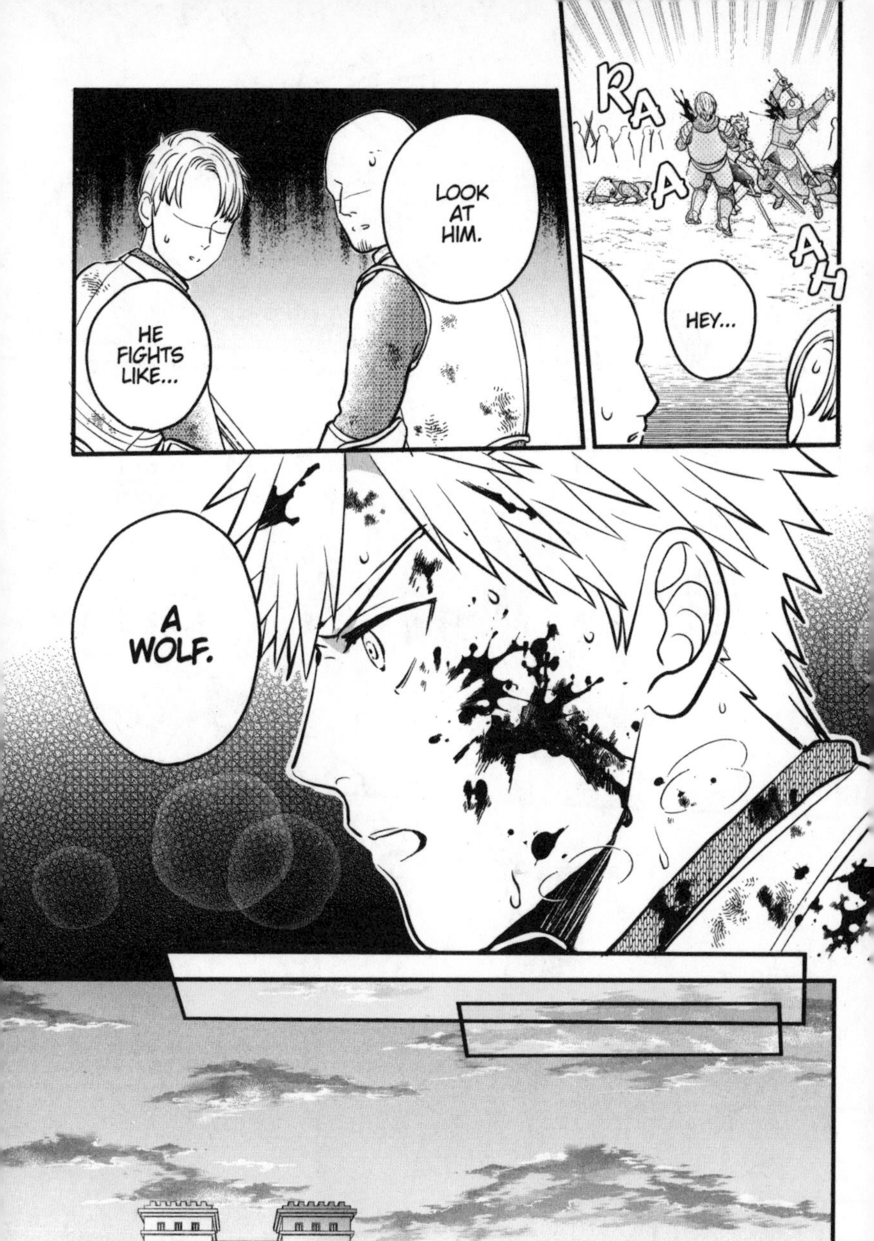
RAAAH
HEY...
LOOK AT HIM.
HE FIGHTS LIKE...
A WOLF.

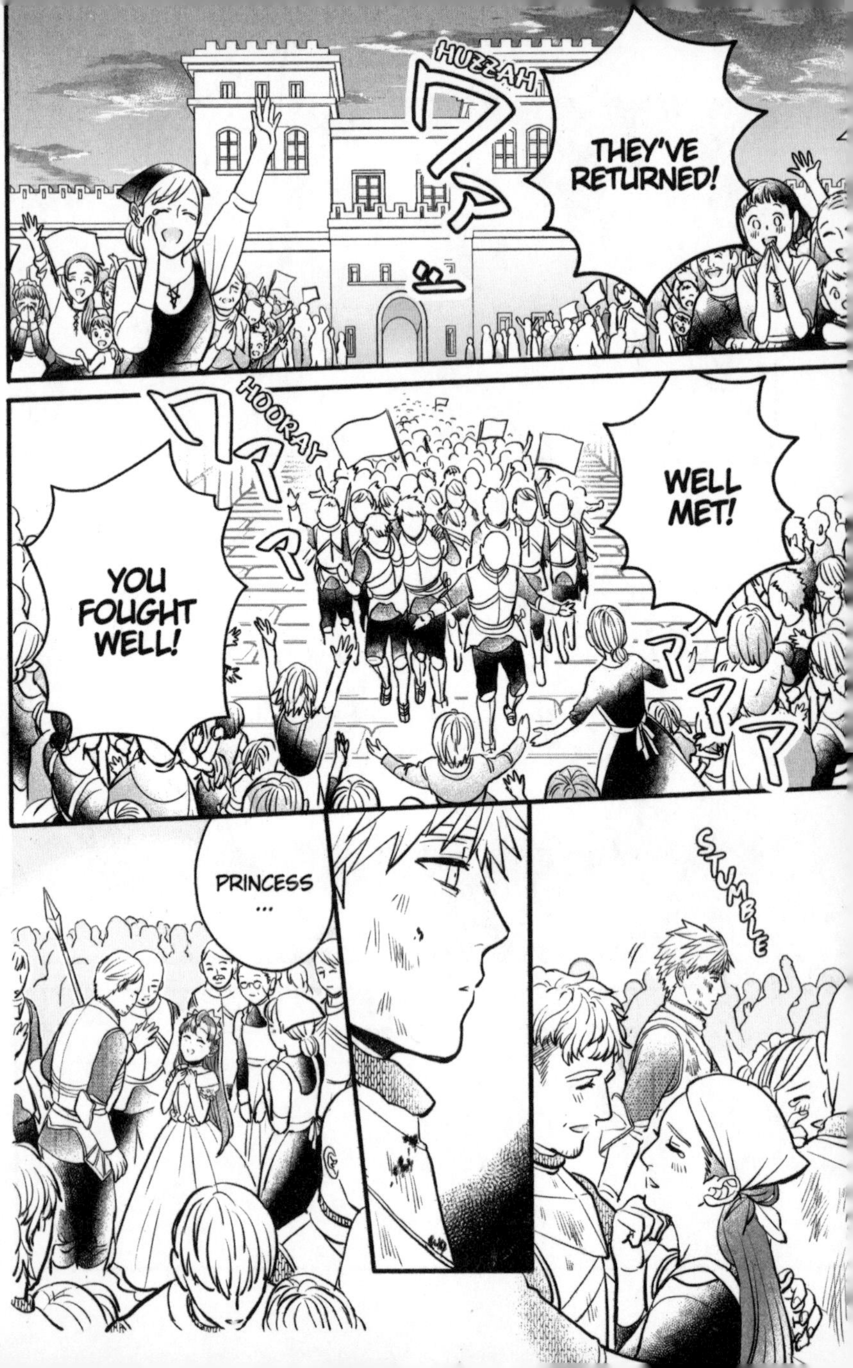
HUZZAH
THEY'VE RETURNED!
WELL MET!
HOORAY
YOU FOUGHT WELL!
STUMBLE
PRINCESS ...

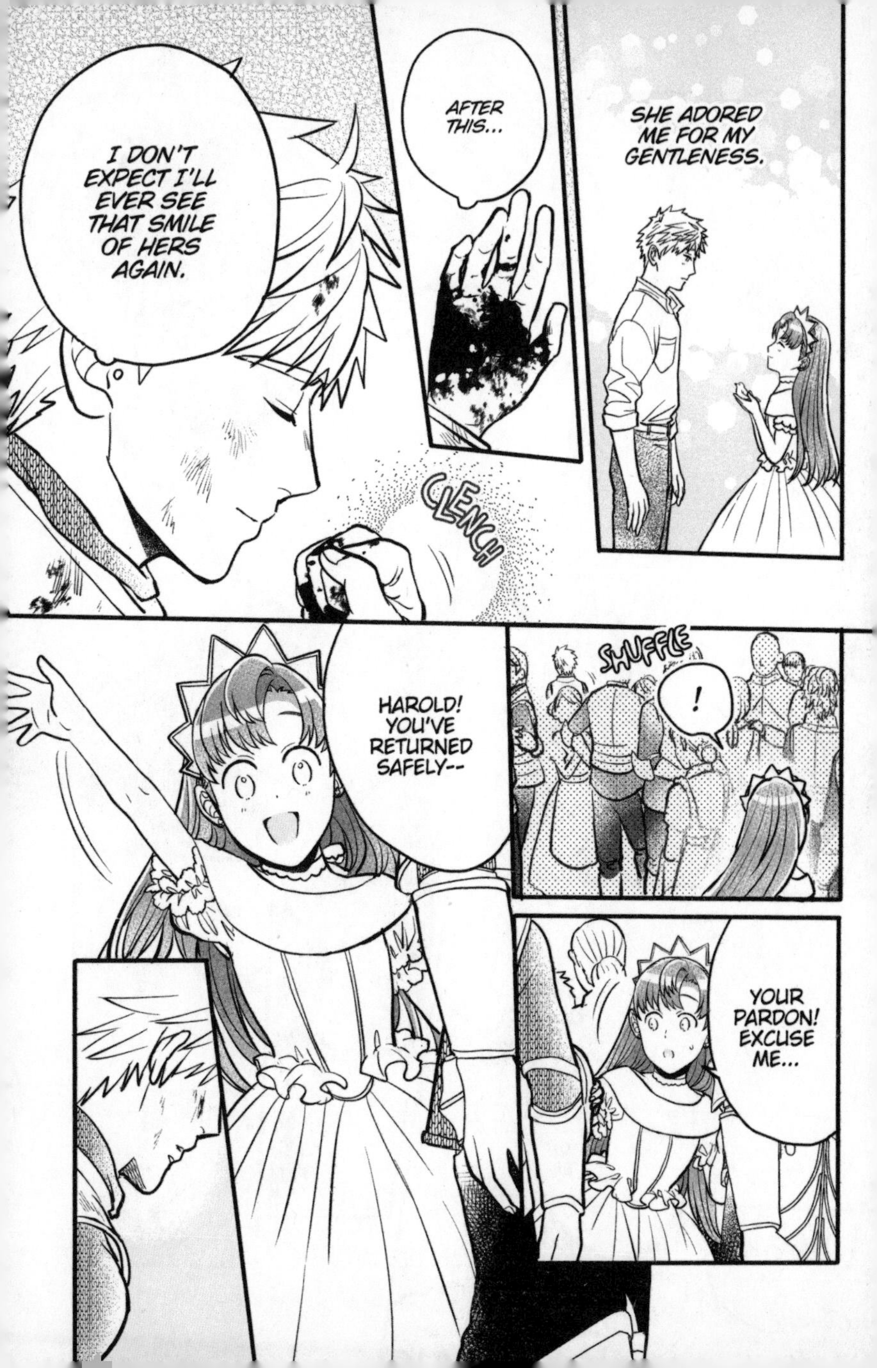
SHE ADORED ME FOR MY GENTLENESS.
AFTER THIS...
CLENCH
I DON'T EXPECT I'LL EVER SEE THAT SMILE OF HERS AGAIN.
SHUFFLE
!
YOUR PARDON! EXCUSE ME...
HAROLD! YOU'VE RETURNED SAFELY--

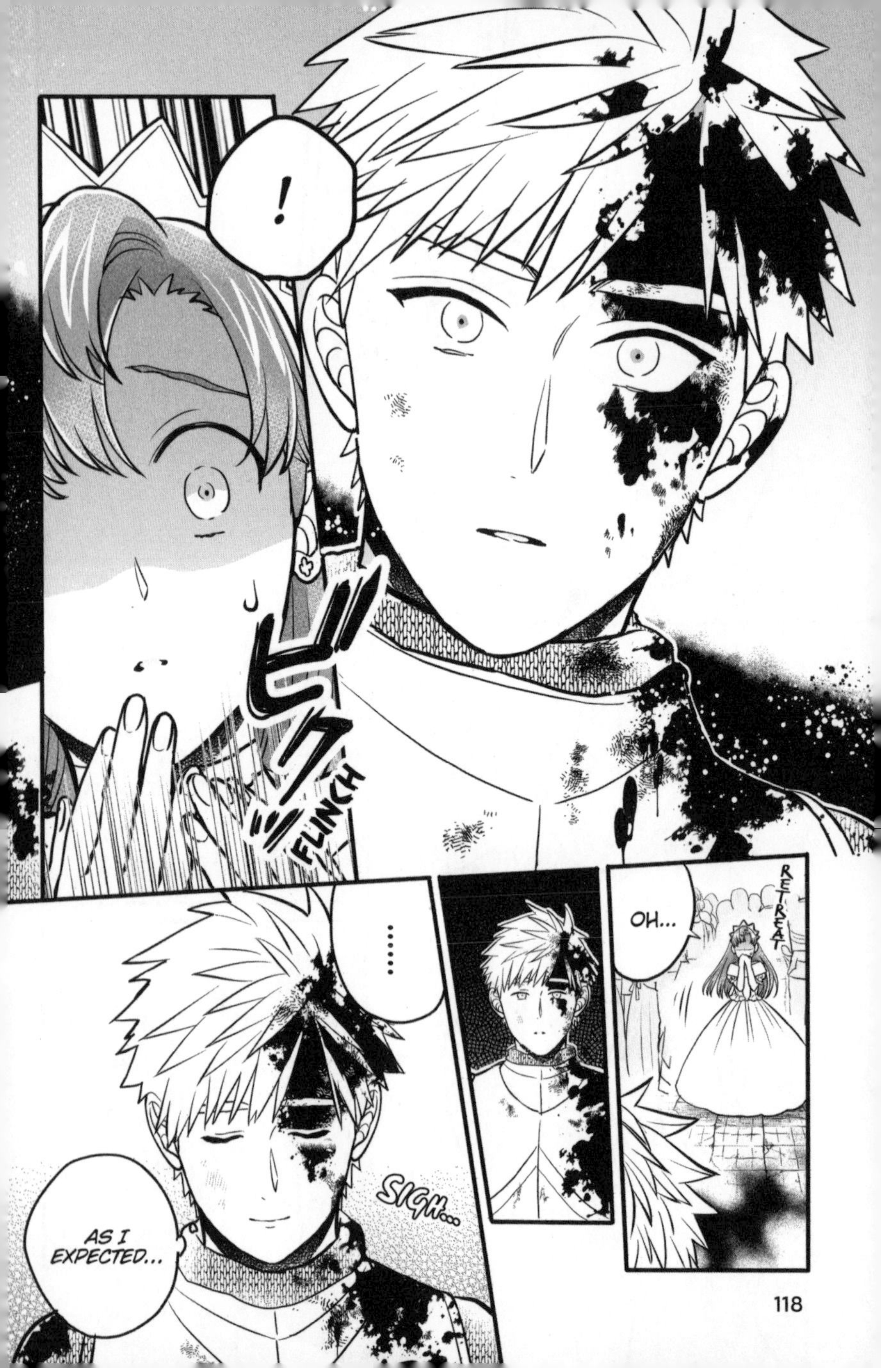
!
FLINCH
OH...
RETREAT
......
SIGH...
AS I EXPECTED...

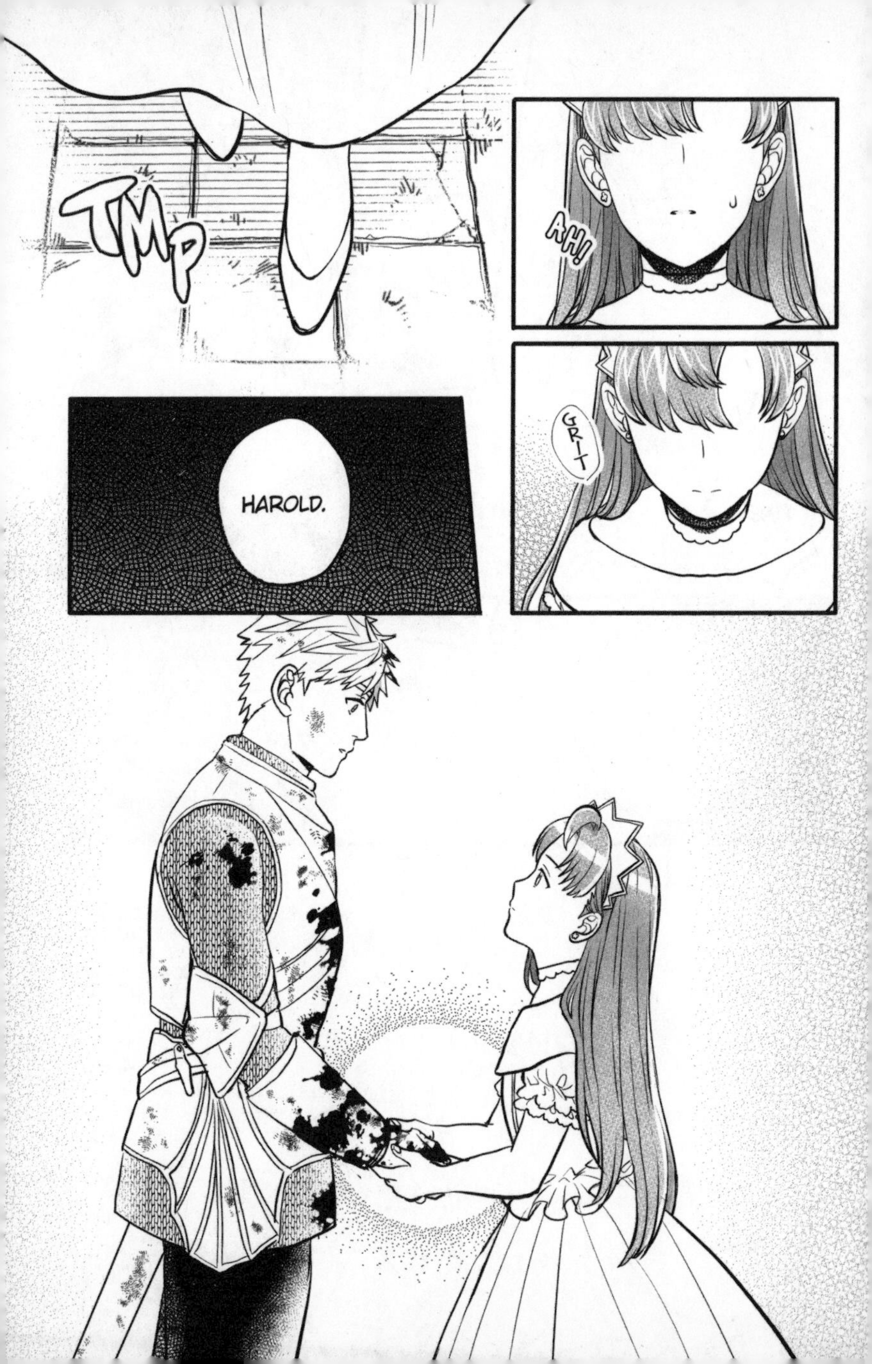
AH!
GRIT
TMP
HAROLD.

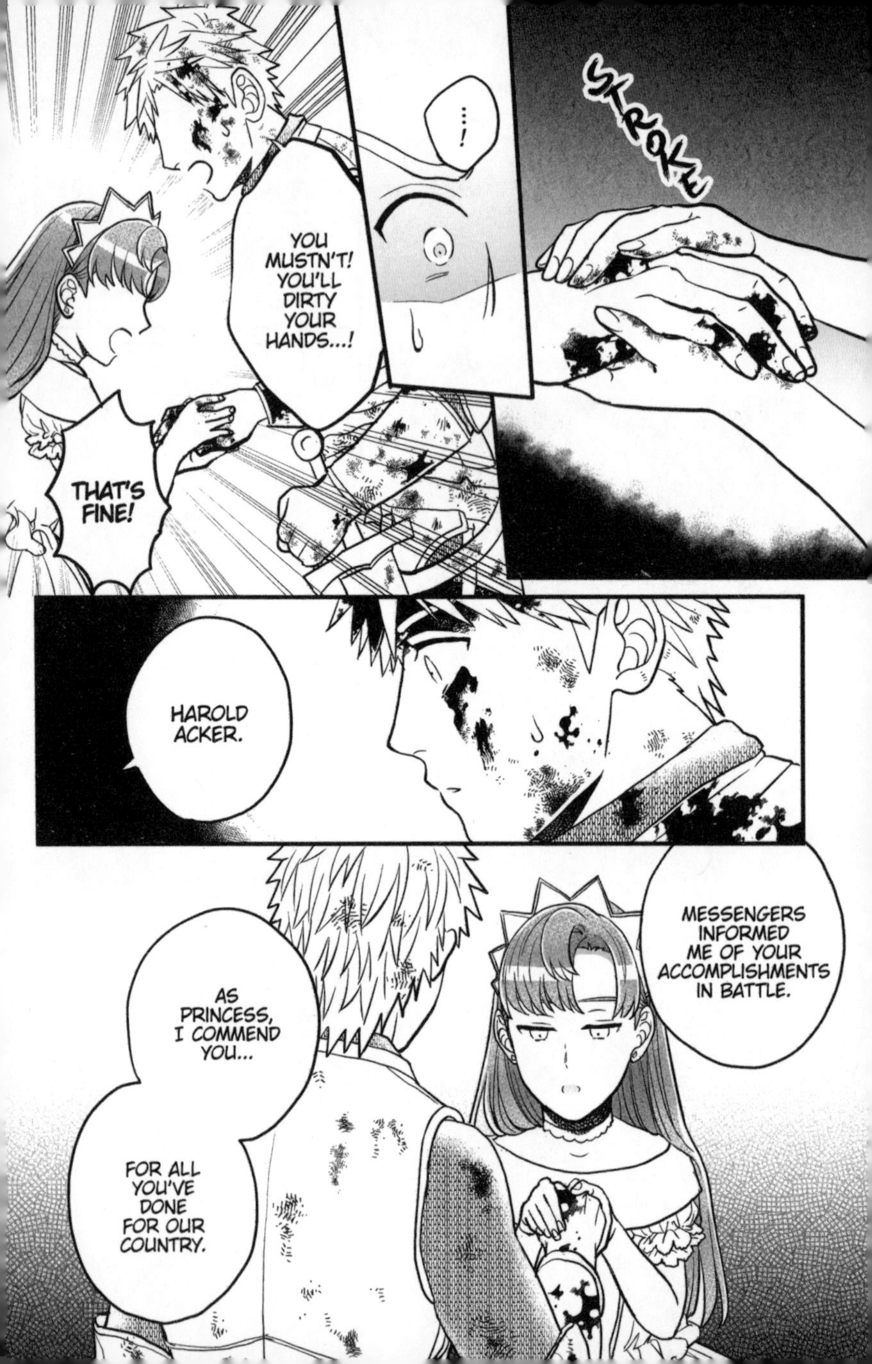
STROKE
...!
YOU MUSTN'T! YOU'LL DIRTY YOUR HANDS...!
THAT'S FINE!
HAROLD ACKER.
MESSENGERS INFORMED ME OF YOUR ACCOMPLISHMENTS IN BATTLE.
AS PRINCESS, I COMMEND YOU...
FOR ALL YOU'VE DONE FOR OUR COUNTRY.

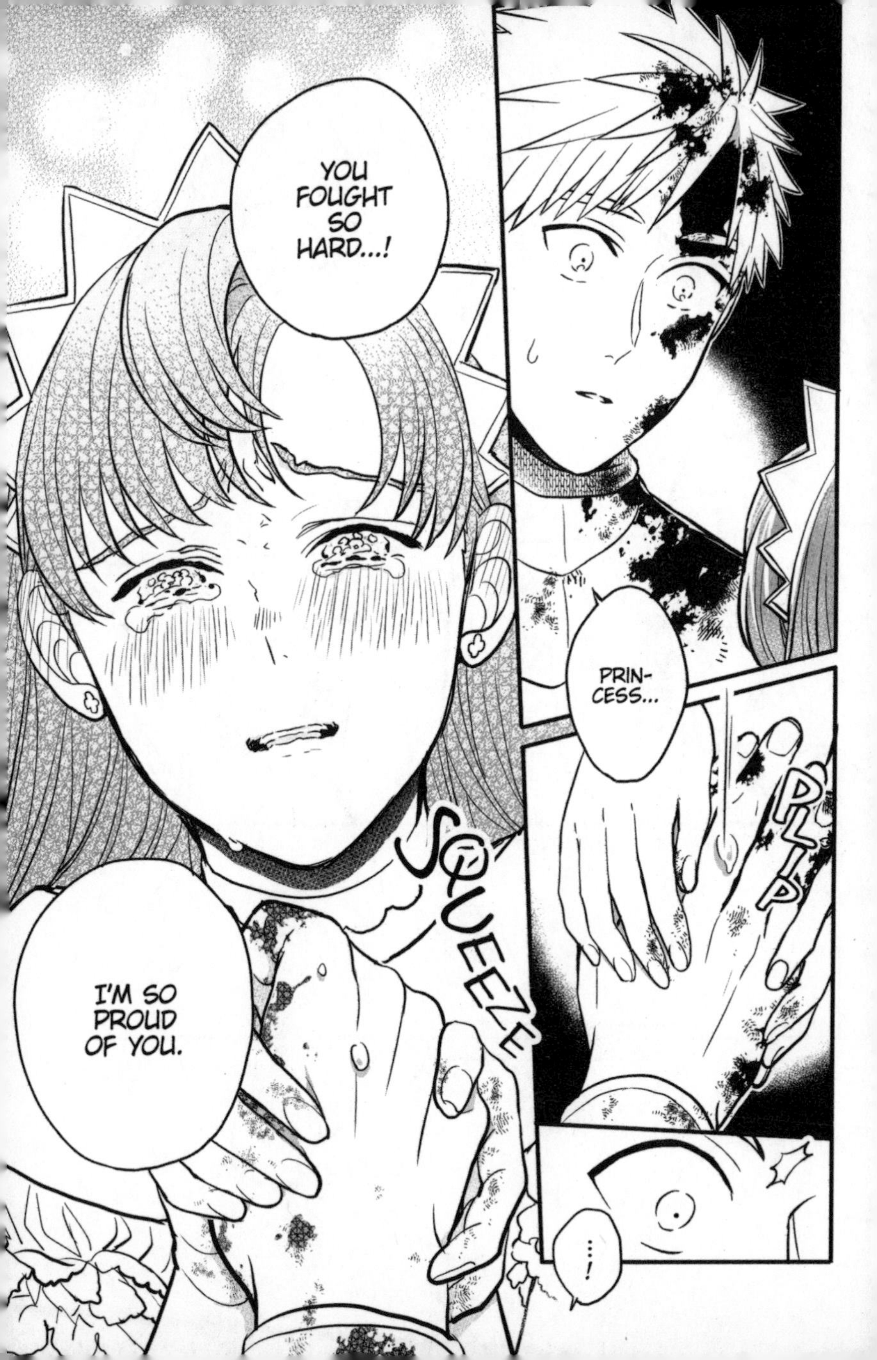
PRIN-CESS...
PLIP
...!
YOU FOUGHT SO HARD...!
SQUEEZE
I'M SO PROUD OF YOU.

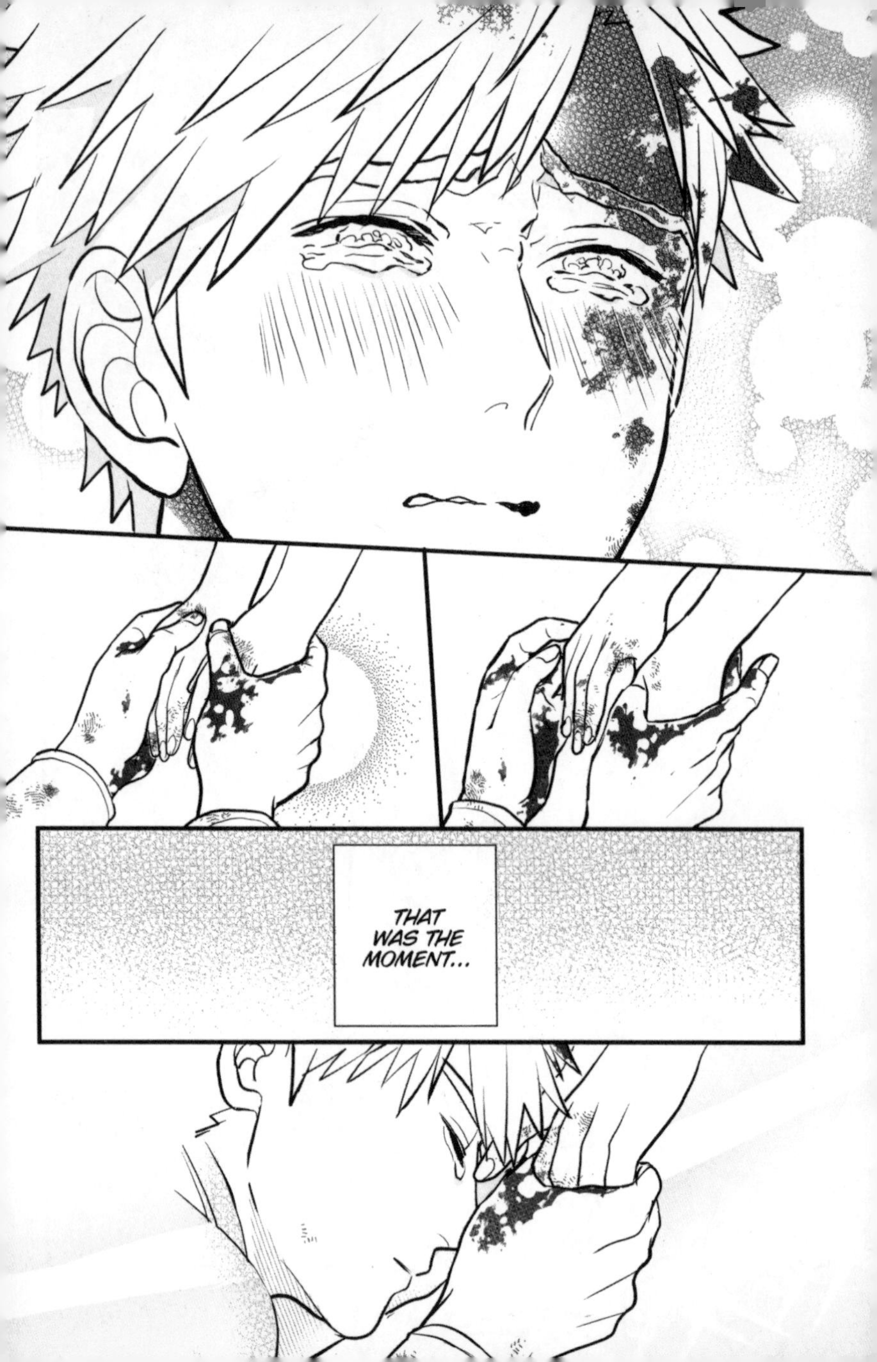
THAT WAS THE MOMENT...

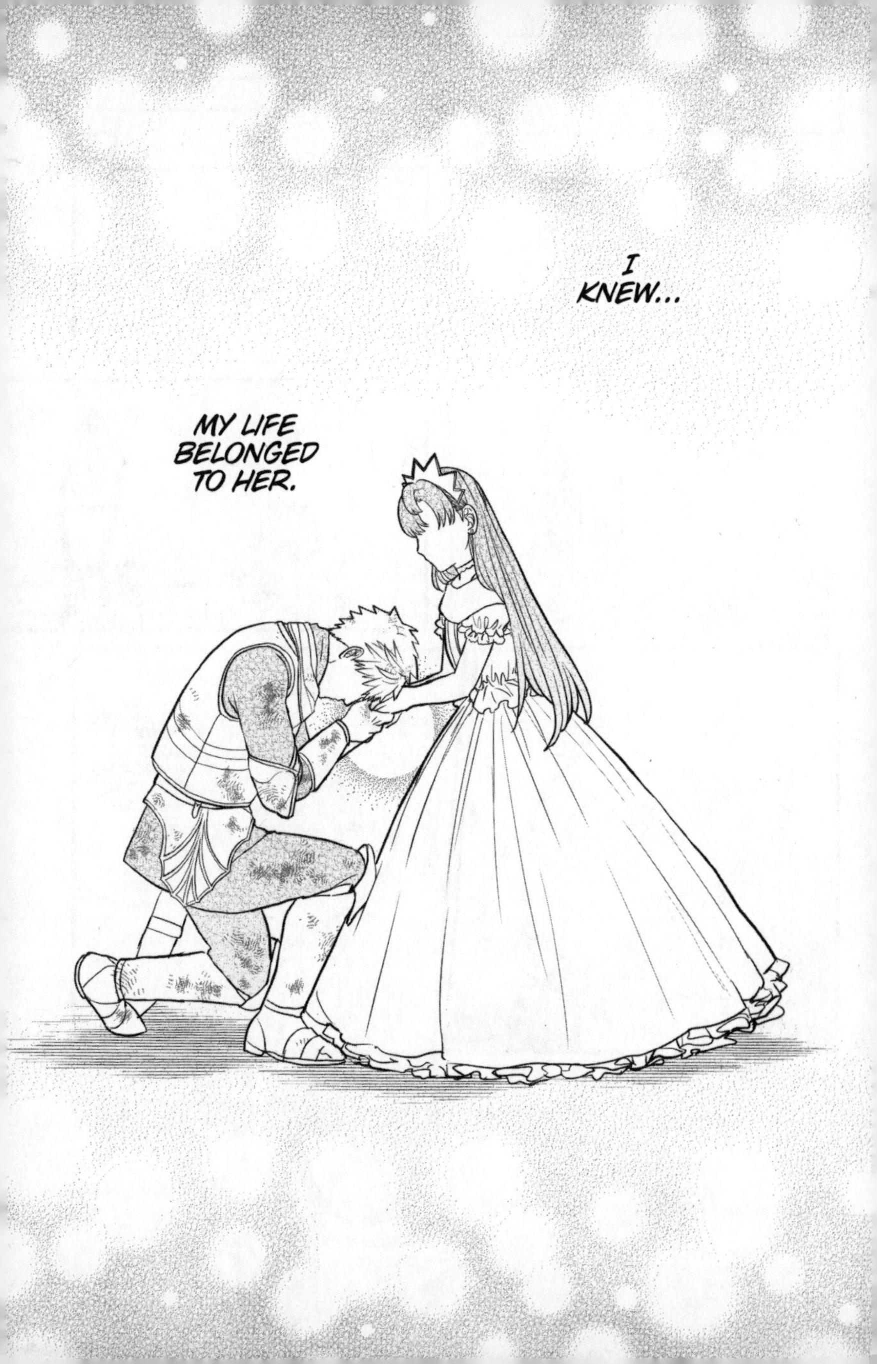
I KNEW...
MY LIFE BELONGED TO HER.

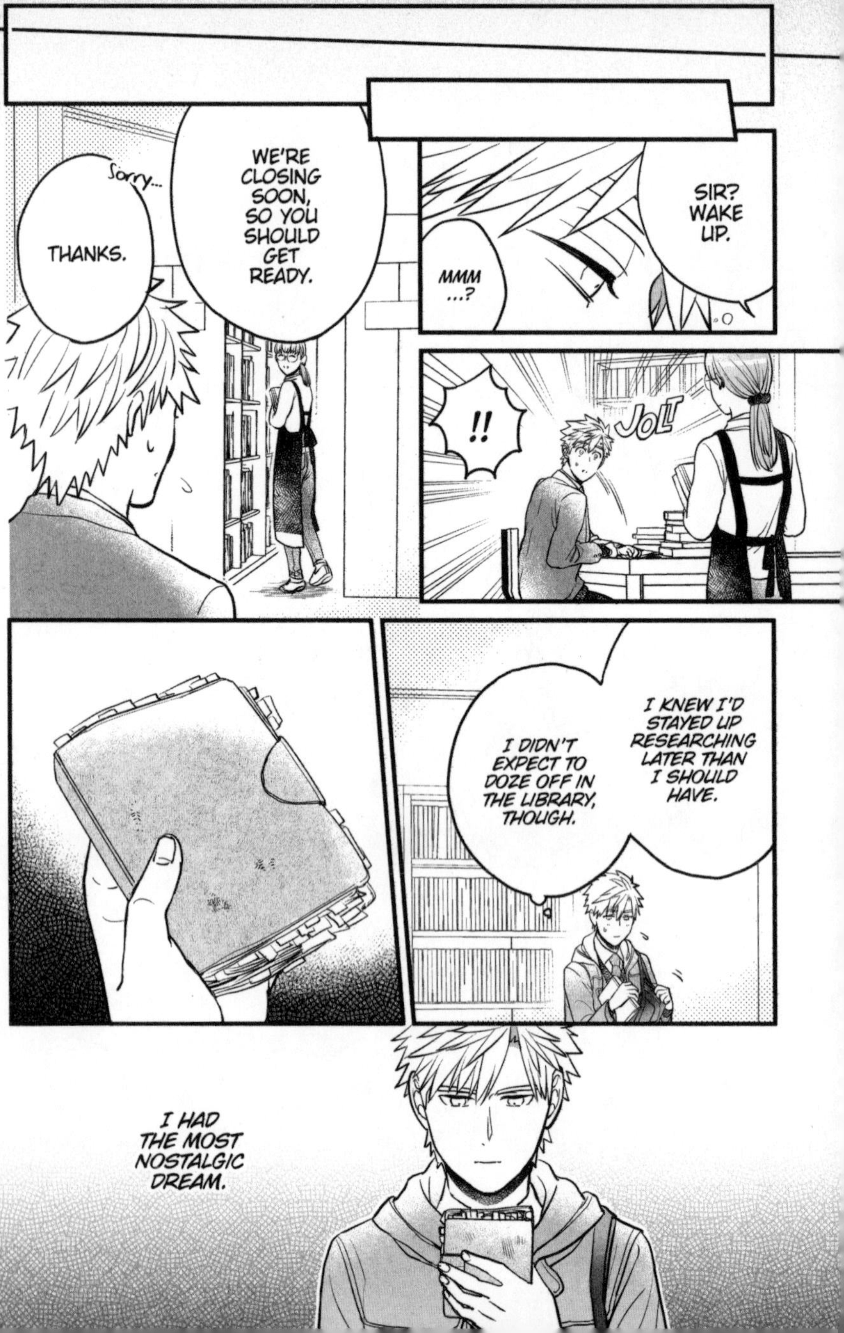
SIR? WAKE UP.
MMM ...?
!!
JOLT
WE'RE CLOSING SOON, SO YOU SHOULD GET READY.
Sorry...
THANKS.
I KNEW I'D STAYED UP RESEARCHING LATER THAN I SHOULD HAVE.
I DIDN'T EXPECT TO DOZE OFF IN THE LIBRARY, THOUGH.
I HAD THE MOST NOSTALGIC DREAM.

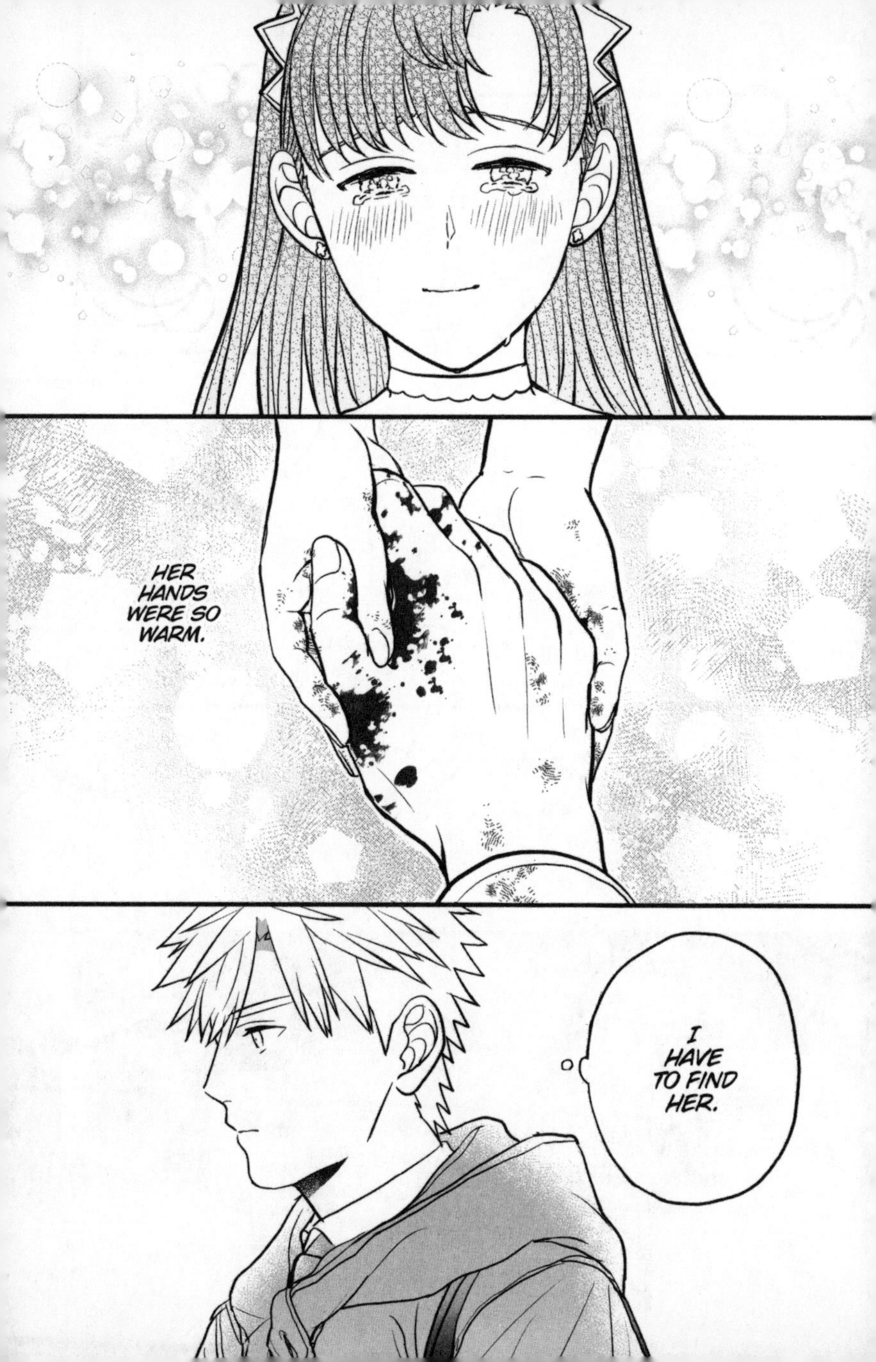
HER HANDS WERE SO WARM.
I HAVE TO FIND HER.

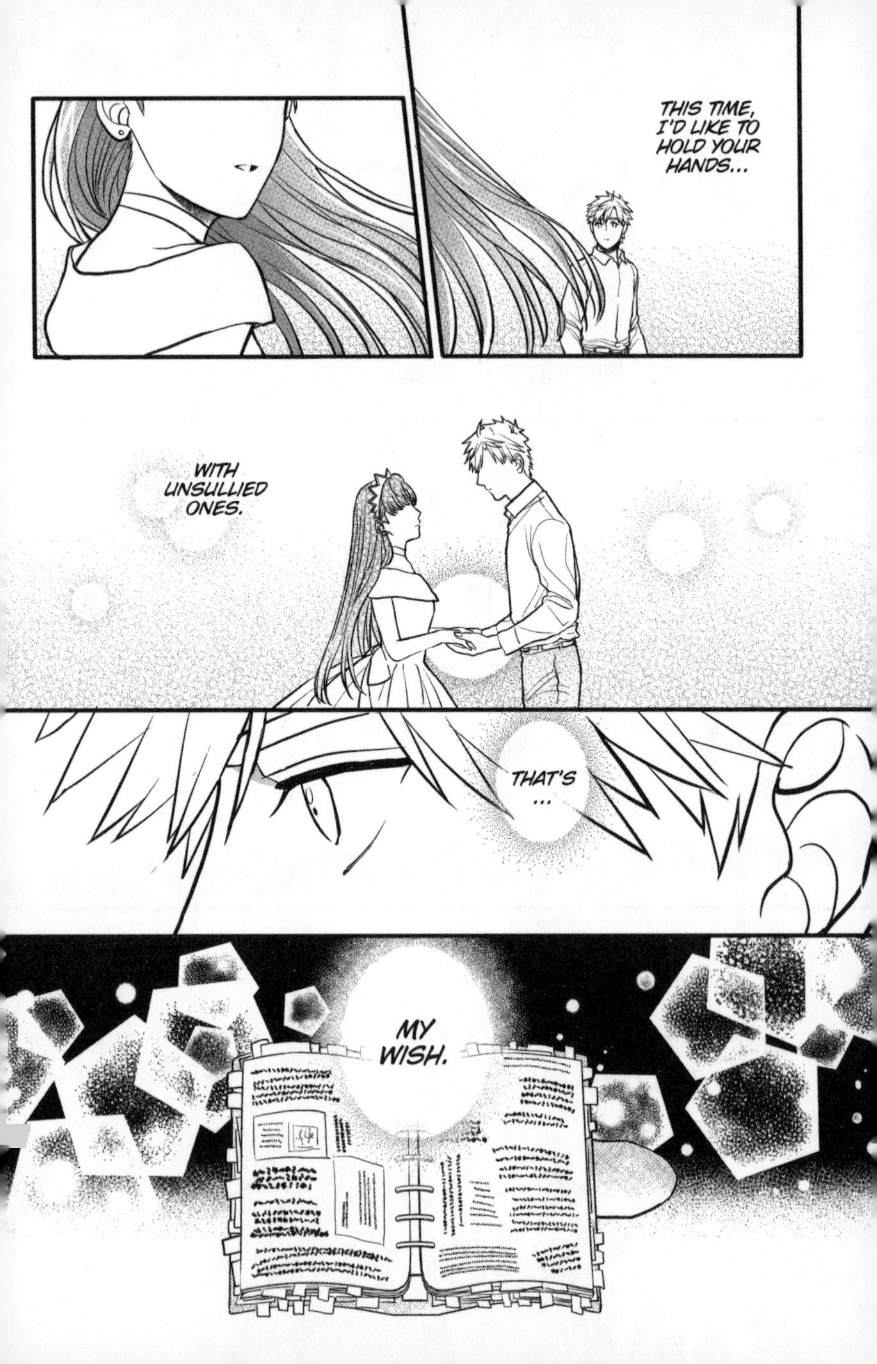
THIS TIME, I'D LIKE TO HOLD YOUR HANDS...
WITH UNSULLIED ONES.
THAT'S ...
MY WISH.

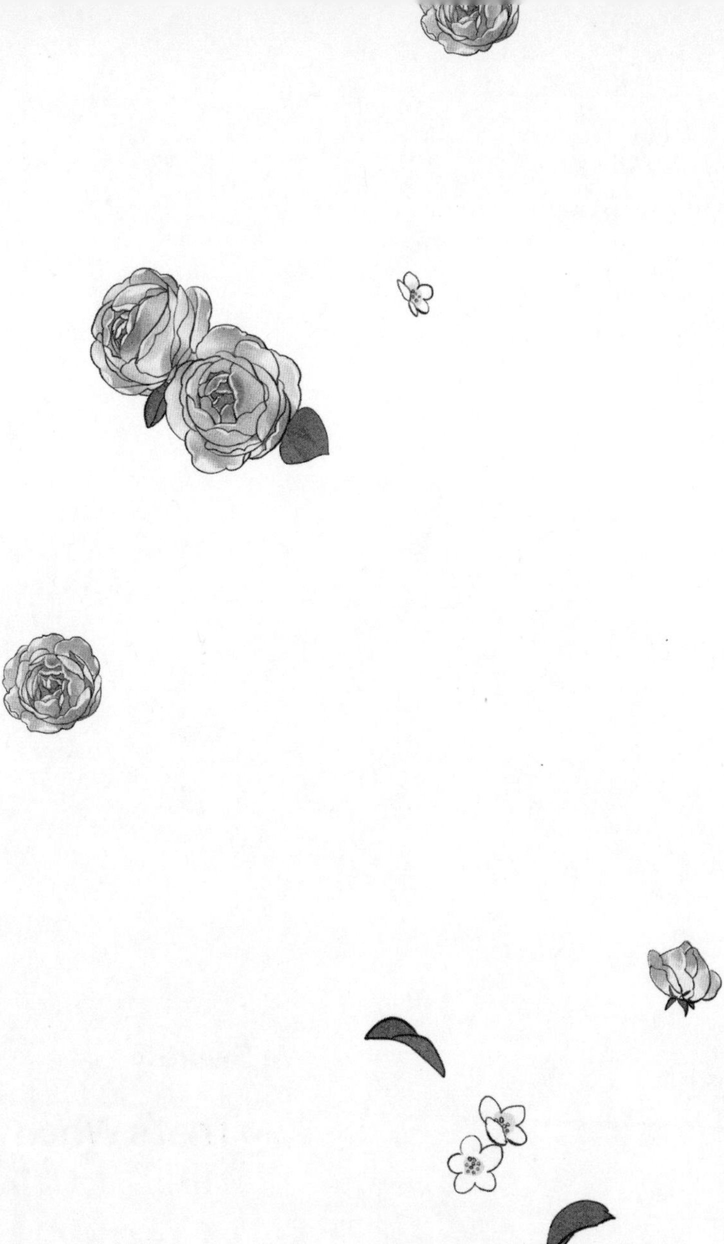

We Swore to Meet in the Next Life and That's When Things Got Weird!

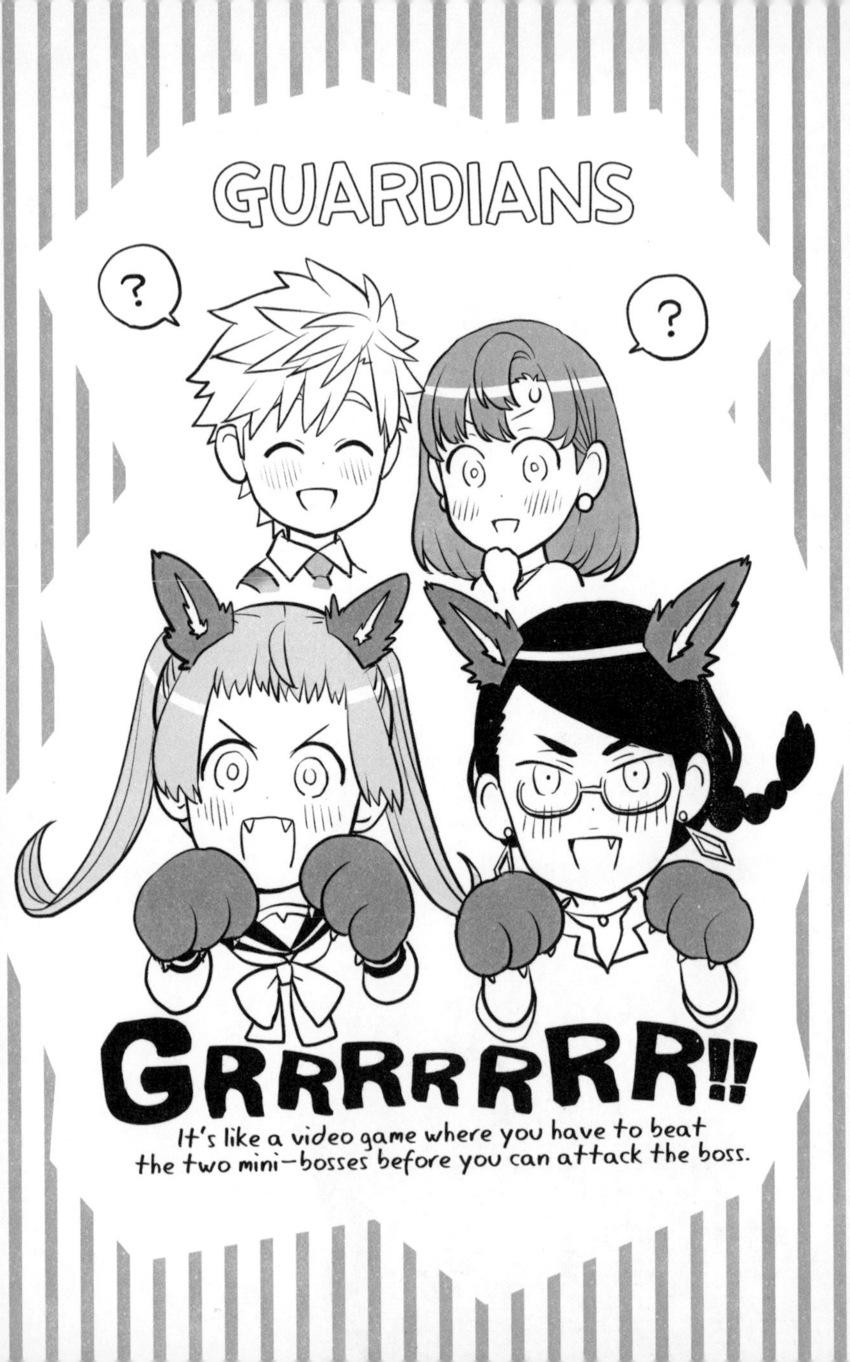
GUARDIANS
?
?
GRRRRRRR!!
It's like a video game where you have to beat the two mini-bosses before you can attack the boss.

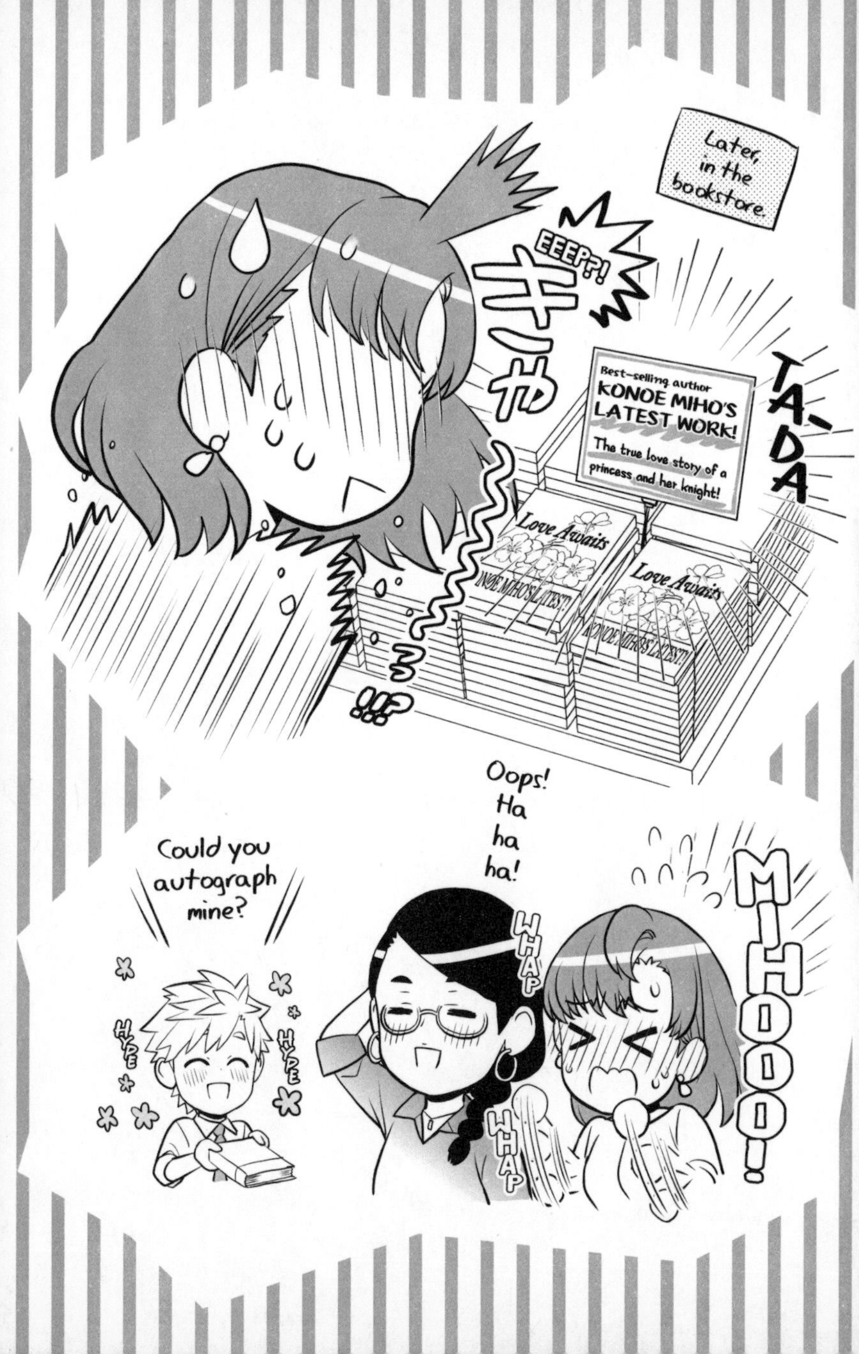
Later, in the bookstore.
EEEP?!
TA-DA
Best-selling author
KONOE MIHO'S LATEST WORK!
The true love story of a princess and her knight!
Love Awaits
Love Awaits
KONOE MIHO'S LATEST!
!!?
MIHOOOO!
WHAP
Oops! Ha ha ha!
WHAP
Could you autograph mine?
HYPE
HYPE

We Swore to Meet in the Next Life and That's When Things Got Weird!

We Swore to Meet in the Next Life and That's When Things Got Weird!

SEVEN SEAS ENTERTAINMENT PRESENTS

We Swore to Meet in the Next Life and That's When Things Got Weird!

story and art by **HATO HACHIYA** **VOLUME 2**

TRANSLATION
Nova Skipper

ADAPTATION
Ysabet Reinhardt MacFarlane

LETTERING AND RETOUCH
Annaliese "Ace" Christman

COVER DESIGN
Nicky Lim

PROOFREADER
Kurestin Armada, Dawn Davis

EDITOR
Peter Adrían Behravesh

PREPRESS TECHNICIAN
Rhiannon Rasmussen-Silverstein

PRODUCTION ASSISTANT
Christa Miesner

MANAGING EDITOR
Julie Davis

ASSOCIATE PUBLISHER
Adam Arnold

PUBLISHER
Jason DeAngelis

We Swore to Meet in the Next Life and That's When Things Got Weird! Vol. 2
Raise wo chikatte Tenseishitara Taihennakotoninatta vol. 2

First published in Japan in 2020 by Ichijinsha Inc., Tokyo.
Publication rights for this English edition arranged through Kodansha Ltd., Tokyo.

Seven Seas press and purchase enquiries can be sent to Marketing Manager Lianne Sentar at press@gomanga.com. Information regarding the distribution and purchase of digital editions is available from Digital Manager CK Russell at digital@gomanga.com.

ISBN: 978-1-64827-110-6
Printed in Canada
First Printing: March 2021
10 9 8 7 6 5 4 3 2 1

FOLLOW US ONLINE: ***www.sevenseasentertainment.com***

READING DIRECTIONS

This book reads from ***right to left***, Japanese style. If this is your first time reading manga, you start reading from the top right panel on each page and take it from there. If you get lost, just follow the numbered diagram here. It may seem backwards at first, but you'll get the hang of it! Have fun!!

1
2
3
4
5
6
7
8
9

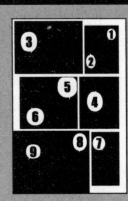